East Asian Social Science Monographs

Foreign Investment and Industrialization in Indonesia

Foreign Investment and Industrialization in Indonesia

Hal Hill

SINGAPORE
OXFORD UNIVERSITY PRESS
OXFORD   NEW YORK
1988

Oxford University Press

Oxford   New York   Toronto
Delhi   Bombay   Calcutta   Madras   Karachi
Petaling Jaya   Singapore   Hong Kong   Tokyo
Nairobi   Dar es Salaam   Cape Town
Melbourne   Auckland
and associated companies in
Berlin   Ibadan

Oxford is a trade mark of Oxford University Press

© *Oxford University Press Pte. Ltd. 1988*

Published in the United States by
Oxford University Press, Inc., New York

ISBN 0 19 588884 7

British Library Cataloguing in Publication Data

Hill, Hal
    Foreign investment and industrialization in Indonesia.
    —(East Asian social science monographs).
    1. Economic assistance—Indonesia
    I. Title   II. Series
    338.91′09598   HC447

    ISBN 0–19–588884–7

Library of Congress Cataloging-in-Publication Data

Hill, Hal, 1948–
    Foreign investment and industrialization in Indonesia.

    (East Asian social science monographs)
    Bibliography: p.
    Includes index.
    1. Investments, Foreign—Indonesia—History—
20th century. 2. Indonesia—Industries—History—
20th century. I. Title   II. Series.
HG5752.H54 1988   332.6′73′09598   87–31367
ISBN 0–19–588884–7

Printed in Singapore by Kim Hup Lee Printing Co. Pte. Ltd.
Published by Oxford University Press Pte. Ltd.,
Unit 221, Ubi Avenue 4, Singapore 1440

Preface

THERE are several reasons for a book-length examination of foreign investment and industrialization in Indonesia. First, the role of foreign involvement in its manufacturing sector is something of a puzzle. It is clear to any observer that the 'foreign presence' is ubiquitous in the modern sector, and yet all available statistical information points to comparatively modest foreign investment inflows and foreign ownership. A second reason is that Indonesian manufacturing experienced extraordinarily rapid growth in the fifteen years after 1967. To better understand this historically unprecedented growth episode, it is important to examine the role of contributing factors, of which foreign investment has undoubtedly been one.

There is, third, the fact that foreign investment in Indonesia has been a contentious issue. When critics of the current regime—both local and foreign—list their grievances, the government's alleged 'open-door' policy towards foreign investment is generally prominent. Finally, the book is in part a response to the challenge that the subject is not worthy of examination because the research and statistical data base is so weak. When I commenced work on the book, it was surprising how *much* had been written on foreign investment in Indonesia, even if much of the material was not easily accessible. Moreover, the range and quality of Indonesian economic statistics have improved enormously in the last decade, such that they are now among the best in South-East Asia.

The purpose of this book is to analyse and integrate this material in the framework of the theory of direct foreign investment, and in the context of general economic developments in Indonesia since 1965. It is not my intention to promote a particular set of arguments for or against foreign investment in that country. Indeed, throughout the study I maintain that a more important consideration is the broader macro and industrial policy environment. I believe Indonesia could have secured a much higher proportion of the benefits of foreign investment over the last two decades if these general policies had been more conducive to the emergence of an efficient and internationally competitive manufacturing sector. In this sense, to conduct a debate concerning the benefits and costs of foreign investment, without reference to this general policy environment, is a somewhat sterile exercise.

Although the study is concerned primarily with foreign investment, an underlying theme—perhaps paradoxically—is the role of the state in

Indonesian industrialization. I accord a central role to the state for three reasons. First, the state is a major investor in the manufacturing sector. State enterprises in Indonesia play a dominant or major role in industries which are often the preserve of foreign investors in less restricted commercial environments. Notable examples include petroleum refining, fertilizers, steel, and aircraft. The second reason is the state's role in the trade regime, itself a critical determinant of the extent, composition, and contribution of foreign investment in Indonesia. For example, Indonesia's high (and highly dispersed) effective protection for much of manufacturing has both induced considerable capital inflow—of an import-substituting nature—and greatly affected the profitability of such investment. Finally, the state has played a key role as a regulator. Investment regulations have determined the entry modalities of foreign firms (for example, some important industries, such as automobiles, are closed to new foreign equity), and the nature of the investment decision.

There are an unusually large number of caveats associated with this book. The first, and most obvious, is that the study has proved to be a data-intensive exercise, and the conclusions are only as sturdy as the data base permits. As noted, Indonesian economic statistics have improved immeasurably in the last decade, but there are still many gaps. I have been careful to highlight existing shortcomings and, where these remain considerable, I hope I have not 'pushed' the data further than warranted. Similarly, Indonesia is in a state of flux, and some parts of the study will date fairly quickly. Two recent, inter-connected events illustrate this proposition. When I first commenced serious work on the subject, in 1984, Indonesia's foreign investment policy was a fairly restrictive one and manufactured exports were miniscule. At the time of final drafting, in the first half of 1987, there had been major changes: investment policies had become a good deal more liberal, and manufactured exports had grown substantially.

The book is primarily an examination of the economics of foreign investment. As an outside (but I hope sympathetic) observer, I am acutely conscious of the fact that foreign investment—and foreign involvement more generally—raises a wide range of complex social, political, and cultural issues, especially so for a country little more than forty years after Independence. I recognize the strength of nationalist sentiment in Indonesia, and the fact that domestic ownership is considered by many to be a 'public good'. I also recognize that political structures—in Indonesia as much as elsewhere—not infrequently impede the adoption of 'first-best' economic policy prescriptions. All an outsider can offer is an analysis of current policies and implications of alternative scenarios, for the consideration of domestic policy-makers.

I hope this book will be of interest to three groups of readers. The first is a scholarly audience, including those with an interest in the Indonesian economy, and industrialization and business in developing countries. The second group is what might be termed the 'development industry'—international organizations and development agencies—for whom I hope I have provided a reasonably complete account of an important facet of

Indonesian development in the last twenty years. Finally, in return for the generous co-operation of the domestic and foreign business community in Indonesia, the book may perhaps provide an overview of a system which they obviously understand far better than a non-participant.

It is appropriate to end an introduction to a study of foreign investment with an acknowledgement of the many debts I have incurred in researching and writing the manuscript. Many Indonesian officials have assisted in providing information or explaining policies. Without naming individuals, I wish to thank staff at the Capital Investment Coordinating Board (BKPM), Bank Indonesia, and the Department of Industry. I am particularly appreciative of the support given by staff of the Central Bureau of Statistics (BPS). The Head of the Industry Section, Mr Sugiarto, generously provided access to unpublished industrial statistics.

Parts of the book have been presented to seminars at the Institute for Economic and Social Research (LPEM), University of Indonesia; the ESCAP/UNCTC Joint Unit on TNCs in Bangkok; the Department of Economics and Statistics, National University of Singapore; and to my Department at the Australian National University. I am very grateful to seminar participants for many useful comments.

I have benefited greatly from the constructive comments of several people kind enough to read all or part of earlier drafts. These people include Heinz Arndt (whose comments, as usual, were unsurpassed in quality and range), Bruce Glassburner, Mac Hill, Peter McCawley, Chris Manning, Thee Kian Wie, Louis Wells, and Kunio Yoshihara. Needless to say, I alone am responsible for remaining errors of fact and interpretation.

I am equally grateful to the many other people who assisted. These include Anne Armstrong, who typed much of the first draft of the manuscript and generally made life pleasant; Kris Bowmer and Libby Giugni, who also cheerfully assisted with typing; Corrine Condie, who ably assisted with the data analysis in Chapter 7; and Hazel Richter, who cast a characteristically eagle eye over the penultimate draft.

Department of Economics   HAL HILL
Research School of Pacific Studies
Australian National University
Canberra
June 1987

Contents

Tables

Figures

Abbreviations and Glossary

ABRI	(*Angkatan Bersenjata Republik Indonesia*) armed forces of the Republic of Indonesia
ASEAN	Association of South-East Asian Nations
BI	Bank Indonesia
BKPM	(*Badan Koordinasi Penanaman Modal*) Capital Investment Coordinating Board
BPS	(*Biro Pusat Statistik*) Central Bureau of Statistics
BRO	*Bedrijfs Reglemeenterings Ordannantie*
CKD	Completely Knocked Down
CSIS	Center for Strategic and International Studies
DAC	Development Assistance Committee (of the OECD)
DPR	(*Dewan Perwakilan Rakyat*) People's Representative Assembly
DSP	(*Daftar Skala Prioritas*) Investment Priority List
EPR	Effective rate of protection
EPZ	Export processing zone
ESCAP	Economic and Social Commission for Asia and the Pacific
GDP	Gross domestic product
Golongan ekonomi lemah	Weak economic groups
IMF	International Monetary Fund
ISIC	International Standard Industrial Classification
Kabupaten	Sub-provincial administrative district
KP	(*Keputusan Presiden*) Presidential Decree
Kretek	Indonesian clove cigarette
MITI	Ministry of International Trade and Industry, Japan
MVA	Manufacturing value added
NICs	Newly industrializing countries
Non-*pribumi*	Non-indigenous Indonesians (mostly Chinese)
NTB	Non-tariff barriers
OECD	Organization for Economic Cooperation and Development
OPEC	Organization of Petroleum Exporting Countries
Orde Baru	New Order (the period from 1966)
Orde Lama	Old Order (the period up to 1966)

Pertamina	State-owned oil company
PLN	(*Perusahaan Listrik Negara*) State Electricity Corporation
PMA	(*Penanaman Modal Asing*) foreign investment
PMDN	(*Penanaman Modal Dalam Negeri*) domestic investment
PN	(*Perusahaan Negara*) state enterprise
Pribumi	Indigenous Indonesian
PT	(*Perseroan Terbatas*) limited liability
PTPM	(*Panitia Teknis Penanaman Modal*) Technical Team for Investment
PUSRI	State-owned fertilizer company
Repelita	(*Rencana Pembangunan Lima Tahun*) Five-Year Development Plan
RUP	(*Rencana Urgensi Perekonomian*) Economic Urgency Plan
Santri	Devout Moslem
SE	(*Sertifikat Ekspor*) Export Certificate
Sensus Industri	Industrial Census
SI	(*Statistik Industri*) Industrial Statistics
SK	(*Surat Keputusan*) (Regulation), *Menteri* (of the Minister), *Direktur Jenderal* (of the Director-General)
Supas	Intercensal survey
UNCTC	United Nations Centre on Transnational Corporations

Notes

Spelling of Indonesian words: In all cases the new (post-1972) spelling is employed.

Currency: US dollars are quoted unless otherwise stated.

Exchange rate: Since the April 1983 devaluation there has been a 'managed float' of the rupiah. The average rupiah : US$ rate in 1984 was Rp 1,026; in 1985 it was Rp 1,111. The rate shortly after the September 1986 devaluation was Rp 1,640.

The Indonesian financial year is 1 April to 31 March.

Introduction

FROM 1967 to 1984, the Indonesian economy grew remarkably quickly, with gross domestic product (GDP) increasing at an annual average rate of almost 8 per cent. Such a period of sustained and rapid growth was unparalleled in the country's history. It was in marked contrast to the patchy record of the 1950s and, especially, to the economic decline and soaring inflation of the first half of the 1960s. Moreover, not only has Indonesia's performance since 1967 been very good in historical perspective, it has also compared favourably with its dynamic neighbours in ASEAN and North-East Asia.

Industrialization has been an integral part of Indonesia's economic recovery and growth. In the mid-1960s, Indonesia was perhaps the least industrialized among the large developing countries, certainly compared to Asia's other two giants, China and India. The manufacturing sector consisted primarily of simple consumer goods and resource-processing activities; much of the small factory sector was state controlled; and in many respects manufacturing had changed little since the country's first period of industrial growth in the 1930s. After 1966, manufacturing production expanded rapidly, so much so that this sector's share of a fast-growing GDP increased by about 50 per cent in less than two decades. In the first decade after 1966, manufacturing growth was concentrated in a wide range of consumer and intermediate goods—the so-called 'easy phase' of import substitution. More recently, since about 1980, the first serious push for backward integration into capital goods production and for labour-intensive and resource-based manufactured exports got under way.

Indonesia's industrialization since 1966 has been fuelled by the rapid import and dissemination of foreign technologies and products. The adoption of more liberal economic policies facilitated these imports, but they were hastened in particular by the promulgation of the Foreign Investment Law of 1967. The Law represented an almost complete reversal of Indonesia's policy towards foreign investment. Perhaps even more important, it was symbolic: it was a major signal to potential foreign investors, and to the domestic business community, of the 'New Order' government's economic and development priorities.

During the last half century, foreign investment policy in Indonesia has encompassed virtually the entire spectrum of postures, from an 'open-door' position, to hostility and to expropriation of foreign capital. The late colonial

era was characterized by extensive Dutch and other foreign investment—
primarily but not exclusively—in the extractive and commercial sectors.
The 1940s, the decade of war and revolution, saw no new foreign (or, in
fact, any) investments; indeed, capital consumption was almost certainly
extensive. In the years immediately after Independence, successive governments gave qualified but cautious support to modest and strictly regulated
capital inflows. However, the initial pragmatic attitude was overtaken,
after the mid-1950s, by the rising tide of nationalism during the era of
Guided Democracy. In 1957, Dutch capital was expropriated, and in the
next seven years most other foreign enterprise came under government
control. The 1967 Law thus represented a sharp and sudden change of
direction, which ushered in a period of relatively liberal policies. This
'liberal era' was to last for only about five years: by the mid-1970s, the
government had become a good deal more restrictive and selective, a move
triggered in part by the political protests of January 1974.

What role has foreign investment played in Indonesian industrialization
after 1966? What would the manufacturing sector look like in the 1980s if
there had not been a large inflow of private equity capital? Given that
Indonesian industry required large injections of foreign capital, technology, and managerial expertise, was the mix of policies adopted after 1966
broadly appropriate? The purpose of this book is to address these questions,
in the context of the New Order's industrial policies.

The fundamental economic and political parameters of the Soeharto
regime provide important clues to answering these questions. In essence, a
strong, centralized, and authoritarian government has presided over an era
of (until very recently) unprecedented economic growth. The economy
has been propelled by large capital inflows and by the boom in primary
commodity exports. Macro-economic policy has generally been orthodox,
and even conservative, except for inflationary episodes which accompanied
the two international oil shocks. Large resource flows have financed huge
public investment in infrastructure and social overhead capital. While the
foreign capital market has remained open, and trade policies a good deal
more liberal than those of the Old Order, the trade regime has been
inward looking, and there has been extensive and increasing resort to a
plethora of non-tariff barriers. Finally, government regulation of the
domestic economy is pervasive, even though bureaucratic resources are
limited. Much of this regulation, moreover, takes the form of direct intervention through controls, rather than indirect manipulation through taxes
and prices.

The outcome, in terms of industrial progress, has broadly accorded with
a priori expectations. Political stability, macro-economic orthodoxy, and
large capital inflows have produced rapid industrial growth. Protectionist
policies have given rise to a 'hot-house' effect, which has stimulated production still further in the short term. But these policies have also
bequeathed a manufacturing sector in which important subsectors are
inefficient and internationally uncompetitive. The response of foreign
investors, and their contribution to industrialization, have been conditioned
by the domestic policy environment. Foreign investors were attracted by

the new business opportunities and they brought in much-needed capital and technology. But it will be argued that their development contribution has been greatly inhibited by the trade regime, and by a comparatively weak bureaucracy which has appropriated, for the country as a whole, a lower share of the 'rents' to foreign investment than could have been the case under alternative policy scenarios.

Why study foreign investment and industrialization in Indonesia? The first reason is, simply, that Indonesia is the world's third largest developing country, and it has been a major recipient of capital since the late 1960s. Any study of the subject in the Third World can therefore hardly afford to ignore Indonesia. Secondly, and related to the first point, Indonesia exemplifies a particular policy environment—common to many developing (and not a few developed) countries—which, as noted, limits the potential gains from foreign investment: a comparatively liberal policy towards these investments, accompanied by a highly regulated and protected manufacturing sector, and by authoritarian political structures. Indonesia's experience with foreign investment is thus of relevance to many other developing countries, not only because of the magnitude of investment flows but also because the essential elements of the policy environment are replicated in many other countries.

A third reason is that the role of foreign investment in Indonesia continues to be a controversial issue. Opinion on the matter, in the popular press and in the research community, is sharply divided. Whenever criticism of the government has surfaced during the New Order, it has invariably focused on the alleged excessive dependence on foreign capital, on foreign (often meaning domestic Chinese) control over the economy, and on concessions to foreign enterprise. Not infrequently the debate has generated more heat than light. It is now almost two decades since the 1967 Law was introduced, and an assessment of the costs and benefits of foreign investment is therefore timely.

A final reason for the study is that the secondary data base is now much improved, notwithstanding the considerable deficiencies which still exist. There is, moreover, a substantial body of literature on foreign investment in Indonesia, particularly in the manufacturing sector. Much of this literature is not widely accessible, however, and a good deal of the survey research on which it is based was conducted before 1980. One aim of this study is to review and distil the main findings from this work, and to point to new areas where research is required.

Foreign investment in manufacturing is the primary focus of this book. In fact, foreign investment in the petroleum industry has been a good deal larger since 1966. But data on the latter investments are extremely poor, and the policy issues (for example, optimal exploitation, taxation, and production-sharing arrangements) differ somewhat. Manufacturing was also chosen for other reasons. One, as noted, is that it has already been the subject of scrutiny, including several informative field surveys. Another is that foreign investment in manufacturing is *visible*—in contrast to enclave investments in petroleum—and therefore invites public comment. Foreign investors' interaction with the domestic business community, in addition, raises important issues of technology transfer and the development of indigenous entrepreneurship. Yet another reason for selecting manufacturing is that it has been the largest recipient of foreign investment among sectors within the jurisdiction of the Capital Investment Coordinating Board (*Badan Koordinasi Penanaman Modal*, hereafter referred to as BKPM). Lastly, the choice was influenced by the author's research interest in industrialization in Indonesia and the ASEAN countries.

This book concentrates mainly on the period after 1966, but we begin, in Chapter 1, with a brief review of developments during the colonial era and the first two decades of Independence. The story before 1966 is relatively straightforward. Extractive and plantation investments were dominant up to 1939, while political developments effectively deterred foreign investors after 1945. Chapter 2 provides an overview of industrialization in the New Order period, to set the stage for later discussion. Particular emphasis is given to the growth in production, and to the equally rapid structural transformation of industry.

The analysis of foreign investment after 1966 begins in Chapter 3, with an examination of the policy environment towards foreign investors. After a brief episode of very liberal policies, from 1974 the environment became a good deal more restrictive, and it remained so until the mid-1980s, when economic stagnation forced the government to offer more concessions to foreign firms. Later in this chapter, there is an examination of aggregate trends in foreign investment since 1967, and their relation to the policy environment. The importance of foreign investment in Indonesia compared to other developing countries is also assessed.

The following two chapters investigate the composition of foreign investment. Chapter 4 looks at the major investors in manufacturing. Japan is dominant, but sizeable investments have also come from other countries. The discussion of source countries is related also to the general literature on major characteristics of investing countries, focusing especially on Japan and the United States, and developed and developing countries. Next, in Chapter 5, the distribution of foreign investment within the manufacturing sector is examined. Using unpublished data from the annual *Statistik Industri* (SI, or Industrial Statistics) series, it is also possible to identify the industries in which foreign investors play a major role, as compared to state and domestic private firms.

Chapters 6 and 7 address two of the more contentious issues concerning foreign investment. Chapter 6 seeks to determine whether the factor proportions of foreign-owned firms differ significantly from those of other ownership groups. It is frequently argued that foreign firms adopt excessively capital-intensive technologies in developing countries, thereby making little contribution to employment generation. The Indonesian data, though limited, throw some light on this issue. The diffusion of technology from foreign to domestic firms is examined in Chapter 7. Unlike the previous chapter, it is far more difficult to reach strong conclusions. The 'development contribution' of foreign firms is a complex subject, because the so-called 'linkages and leakages' are very difficult to identify and measure. There have, however, been a number of useful firm surveys in Indonesia which, while not definitive, are at least suggestive.

Chapter 8 critically assesses the Indonesian government's policies towards foreign investment, in the context of the country's industrial programme. The main argument is that these policies represent an understandable response to political pressures. Nevertheless, the economic rationale for many of these policies is weak, and the same ends could be achieved more effectively through alternative measures. Finally, Chapter 9 summarizes the main findings of the book, and considers future prospects for foreign investment in the subdued economic environment of the late 1980s and beyond.

It hardly needs to be emphasized that foreign investment data for Indonesia—or, for that matter, most countries—need to be interpreted with great care. The most widely accessible data on Indonesia are approved foreign investments for sectors within the jurisdiction of the BKPM. These data are frequently cited by researchers unfamiliar with Indonesian statistics, even though they give an entirely misleading impression concerning the magnitude and composition of these investment flows. Indonesian economic statistics, including those on foreign investment, have improved immeasurably since the mid-1960s. But important deficiencies remain. These are summarized briefly in Chapters 2 (on manufacturing) and 3 (on foreign investment); an Appendix sets out these limitations in more detail.

1 The Colonial Era and Early Independence

The foreign investment community still awaits the promulgation of the long-promised regulations governing foreign enterprise in Indonesia and clarification of the general conditions under which foreign enterprise can expect to operate. (Higgins, 1957, p. 80.)

The Colonial Era

INDONESIA'S modern industrial sector in the colonial era was very small and largely foreign owned. Before 1920, what little manufacturing there was consisted almost entirely of seasonal cottage activities (rice milling, textiles, and so on), and estate-based activities. The disruption of trade flows during the First World War had induced some limited import substitution, but the effects were short-lived. In fact, in the 1920s there were only two large industrial establishments in the entire country, apart from processing facilities on the estates. Both these establishments were foreign owned—a cigarette manufacturing plant owned by British-American Tobacco, and a General Motors car assembly plant (Soehoed, 1967, p. 66).

The Great Depression was the initial catalyst for industrialization in Indonesia. The depression had a catastrophic effect on the economy: the colony's exports declined from 1,488 million guilders in 1929, to 505 million guilders in 1935 (*Statistical Pocketbook of Indonesia, 1941*), while plantation employment over the same period more than halved (Wertheim, 1956, chap. 5, part 3B). In the circumstances, the government had little alternative but to encourage industrialization, despite the earlier vigorous opposition to it from interests associated with the plantation sector. The removal of some restrictions on establishing plants and the introduction of limited protection against import competition, both enacted in the Crisis Import Ordinance of 1933, were the main spurs to industrial growth in the 1930s. By 1939, according to the colony's first Manufacturing Census, the 'factory sector' employed about 173,000 persons, primarily in the food, textiles, metal goods, and repair industries (Broek, 1942). Although detailed estimates of the ownership composition of manufacturing were not available, anecdotal evidence indicates that foreign firms were dominant.[1]

The structure and sources of foreign investment in the then Netherlands

East Indies resembled those in many other colonies. Data are incomplete, but Callis (1942, p. 36) estimated that the stock of total foreign investment rose from $318 million in 1900 to $2,264 million in 1937. A little over half ($1,411 million) was what Callis termed 'entrepreneur'—direct in modern parlance—investment; portfolio investment made up the remainder. Polak (1942) provides the most complete series of annual estimates of investments, based on his pioneering construction of balance of payments data (see Table 1.1). The estimates suggest that new foreign investments peaked at almost $100 million in 1934, and that there were large inflows in the late 1920s and early 1930s. Such substantial investments during the depression may on first sight appear surprising, but it needs to be remembered that these are gross data and that there were also sizeable outflows over the same period. It is possible that Callis' stock estimate for 1937 is an over-estimate, in view of these outflows.

The Netherlands was the major source of foreign investment,[2] and this investment was concentrated in the 'export enclaves', mainly plantations, extractive industries, and associated activities. Callis (1942, p. 34) esti-mated that, at the outbreak of the Second World War, the Netherlands accounted for 63 per cent of all direct foreign investment, followed by the United Kingdom (14 per cent), 'island Chinese' (11 per cent), and the United States (7 per cent). These figures are very approximate, especially for the Chinese. Moreover, no breakdown is provided for portfolio investment.

Estimates of the industrial composition of foreign investment in Indonesia are available only for Dutch capital (see Table 1.2). Agricultural plantations accounted for almost half (45 per cent) of the total, and petroleum another one-fifth. These and other activities developed to serve Dutch interests in the colonial economy—agricultural banks, transport, and public works—constituted almost 90 per cent of Dutch investments. Although Dutch manufacturing investments were an important component of the newly emerging industrial sector, they accounted for a tiny fraction of the total from that country.

TABLE 1.1

Foreign Investment in the Netherlands East Indies, 1925–1939

Year	$m	Year	$m
1925	33	1933	59
1926	19	1934	99
1927	14	1935	5
1928	42	1936	7
1929	24	1937	14
1930	73	1938	7
1931	41	1939	10
1932	37		

Source: Polak, 1942, pp. 65–65a.

Note: These figures refer to 'new long-term investments'. They are gross data. They have been converted to US dollars at the prevailing guilder–dollar exchange rate.

TABLE 1.2

Composition of Foreign Investment in Colonial India and Indonesia
(percentage of total)

Sector	British Investment in India, 1938	Dutch Investment in Indonesia, 1940
Sugar	⎧	15
Rubber	⎨ 16	17
Other agriculture	⎩	13
Mining	18	19
Transport and public utilities	24	14
Manufacturing	15	2
Agricultural banks	n.a.	10
Managing agencies	16	n.a.
Miscellaneous	12	10

Sources: Tomlinson, 1985, p. 12. The Indonesian data are from Callis (1942).
Note: Refers to stock of foreign investment; mining for Indonesia refers only to petroleum.
n.a. = Not available.

Indeed, it is instructive to compare the pattern of British investments in India with that of Dutch investments in Indonesia during this period (see Table 1.2). The share of manufacturing (mainly in jute and cotton textiles, and engineering) in British investment in India was over seven times the corresponding Dutch share. Moreover, in the case of India, there was a far greater diversification out of the plantation agriculture in response to the depression than occurred in Indonesia. These differences were attributable, in part, to the nature of the respective colonial regimes. The Dutch view of the Netherlands East Indies was more mercantilist, while the 'institutional infrastructure' (including education) was stronger in colonial India.[3]

The First Two Decades of Independence, 1945–1965

The Second World War provided an initial impetus to industrialization, but for most of the 1940s manufacturing output and investment declined. The Japanese occupation devastated the economy, especially the manufacturing sector. Many raw material imports were prohibited, equipment was shipped out, and labour supplies disrupted. Not surprisingly, there was no new foreign investment during this decade. Foreign assets taken over by the Japanese were returned, either in 1945 or after the cessation of hostilities between the Netherlands and Indonesia in 1949. (An estimate of foreign investment of $2.24 billion in 1952 (Oei, 1969, p. 42) broadly confirms the absence of any new investments in the preceding decade and a half.) For the next seventeen years, Indonesia was a large importer of capital and technology, but virtually none came in the form of direct foreign investment.

The government of the newly independent republic accorded a high priority to industrialization. The prevailing 'terms of trade pessimism' after the Korean War commodity boom led many policy-makers to believe that industry was the key to progress. This view was reinforced by nationalist sentiment to the effect that the colonial government had deliberately retarded manufacturing. The first push for industry was manifested in the Economic Urgency Plan (*Rencana Urgensi Perekonomian*, RUP), introduced in 1951. The RUP was essentially a pragmatic programme intended to promote the twin objectives of small industry and *pribumi* (indigenous) entrepreneurship. Direct government intervention in the form of state enterprises was to be minimal, being restricted to a few areas of heavy industry.

The emphasis on domestic—especially *pribumi* and state—ownership was understandable for, as noted, indigenous control over modern industry was very limited. While there were a few large *pribumi* firms in traditional industries like textiles, Paauw's observation regarding ownership patterns at the time of the Dutch withdrawal in 1949 aptly summarized the situation: 'Small-scale handicraft industry was almost completely the domain of the Indonesian, while industrial processing for export was dominated by foreigners. Modern industries producing consumer goods such as textiles for the domestic markets were owned by Europeans and the Chinese minority.' (Paauw, 1963, p. 180.)[4] Despite the sometimes bitter struggle for independence, the RUP was not hostile towards foreign investment. In fact, it formally encouraged it, subject to a 51 per cent Indonesian ownership requirement, and the reservation of certain areas for exclusive domestic ownership.

In the event, no new foreign investment was forthcoming. By the mid-1950s, there was little prospect of Indonesia attracting such investments. For one thing, the results of the RUP were disappointing, and there was little evidence of an emerging *pribumi* business sector.[5] Consequently, in formulating the Five-Year Plan, 1955–60, the government maintained the emphasis on industry, but accorded less priority to the private sector and more to state enterprises. In addition, political attitudes were changing, particularly towards the role of foreign capital. As Weinstein (1976a, p. 211) observed, '. . . the Cabinets that held office in 1953 and thereafter, though still committed to seeking foreign investment, did so with markedly less enthusiasm, especially as they became inclined to blame Indonesia's economic difficulties on foreign control of the economy'.

A foreign investment bill, designed to lay down the government's minimum requirements while encouraging foreign investment in certain areas, was drafted in 1953. It was eventually approved by Cabinet in modified form in 1956, and passed by Parliament in 1958. The Foreign Capital Investment Law, as it was known, established the Foreign Investment Board in the same year. As Paauw (1960, p. 355) noted, the Law was 'neither the most generous nor the most hostile of the many drafts through which the bill went prior to passage by Parliament'. The Law precluded foreign investors from certain areas, including utilities, some mining, and 'enterprises usually undertaken by Indonesian nationals'. Although it did not prohibit majority foreign ownership, it did specify that 'joint operations . . . shall be given priority'. Profit transfers were permitted, although the exchange rate to be used (Indonesia by then had a multiple exchange rate system) was not specified.[6]

While largely moderate in tone, the Law conferred enormous discretionary power in the hands of the implementing authorities, and potential foreign investors were, moreover, deterred by growing political uncertainties. In any event, the Law was repealed by President Sukarno in 1959 (Oei, 1969, p. 36). Any prospect of substantial foreign investment was removed with the nationalization of Dutch enterprises in December 1957.[7] Subsequently, British and Malaysian assets were nationalized in 1963 during the confrontation dispute, and in 1965 some American property was taken over.

After 1957, industry stagnated, along with the rest of the economy, and capital flows came mainly from the socialist bloc in the form of loans. An indication of the sluggish industrial growth is that, over the period from 1953 to 1965, manufacturing growth barely kept pace with that of population, and the sector's share of GDP actually declined marginally.[8] While some new plants were established, mainly with foreign capital, capacity utilization rates were low, and supplies—particularly of imported inputs— were erratic.[9] Indeed, among large and medium firms (defined in Table 2.3 below) output fell continuously from 1961 to 1965, and 1961 production levels were not attained again until 1968 (BPS, 1970).

According to carefully constructed estimates of Indonesia's balance of payments from 1950 to 1965, prepared by Rosendale (1978), cumulative *net* private capital inflows (that is, *to* the private sector) totalled only $450 million. Direct foreign investment from 1956 to 1965 was only $84 million, consisting entirely of investments by foreign oil companies; no other long-term investments were recorded (Rosendale, 1978, p. 81).[10] After 1957, aid and private capital flows from North America and Europe virtually dried up, and socialist countries became the major donors. Rosendale (1978, p. 306) estimates that the latter bloc had contributed about $600 million in economic aid by 1966. The industrial composition of this aid is not known precisely, but she estimates that heavy industry was the largest recipient. Half the total aid came from Russia. It took the form of several large projects, including the beginnings of a steel plant at Cilegon, a super-phosphate factory at Cilacap, and initial work on a hydroelectric scheme and aluminium smelter at Asahan, North Sumatra. None of these projects was completed by the end of 1965. But it is worth noting that the first and third of these projects were rehabilitated and continued during the New Order regime, the first amidst considerable controversy (see Arndt, 1975).

Some of these projects took the form of production sharing agreements, which resembled foreign investment in certain respects (Gibson, 1966, parts I and II). These agreements stipulated that foreign partners would provide the foreign exchange component of a project, for which payment would be guaranteed and financed out of future production. Separate technology and marketing agreements were also included, but in all cases the plants were wholly Indonesian owned, usually by the state.

Foreign capital commitments in this programme (from 1962 to 1965) totalled $72 million, more than half of which was from Japan[11] and

Japanese-financed war reparations to Korea, which the latter country used to finance operations in Indonesia. Timber was to be the major recipient industry, in addition to some agricultural processing activities. The results were disappointing. By the beginning of 1966, capital of only $12 million for eight projects had been supplied. The New Order regime regarded some of these projects—especially those from the socialist bloc—as politically inspired and not adequately assessed, and most were shelved (Sadli, 1972).

Some idea of ownership patterns in Indonesian manufacturing is given in the Industrial Census of 1964. The census data, which actually refer to 1963, need to be interpreted with great caution: political disruption affected data collection in some provinces, and monetary estimates in an era of runaway inflation are very approximate. Nevertheless, the results for large and medium firms do warrant some examination because ownership data were provided (see Table 1.3). The census revealed that much of the large factory sector was in government hands. Although government firms numbered only 561 out of a total of over 27,000, they accounted for almost 40 per cent of installed capacity and 20 per cent of employment. Average installed capacity among these firms was nearly 20 times the figure for manufacturing as a whole, while employment per firm was nine times greater. Since government firms also had privileged access to foreign exchange and other rationed inputs, they undoubtedly contributed a disproportionately large share of output.[12] Thus, by the mid-1960s, the 'commanding heights' of Indonesian industry—what little there was of them—were under state control, although foreign capital and expertise had played quite a significant role.

TABLE 1.3

Employment and Power Capacity of Medium and Large Firms by Ownership, 1963

Ownership	Number of Firms	Employment	Installed Power Capacity (hp)	Employment per Firm	Installed Capacity per Firm (hp)	Installed Capacity per Worker (hp)
State	561	173,595	283,738	309	506	1.6
Cooperative	635	28,203	11,935	44	19	0.4
Private						
Incorporated	4,932	313,507	286,722	64	58	0.9
Other	21,289	390,991	133,125	18	6	0.3
All firms	27,417	906,296	715,520	33	26	0.8

Source: BPS, 1970a.
Note: Prior to 1974 medium and large firms were defined to include firms employing at least five workers with power, and at least ten workers without power. The definition thus differs from that adopted subsequently, of twenty or more workers.

1. Sitsen (1942) provides the most detailed account of industrialization in the colonial era.

2. Schmitt (1962, pp. 284–5), for example, cites estimates that just prior to the Second World War only 19 per cent of non-agricultural capital was owned by indigenous Indonesians, while 52 per cent was held by Dutch interests. Polak (1942) provides further information on the distribution of ownership and output.

3. See Tomlinson (1985) for an interesting comparison of foreign investment in the two countries from 1920 to 1960, and an elaboration of these points.

4. Data from the early 1940s (cited in Sutter, 1959, p. 42), immediately prior to the outbreak of war in South-East Asia, support Paauw's contention. For example, in textiles, one of the major industries, European firms owned almost 40 per cent of the country's mechanized looms. Chinese- and Arab-owned firms accounted for a little less than 54 per cent, while the share for indigenous firms was just 7 per cent. Even in the case of handlooms, indigenous firms owned just 35 per cent of capacity. Sutter's chapters on manufacturing (vol. 1, chap. 2; vol. 3, chap. 19) are most informative.

5. Several frank assessments of the RUP were published by economists at the University of Indonesia. See, for example, Sumitro (1954) and Mulia (1958). These articles are particularly instructive, since many of the problems associated with the RUP surfaced again in the early years of the New Order.

6. For further details, see Paauw (1960, pp. 425–30), who provides an unofficial English language translation of the Law.

7. In 1958, the Dutch government estimated the value of Dutch property expropriated to be $1.2 billion. However, it eventually agreed to a settlement in 1967 of $157 million, to be paid over 30 years (Oei, 1969, p. 41).

8. From 1953 to 1959, real manufacturing output grew at 1.9 per cent annually, while from 1960 to 1965 the rate was 2.1 per cent. The corresponding GDP growth rates were 3.2 and 2.0 per cent respectively (McCawley, 1979, p. 6).

9. Detailed industry studies in the Old Order are rare. One exception is Palmer (1972), which contains much useful information about the textile industry. The study also reveals the unimportance of foreign capital, except in the provision of imported machinery and in the establishment of mills under state control. Castles (1967) also provides some useful information on the *kretek* (clove) cigarette industry over this period.

10. A good deal of this foreign oil investment must have come from America. It is worth noting that the United States Department of Commerce data record American investment in Indonesia as $58 million in 1950, rising to $169 million in 1957, but falling to $106 million in 1966 (United States Department of Commerce, 1984, pp. 50 and 56). The decline after 1957 was due to the expropriations and subsequent withdrawals of some American oil investments, although it is not clear how nationalized investments subject to international dispute were treated in the data.

11. Japanese war reparations were a good deal larger than this total. According to Nishihara (1976, pp. 82–4), these reparations totalled $223 million from 1958/9 to 1969/70. Of this, $74 million went to heavy industry (mainly machinery) and $34 million to light industry, including paper mills, plywood plants, and textiles. It is interesting to note that, despite its wartime occupation of Indonesia, Japan was the only major OECD country to maintain cordial relations with the Old Order government, right up to 1965.

12. The status of foreign firms nationalized in 1963 and 1964 is not clear. But to the extent that there were nationalizations in 1964, after the census data were collected, Table 1.3 understates the importance of the state firms.

2 Industrial Transformation, 1967–1985

> To a striking degree, the Indonesian manufacturing sector is composed of industries processing agricultural goods. In the development of a broad industrial base Indonesia is many years behind India and China. (McCawley, 1979, p. 31.)

IN 1965, Indonesia was at the crossroads. The economy was contracting, inflation was out of control, the political environment was increasingly turbulent and uncertain, and the country was becoming more and more isolated in the international community. The state of manufacturing was symptomatic of the general economic decline. The situation was aptly summarized in the New Order government's First Five-Year Plan (*Repelita*[1] *I*):

> . . . many industrial enterprises were taken over from their original owners, thus causing an exodus of managers and foreign skilled labor. The Government began to interfere increasingly in various economic activities. Industrial enterprises were dependent on Government rationing of foreign exchange to meet their demands for raw materials, spare parts, and equipment. Freedom to make managerial decisions became more restricted. . . . Manpower could not be utilized in accordance with economic criteria and politics dominated industry. (*Repelita I*, 1969, chap. 5, pp. 1–2.)

In fact, Indonesia was then one of the least industrialized of the major developing countries. Its manufacturing sector comprised simple consumer goods industries, such as textiles (mainly employing non-mechanized technology), a few agricultural processing activities, such as rice milling and rubber smoking, and a miniscule capital goods sector, consisting primarily of nationalized Dutch factories and a few plants established by socialist bloc countries. Although it was the fourth largest developing country (third largest after the separation of Pakistan), its manufacturing output was less than that of many smaller countries, including Hong Kong, Chile, the Philippines, and Thailand.

Industrial development after 1966 is in marked contrast to that of the previous two decades. The New Order government of President Soeharto, generally dated from March 1966, reversed the political and economic priorities of the previous regime. The two decades 1966–85 witnessed the first period of sustained and rapid industrialization in Indonesia's history. The adoption of orthodox macro-economic policies, the restoration of political stability, large resource inflows—initially in the form of aid and later from the oil boom, and the influx of modern technologies all contributed to an era of extraordinarily fast industrial progress.

The purpose of this chapter is to provide an overview of this industrial transformation,[2] as a prelude to a more detailed examination of the specific role of foreign investment. After a brief review of Indonesia's industrialization in comparative perspective, there is an examination of the policy context, in particular the government's industrial objectives. The next two sections investigate the course of industrialization, focusing on the growth of production and the changing structure of industry. Finally, there is a review of the level of and trends in ownership within the manufacturing sector. This last section is of some importance because it places the role of foreign investors in wider perspective, alongside that of the other two major actors, domestic (private) firms and state enterprises. The latter are particularly significant. Despite the new government's political reorientation, state enterprises dominate much of Indonesia's modern manufacturing, and their role has probably become even more pronounced since the 1973 oil boom. Any discussion of Indonesia's rapid industrialization after 1966, and the contribution to it of foreign investment, is incomplete without reference to the state-owned sector.

Indonesian Industrialization in Comparative Perspective

By the early 1980s, Indonesia had emerged as a significant industrial nation among developing countries, for the first time in its history. From 1970 to 1984, real industrial output more than quadrupled. Its industrial sector in 1984 was still much smaller than that in countries such as Brazil, Korea, and India, but it was perhaps the tenth largest among developing countries.[3]

How does Indonesian industry compare with that of other countries, particularly its neighbours? Its structure differs significantly, since the modern factory sector is dominated by one industry—petroleum refining—which is exclusively state owned. In terms of broad indicators, also, there are important differences (see Table 2.1). The first is Indonesia's extraordinarily rapid growth, until recently. Over the period 1965–73, manufacturing in Indonesia grew quite quickly, albeit from a very small base. But its performance was not exceptional—in fact, it was similar to the World Bank's category of 'lower-middle income economies'—because this period includes the years of stagnation and stabilization, 1965–8. A much sharper contrast emerges in the following eleven years, 1973–84. These were the years of 'hyper-growth', in which Indonesian manufacturing grew faster than that of Korea and Singapore (almost double the latter's rate), and well over twice as fast as that of India and the Philippines, and the lower-middle income group as a whole.

Indonesia now has the largest manufacturing industry in ASEAN, contributing about 30 per cent of the region's output. But in spite of the rapid growth, it still remains the least industrialized of the five countries, apart from the special case of ASEAN's latest entrant, Brunei. In many respects,

TABLE 2.1

Comparative Indicators of Industrialization in Indonesia and Selected Asian Developing Countries

Region/Country	GNP per Capita, 1984 ($)	Manufacturing Growth, Annual Average Percentage		Manufacturing Output, 1984, as Percentage of		Manufacturing Output		Manufactures, 1983, as Percentage of Merchandise		Manufactured Exports, per Capita, 1984 ($)
		1965–1973	1973–1984	GDP	Agriculture	1984 ($m)	1984 Per Capita ($)	Exports	Imports	
Indonesia	540	9.0	14.9	13	50	11,155	70	8	63	11
Other ASEAN										
Malaysia	1,980	n.a.	8.7	19	90	5,756	376	22	72	236
Philippines	660	8.5	4.3	25	100	8,811	165	50	60	50
Singapore	7,260	19.5	7.6	25	2,500	3,994	1,597	57	56	5,485
Thailand	860	11.4	10.0	19	83	8,170	163	32	64	47
Other Asian										
India	260	4.0	5.9	15	43	29,219	39	52	49	7
Korea	2,110	21.1	11.5	28	200	23,691	591	91	51	664
Lower middle income countries	740	8.5	5.9	17	77	n.a.	n.a.	21	63	n.a.

Source: World Bank (annual).

Note: Some data refer to a year earlier than that mentioned. Per capita manufactured exports were derived from 1984 total exports and population, and 1983 shares of manufactures in total exports. n.a. = Not available.

Indonesia's industry is more akin to that of India than to the more outward looking economies of South-East and North-East Asia. The share of manufacturing in GDP is one of the lowest in the region—below that of India and the lower-middle income group. In 1984, per capita manufacturing value added (MVA) was just $70, or less than one-fifth the figure for Malaysia, and less than one-half that for the Philippines and Thailand. Correspondingly, manufacturing output was only half agricultural production, whereas in most neighbouring countries it was greater than, or nearly equal to, the latter sector.

Another distinguishing feature of Indonesia is that its manufacturing exports are still very small. Despite the first signs of significant growth in recent years, manufactures constituted just 8 per cent of merchandise exports in 1983. This is one of the lowest shares in the region, and Indonesia remains, relatively, one of the largest net importers of manufactures. Such a low share is not altogether surprising in view of the country's large oil and gas exports. These exports have compressed both the shares and the absolute values of non-oil exports, the latter through the well-known 'Dutch disease' effects (on which see Corden, 1984). Nevertheless, even on a per capita basis, Indonesia's manufactured exports remain remarkably low.

Industrial Policies and Objectives: The Five-Year Plans

Before looking at the pattern of Indonesia's industrialization since 1966 in a little more detail, it is useful to review the government's industrial objectives. The successive five-year plans, beginning in 1969/70, have become an important feature of the New Order. These plans, it is true, have been largely indicative in nature, concerned primarily with broad targets and policy emphases. But they do illustrate the thinking of the government, and they certainly contain a good deal more economic content than the plans before 1966.

While the plans are only very general expressions of intent, it is possible to detect both continuities and shifts in emphasis in the four issued to date.[4] For example, all four emphasize the importance of industries which 'earn or save foreign exchange', an objective which presumably refers to all activities except those with negative value added at international prices. The promotion of labour-intensive and small-scale industry also figures prominently, as does the goal of regional dispersal.

A closer look at the plans also indicates a shift in the government's underlying objectives. *Repelita I* (1969/70–1973/4), for example, stressed little more than those industries which supported the agricultural sector through forward and backward linkages. In *Repelita II* (1974/5–1978/9), the emphasis shifted to greater support for *pribumi* enterprise and 'weak economic groups' (*golongan ekonomi lemah*), plus a wider range of consumer goods. The next two plans, *Repelita III* (1979/80–1983/4) and *Repelita IV* (1984/5–1988/9), extended the goals of industrial diversification and backward integration, buoyed by expected large oil revenues. 'Linkages' became the key concept, in the last plan especially: 'The development of basic industries, which produce industrial materials, consumer goods, and capital goods, will strengthen forward and backward linkages, as well as linking up basic, miscellaneous, and small industry' (*Repelita IV*, 1984, chap. 11, p. 14; author's translation). As part of the government's push for a larger capital goods industry, *Repelita IV* listed the major priority areas in considerable detail. These included:

a. Machinery and factory equipment, for sugar, rubber, tea, and wood processing.
b. Metal-working equipment.
c. Agricultural equipment.
d. Machinery to produce industrial components.
e. Electrical machinery.
f. Machinery to produce electronic components.
g. Motor vehicles.
h. Railroad equipment and trains.
i. Aircraft.
j. Ships and boats.
k. Steel and structural metal products.
l. Aluminium and aluminium goods.

(*Repelita IV*, 1984, chap. 11, pp. 19–20; author's translation.)

What is to be made of these plans? Are they 'back of the envelope' exercises, written for domestic political (and international) consumption, and consisting of little more than rhetoric? Or are they firm and coherent expressions of intent? The reality falls somewhere in between. The *Repelita* are not comprehensive and consistent macro-economic plans. Some of their objectives are vague and all-embracing. And where others may con-flict—for example, the goals of labour-intensive and heavy industry—there is little indication of priorities. Nevertheless, the plans are a useful indicator of the government's industrial policy objectives, and plan contents have certainly become more specific over time. *Repelita II*, for example, published shortly after the political disturbances of January 1974 and reflecting increased concern with equity objectives, did place more emphasis on *pribumi* enterprise, small-scale industry and employment, and regional development. And the current plan (*Repelita IV*) articulates very clearly the goal of developing a large machinery and equipment industry, together with greater processing of d6mestic resources. Thus the plans do chart the government's overall policy goals, albeit only in a general fashion.

Ownership receives little attention in all four *Repelita*, with a few exceptions. The most important exception, already alluded to, is the *pribumi* sector. But even here, the specific measures to be adopted are not discussed in detail, and ownership targets are not specified. State enter-prises are not discussed in any depth, perhaps surprisingly in view of their importance. Where they are mentioned, it is often in fulfilling a residual role if the desired investments are not forthcoming from the private sector.[5] Foreign investment is rarely mentioned in the context of industrial planning.

Rapid Industrial Growth and Structural Change

It will be useful to examine the record of industrial growth and transformation since 1966 in a little more detail. The range and quality of Indonesian
industrial statistics have improved enormously over this period, and
especially after 1974. Although some shortcomings remain (see Appendix),
it is possible to provide a fairly coherent picture of Indonesian industrial
development since the early 1970s.

Industry did not respond immediately to the change in regime in 1966,
because of erratic foreign exchange supplies, continuing political uncertainty, and a severe credit squeeze. The era of extremely rapid growth
began effectively in 1968, when manufacturing output grew by almost 9
per cent (see Figure 2.1). Thereafter, in almost every year to 1981, manufacturing grew by over 10 per cent, with the result that in the decade
1971–81 real output almost quadrupled. Consequently, although GDP also

FIGURE 2.1

The Growth of Manufacturing and GDP, 1966–1984

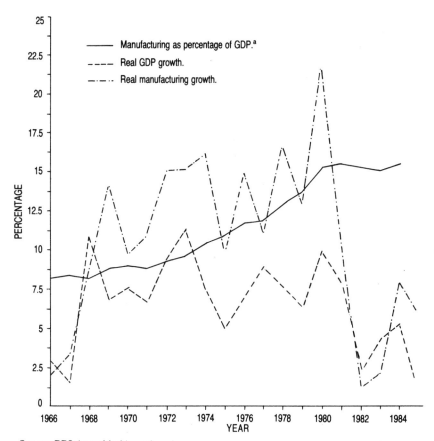

Source: BPS (monthly b), various issues.

[a] Constant 1960 prices, 1966–70; and constant 1973 prices, 1971–84.

grew rapidly, the share of manufacturing in GDP almost doubled from 1966 to 1984.[6] The abrupt about-turn in manufacturing was due primarily to general improvements in the economic climate rather than to industry-specific factors. Government spending began to stimulate domestic demand, the restoration of political stability and control of inflation increased investor confidence, and property expropriated (from foreigners and Chinese) before 1965 was returned to previous owners. To stimulate foreign confidence and investment, the Foreign Investment Law (No. 1, 1967) was enacted, followed by the Domestic Investment Law in 1968.

The oil boom proved a major bonanza for manufacturing. Two of the highest growth rates for manufacturing were registered in 1974 and 1980, that is, in the years following large oil price increases. Clearly the resulting squeeze on tradable goods industries, such as manufacturing, was more than compensated for by large 'expenditure recycling' effects of the central government, and by restrictive trade policies which, in effect, converted some manufacturing into 'non-tradable' sectors.

After 1981, there was a sharp deceleration in Indonesian industrial growth, to between 1 and 2 per cent in 1982 and 1983. The downturn illustrated the heavy dependence of manufacturing on domestic demand growth.[7] In the wake of declining real oil prices, the government postponed a number of large industrial projects, and introduced tight fiscal and monetary policies, greatly reducing economic growth. These cutbacks also coincided with the completion of much of the 'easy phase' of import substitution. In sum, domestic demand declined, the oil revenues which were to have financed the second round of import substitution fell, and there was no established export base. The combined effects of these three factors resulted in sluggish industrial growth. Manufacturing picked up in 1984, but it reflected the once-and-for-all impact of greatly expanded oil refining capacity coming on stream.

The index of manufacturing production, published from 1975, broadly corroborates these trends, and indicates the areas of rapid growth (see Table 2.2). For example, most of the growth after 1975 has been in intermediate and capital goods production. The index for all groups rose to 259 per cent by 1985 but, with the conspicuous exception of *kretek* cigarettes, production of consumer goods has grown slowly, and actually *declined* after 1981. The record for capital goods industries is also patchy. They expanded rapidly until the early 1980s, but thereafter production of appliances and motor vehicles has also declined. Both demand and supply effects explain this trend. Slower economic growth resulted in the deferred purchase of luxury goods—such as these—and the devaluation of the rupiah in 1983 and 1986 translated into large and immediate price increases in local currency terms, because these industries are still highly import intensive. 'Mandatory deletion programmes', as policies to enforce local sourcing of components are termed, also contributed to slower growth in that they increased costs.

Indonesia's really rapid industrial growth has occurred in intermediate goods. Some of these industries have recorded extremely high growth rates, in many cases because of the effects of government policies. For

TABLE 2.2

Index of Manufacturing Production in Selected Industry Groups, 1975–1985 (1975 = 100)

	Number of Establishments[a]	1976	1977	1978	1979	1980	1981	1982	1983	1984	1985
Consumer Goods											
White cigarettes	13	104	105	116	131	130	124	115	120	117	97
Clove cigarettes	20	104	125	122	120	151	180	186	196	225	251
Yarn	20	109	101	112	111	118	126	121	114	124	111
Weaving	193	108	109	112	122	126	138	130	121	125	127
Intermediate Goods											
Plywood	6	118	197	218	220	392	471	424	438	418	387
Paper	8	98	107	134	151	153	152	148	129	164	182
Basic chemicals	13	97	97	87	124	128	127	130	132	147	149
Fertilizer	3	83	161	192	336	466	492	496	560	706	850
Tyres and tubes	12	137	168	203	227	257	301	294	300	300	311
Glass	17	94	139	160	171	208	257	259	227	247	250
Cement	7	125	178	255	314	367	391	419	566	616	686
Iron and steel	15	137	141	180	443	1,034	1,247	970	1,147	1,165	1,158
Capital Goods											
Structural metal products	24	109	133	154	158	172	188	196	203	198	214
Electrical appliances	16	125	180	232	230	340	349	333	351	279	243
Motor vehicles	17	108	122	136	117	194	248	226	198	179	183
Motor cycles	5	89	76	89	75	114	164	187	130	92	100
All Groups		109	126	146	158	194	213	213	226	240	259

Source: BPS (monthly, b).
[a] As at 1986.

15

example, plywood expanded quickly until recently because of the government policy of enforced export substitution, through the ban on log exports. Fertilizer production, dominated by state enterprises, rose ninefold from the mid-1970s, as the government recycled oil revenues into an ambitious programme of capacity expansion. Cement and iron and steel, in which state enterprises also play a prominent role, have grown extremely fast.

The pattern of industrial policies since 1966 has therefore reflected the government's changing priorities. In the first decade or so of the New Order, rapid economic growth and extensive (largely indiscriminate) protection were the under-pinnings of industrial expansion. During the second decade, industry-specific intervention—through regulations and ownership—has become a good deal more important.

These changes are reflected in the changing composition of industrial output from 1972 to 1984. Light industry, much of it food processing and textiles, dominated Indonesian industry in the early 1970s, accounting for about four-fifths of industrial production (see Figure 2.2). By 1984, its share had fallen appreciably, although it still accounted for more than half the total. Correspondingly, the share of heavy industry rose substantially, to over 40 per cent. It is useful to divide the latter into the more capital— and often scale—intensive processing activities, such as paper, cement,

FIGURE 2.2

The Changing Composition of Industrial Output, 1972–1985

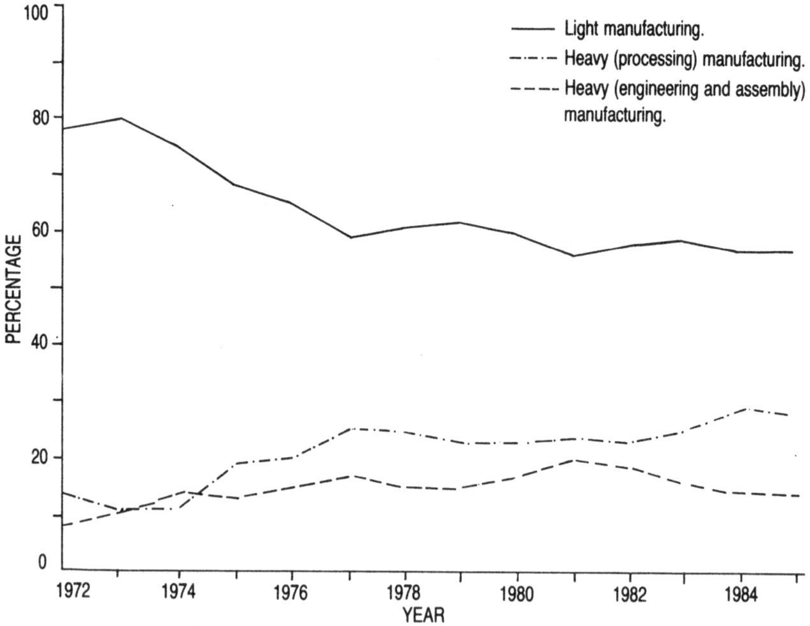

Source: BPS, Statistik Industri, various issues.
Note: The following classification of industries is adopted (for description of industries see Table 2.6):
Light industry: ISIC 31, 32, 33, 342, 355, 356, 39.
Heavy (processing) industry: ISIC 341, 351, 352, 36, 37.
Heavy (engineering & assembly) industry: ISIC 38.

chemicals, and iron and steel, and engineering and assembly activities. While the share of the latter has approximately doubled over the period, the largest absolute increase has occurred in the processing industries, as discussed above. Of course, the share and rate of increase in the latter groups would be much larger still if petroleum refining were included in the data.

By almost any other indicator, structural change in Indonesian industry has been extremely rapid. The magnitude of these changes does not need to be elaborated here in any detail.[8] But it might be useful to summarize a few key indicators. First, many new products were produced domestically for the first time, and the quality of existing products improved substantially. Secondly, there was a consolidation towards larger industrial units, as indicated by the average size of firms in the factory sector. Thirdly, labour productivity grew significantly, particularly in the case of traditional industries, such as textiles and food processing (see McCawley, 1984). In some activities, including rice milling and weaving, a virtual technological revolution occurred, as new mechanized equipment replaced existing manual production methods.[9] Fourthly, the structure of manufacturing output in Indonesia, as indicated by an index of structural change for the 3-digit industry groups, changed most rapidly in ASEAN between 1971 and 1980, and even exceeded that of Korea.

Only in the case of manufactured exports were the changes less evident, until very recently. As noted above, Indonesia's exports of manufactures are very small by regional standards. In 1975, they totalled just $85 million (see Table 2.3). This figure rose to $500 million in 1980, stimulated in part by the November 1978 devaluation, but they still accounted for just 2 per cent of the country's merchandise exports. The 1980s have witnessed the first major outward push, such that by 1985 these goods were 10 per cent of the total. The increased share is partly attributable to declining oil export prices, but the value of manufactured exports also rose sharply, by almost fourfold in nominal terms from 1980 to 1985. These exports remain highly concentrated—plywood contributes one-half, and the next three largest items another 30 per cent. Nevertheless, the increase is indicative of a more outward-looking manufacturing sector, and the principal items do accord with Indonesia's comparative advantage in resource-based and labour-intensive industries.

An Overview of Ownership Patterns

Little has been said in this chapter concerning ownership. The following chapters will concentrate mainly on foreign investment, but it needs to be emphasized that state enterprises, along with (domestic) private firms, are very significant. The New Order regime quickly discarded much of the political symbolism and rhetoric of the Sukarno regime, including a commitment to socialism, and returned to their previous owners many enterprises nationalized before 1966. But nationalist sentiment has remained very powerful. One manifestation of this sentiment has been continuing state ownership in certain designated 'key' industries.

TABLE 2.3

Manufactured Exports, 1970–1985 ($'000, or percentage)

	1970	1975	1980	1981	1982	1983	1984	1985
Manufactured exports[a]	12,153	85,348	500,637	672,339	808,391	1,372,697	1,839,257	1,833,744
Percentage of total merchandise exports	1	1	2	3	4	7	8	10
Major items								
Plywood (631)	0	360	68,490	194,660	316,442	737,671	791,395	941,276
Clothing (841)	0	2,432	98,274	95,257	116,938	157,159	295,743	339,079
Electronics[b]	0	4,736	94,015	73,794	116,854	116,781	135,828	73,084
Textiles (652–653)	1,482	464	30,116	27,393	32,837	88,603	145,381	154,271
Percentage of major items in manufactured exports	12	9	58	58	72	80	74	82

Sources: International Economic Data Bank, Australian National University; and BPS (monthly, a), various issues.

[a] Refers to SITC 5–8 less SITC 68. Figures in parentheses after each major item refer to SITC code.
[b] Up to 1982, SITC 729; after 1982, SITC 776 and 778.

Although ownership has been a contentious issue in Indonesia since 1966, popular debate has had little empirical basis. One reason has been, simply, the paucity of ownership statistics. The 1974/5 Industrial Census provided the first detailed information on ownership since the late colonial era (for an analysis see McCawley, 1981). Useful as these data are, they provide a snapshot picture of manufacturing, after only five years of rapid growth during the New Order, and before the government's push for heavy industry. Unpublished tabulations from the *Statistik Industri* (SI) series obtained recently provide a more complete picture. The SI data report employment and value added for each 5-digit industry group, and for seven ownership categories: government, private, foreign, the three joint venture 'pairs', and firms in which all three have equity. The data have been obtained for two years, 1975 and 1983.

In both years, privately owned domestic firms were by far the largest group, accounting for over half of value added and about three-quarters of employment (see Table 2.4). If the joint venture shares are allocated equally between partners, private firms are even more dominant, their share of value added rising from 57 to 68 per cent over the period 1975–83. By contrast, output and employment shares of both foreign and government firms have declined, the latter substantially.

Does this mean that most of Indonesian manufacturing is effectively in the hands of private domestic firms? In some industries this is undoubtedly the case, but the conclusion that these firms dominate industry must be qualified, in at least three respects. First, the assumption that the large private–foreign group (21 per cent of value added in 1983) is a 'partnership of equals' is erroneous, as we shall see later. Secondly, several large and predominantly state-owned industries are excluded from the SI series. One of these is oil refining, which alone accounts for over 15 per cent of manufacturing output. Inclusion of this and other industries would almost double the share of state enterprises.[10] Thirdly, many of the larger private firms are so inextricably linked to the state apparatus that they hardly qualify for the label 'private' in the usual sense of the term. These links refer not only to dependence on bureaucratic largess and patronage, but also to the so-called *cukong*, arrangements involving close ties between Chinese business interests and senior armed forces officials.

There are important differences between ownership groups in terms of relative size (see Table 2.5). Private firms are by far the smallest, whether in terms of value added and employment per firm, or value added per worker. In 1983, for example, each state enterprise generated on average six times as much MVA as each private firm, and employed four times as many workers. Foreign firms were larger also, by a similar margin. The differentials for joint ventures containing a foreign partner, in terms of value added per firm, were generally greater still. On the other hand, the size differential between private and other firms has narrowed over time: in 1975, MVA per firm for industry as a whole was 80 per cent higher than that for private firms; by 1983, it had declined to 60 per cent. But it is still the case that much of the large-scale manufacturing in the factory sector is state or foreign controlled.

TABLE 2.4

Output and Employment Shares by Major Ownership Groups, 1975 and 1983

	Government	Private	Foreign	Government/ Private	Government/ Foreign	Private/ Foreign	Government/ Private/ Foreign	All Firms
1983								
Value added	14.4	56.9	1.5	1.0	4.2	21.1	0.9	100
Employment	13.0	74.0	1.1	1.1	1.1	9.4	0.3	100
1975								
Value added	25.0	50.8	10.2	1.1	2.1	10.5	0.4	100
Employment	15.8	74.5	2.0	1.2	0.7	5.5	0.2	100

Source: Unpublished BPS data, based on the *Statistik Industri* series.

TABLE 2.5

Indicators of Relative Size by Major Ownership Groups, 1983

	Total	Government	Private	Foreign	Government/ Private	Government/ Foreign	Private/ Foreign	Government/ Private/ Foreign
Number of firms (percentage of total)	100	3.7	91.3	0.4	0.8	0.2	3.4	0.1
Value added/firm								
Rp million	497	1,915	310	2,046	582	8,408	3,047	7,207
Index, private = 100	160	618	100	660	188	2,710	983	2,325
Employment/firm	140	486	113	413	180	590	383	620
Index, private = 100	124	430	100	365	159	522	339	549
Value added/worker								
Rp '000	3,565	3,943	2,740	4,948	3,236	14,254	7,957	11,625
Index, private = 100	130	144	100	181	118	520	290	424

Source: As for Table 2.4.

Finally, what of the pattern of ownership among manufacturing industries? Presenting the SI data at the 5-digit level for all seven ownership groups and two years generates a huge number of observations. To simplify the analysis, the joint venture groups could be collapsed into single ownership groups by apportioning shares equally (that is, half the 'foreign/private' groups go to 'foreign' and the other half to 'private', and so on). Such an approach would be somewhat misleading, however. Many case studies— as documented in later chapters—suggest strongly that local partners play a subordinate role in joint ventures, even when they (the local partners) own more than half the equity capital. The large increase in the foreign/ private share between 1975 and 1983, and the corresponding decline for foreign firms (see Table 2.4), simply reflects the fact that wholly foreign-owned investments were not permitted after 1974, and there was considerable pressure on existing foreign firms to divest part of their equity.

A more satisfactory summary is one which combines foreign/private and the now very small pure foreign group into one category, termed 'foreign' in Table 2.6. This classification may result in some understatement of the relative importance of the domestic private business group. Nevertheless, it needs to be remembered that the role of foreign firms is also understated, because they are quite crucial in several industries closed to new foreign investments, but in which there are extensive licensing arrangements. (Motor vehicles and motor cycles are two of the most important examples.) For the purposes of simplification, also, the small government/private group is assigned to 'government' firms, reflecting the realities of control in most such cases. Finally, a separate category is maintained for government firms in partnership with foreign firms, together with the joint ventures between all three groups. These firms appear to be distinctive enough, in terms of management control and operations, to warrant their own category. Ownership shares for all four groups are presented in Table 2.6.

It is clearly quite misleading to assert that foreign investors dominate Indonesian manufacturing. We will examine their role in detail in Chapter 5, but here it will be useful to draw attention to the significant position of private and government firms.

Private firms dominate much of manufacturing. Their share of output has been increasing over time, and in sixteen of the 28 main industry groups they contributed over half of value added by 1983; in a further two cases they were the largest single group. Moreover, their dominance is not confined to small and slow-growing industries. They have complete control of the largest industry (at the 5-digit ISIC level), *kretek* cigarettes, and they are by far the most important in the fastest growing industry, plywood. In a range of other significant industries—most food products, textiles, garments, rubber products, and most non-metallic minerals industries— they are the dominant actors. As would be expected, their contribution is more substantial in consumer goods and labour-intensive industries.

Government firms play a more significant role in Indonesia than in any other developing market economy of East and South-East Asia. As noted, the importance of these firms is greatly understated by the omission of the huge, state-owned petroleum refining industry. It is also thought that

TABLE 2.6

Ownership Shares by Industry, 1975 and 1983 (percentage of each industry's value added)

	Industry	1975				1983			
		Government	Private	Foreign	Government–Joint Ventures	Government	Private	Foreign	Government–Joint Ventures
311	Food	64	28	8	0	48	36	16	0
312	Manufacturing	8	71	10	11	7	69	24	0
313	Beverages	n	63	7	30	n	18	51	31
314	Tobacco	1	69	30	1	n	90	10	n
321	Textiles	14	66	18	2	9	63	27	1
322	Garments	n	100	n	0	n	97	3	0
323	Leather	7	91	2	0	29	71	0	0
324	Footwear	0	15	85	0	7	18	76	0
331	Wood products	6	69	26	0	3	77	19	n
332	Furniture	6	91	2	0	1	87	12	0
341	Paper products	37	38	25	0	26	51	24	0
342	Printing and publishing	37	52	5	7	14	75	2	10
351	Industrial chemicals	93	5	2	1	72	8	18	3
352	Other chemicals	4	45	50	1	3	34	61	2
355	Rubber products	34	15	51	0	5	74	22	0
356	Plastic products	n	86	14	0	0	71	29	0
361	Pottery	23	7	71	0	3	50	47	0
362	Glass	22	44	35	0	4	26	70	0

(continued)

TABLE 2.6 (continued)

Industry	1975				1983			
	Government	Private	Foreign	Government–Joint Ventures	Government	Private	Foreign	Government–Joint Ventures
363 Cement	74	14	9	3	49	22	11	19
364 Structural clay products	3	97	1	0	8	92	0	0
369 Other non-metallic minerals	19	81	0	0	12	88	0	0
371 Basic metals	1	83	16	0	36	9	8	47
381 Fabricated metals	15	42	38	6	7	45	37	10
382 Machinery (excluding electrical)	57	26	10	8	23	34	32	11
383 Electrical machinery	6	51	35	8	3	40	54	4
384 Transport equipment	15	83	2	0	12	66	23	0
385 Professional and scientific equipment	0	100	0	0	0	100	0	0
390 Other	50	48	2	0	1	41	58	0
Total	26	51	21	2	15	57	23	5

Source: As for Table 2.4.
Notes: 'Government' includes government–domestic joint ventures; 'Foreign' includes foreign–domestic joint ventures; 'Government–Joint Ventures' includes government–foreign and government–foreign–private joint ventures. Numbers do not always add to 100 owing to rounding. n = Negligible (less than 1 per cent).

some other state enterprises have not been enumerated in the *Statistik Industri* series, at least until recently.

The contribution of state enterprises has been shaped by two broad sets of factors. The first, and by far the more important, is government-determined investment priorities in the New Order, especially following the huge growth in oil revenues in the 1970s. In successive *Repelita*, the government accorded high priority to certain strategic industries, which were regarded as essential to the development of a modern industrial sector. According industries such a status provided the rationale for direct state investment. It also had the effect of deterring the entry of private investors, other than through joint ventures with the state.

The number of industries in which state enterprises figure prominently is small, but in most cases they are important industries. One such example is the huge fertilizer industry, which has been regarded as a strategic input into the rice self-sufficiency programme. In 1983, the huge PUSRI conglomerate and other state firms accounted for 99.6 per cent of output. Subsequently, their share must have declined somewhat following the establishment of the Aceh plant—Indonesia's contribution to the ASEAN Industrial Joint Ventures—but in any case the government has a 60 per cent equity stake in this plant. The cement industry has also been considered particularly important during the building boom which characterized much of the New Order. In 1983, government firms contributed 55 per cent of output and, in joint ventures with foreign firms, a further 21 per cent. The government's share must now be considerably higher, following the bail-out by the state banks of the large Indocement conglomerate in 1985. A third industry in which the government is the major actor is basic metals. The government's share of this industry rose rapidly after 1975 because of two major investments: the rehabilitation of PT Krakatau Steel, in West Java, and related plans for further developments jointly with (domestic) private and foreign interests; and the huge Asahan hydroelectric and alumina plant in North Sumatra, in association with a Japanese consortium.

State enterprises therefore dominate much of Indonesia's processing industries, providing inputs to end-use consumer industries. For this reason, Thee and Yoshihara (1987) accurately characterize the division of ownership as being one of 'upstream socialism, downstream capitalism'.

The second factor shaping the industrial composition of state enterprises is history. The most important example is sugar refining, in which government firms produced 86 per cent of the output in 1983. The government acquired sugar plantations and their mills when the Dutch estates were nationalized in the late 1950s. These mills have remained in government hands during the industry's growth and modernization since 1970. Government firms also remain quite significant in some machine and metal goods industries, especially non-electrical machinery. But their role has diminished considerably since 1975 (their share of ISIC 382 declining by more than one-half), as new private and foreign firms have provided most of the growth. A final group of significant state enterprises is that under the control of the Minister for Research and Technology,

Dr Habibie. These firms include the well-known aircraft manufacturer, PT Nusantara, as well as ship-building, ammunitions, and electronics plants. (It is, however, thought that these firms have been under-enumerated in the industrial statistics.)

Conclusion

A number of themes emerge from this analysis of Indonesian industrialization since 1966. The first and most important is extremely rapid growth and structural change, until the slow-down in the early 1980s. The second is a strong government predisposition towards intervention, both indirectly through regulation and directly through ownership. A third theme is that, despite the record of growth, Indonesia is still the least industrialized of the developing market economies of North-East and South-East Asia; the standard 'industrialization indicators', in the Chenery patterns-of-growth sense, are still below expected figures. Finally, private firms feature prominently in manufacturing, but state and foreign firms are more significant in their control over the 'commanding heights' of Indonesian industry. Each of these points is important as we focus specifically on the role of foreign investment in the following chapters.

1. *Repelita* is the acronym for *Rencana Pembangunan Lima Tahun* (Five-Year Development Plan).

2. Despite the size of the country and the pace of industrial progress, surprisingly little attention has been paid to Indonesian industry. The major exceptions are McCawley (1981, based on a more detailed exposition in 1979) and Donges *et al.* (1974). Some of the material in this chapter is based on the author's own work in progress (Hill, forthcoming). The section on manufacturing in each 'Survey of Recent Developments' of the *Bulletin of Indonesian Economic Studies*, published since June 1965, contains useful information.

3. It is worth noting that national accounts data measure the contribution of manufacturing at domestic prices. In Indonesia, as in most developing countries, the share of manufacturing is overstated because this sector receives above average protection. (Indeed, as shown below, a number of industries contribute *negative* value added if measured at international prices.) Manufacturing protection in Indonesia is probably relatively greater than that of other developing countries with large manufacturing sectors, but the difference is unlikely to have an appreciable effect on the country rankings.

4. The following is a very brief summary of the industry chapters in each plan. This chapter, especially in the last three plans, contains a quite detailed review of developments in the previous plan period, together with broad production targets and policy discussion for the next plan period.

5. The following statement, in *Repelita I*, is indicative: 'An investment plan will be worked out to make possible increased production in the respective industries. . . . If, after a certain period of time, no private capital is invested in a vital branch of industry, the Government will decide to make its own investment.' (*Repelita I*, 1969, chap. 5, p. 9.)

6. In current prices, of course, the increased share of manufacturing was a good deal less, because of the huge price effects of the petroleum sector. This factor also accounts for the difference in shares between Table 2.1 and Figure 2.1. Note that the data for the years 1971–84 in Figure 2.1 refer to 1973 constant prices. In August 1985, new estimates were released using 1983 prices, based on the results of the 1980 Input–Output Table. In the new data, current price estimates of manufacturing output have been revised downwards somewhat (Dick, 1985).

7. Poot (1981, p. 81) attempted a statistical decomposition of the sources of industrial growth for 1971–5 for major industry groups. As expected, domestic demand contributed at least two-thirds of the growth in practically all industries, while in all cases the contribution of exports was less than 10 per cent. The effects of import substitution were large (greater than 50 per cent) only in paper, fertilizer and machinery.

8. See Ariff and Hill (1985, chap. 5) for further discussion and comparisons with the other ASEAN countries.

9. These two industries are important because they were both large employers of labour and technological changes were particularly sudden. See Timmer (1973) and Hill (1983) for case studies. Elsewhere the changes were perhaps equally rapid, but less well documented.

10. Including these omitted industries together with small and cottage industry, the author has elsewhere estimated that the effective share of state enterprises in 1983 rises from 17 per cent of value added (Table 2.6) to 29 per cent (see Hill, 1987).

3 Foreign Investment after 1966: The New Regime

> When we started out attracting foreign investment in 1967 everything and everyone was welcome. We did not dare to refuse; we did not even dare to ask for bonafidity of credentials. We needed a list of names and dollar figures of intended investments, to give credence to our drive. The first mining company virtually wrote its own ticket. Since we had no conception about a mining contract we accepted the draft written by the company as a basis for negotiation and only common sense and the desire to bag the first contract were our guidelines. (Sadli, quoted in Palmer, 1978, p. 100.)

THE early years of the New Order government witnessed a remarkable change in policy towards foreign investment. After a decade of nationalization and increased hostility towards foreign investors, especially from the West, one of the first decisions of the new government was to introduce the Foreign Investment Law No. 1/1967. Anxious to restore the country's credibility abroad—and to attract foreign capital—the government's new Law was an invitation to foreign investors with minimal conditions attached. Indeed, the new regulations were far more liberal than those in the aborted Law of 1958. In addition, the new government signed Investment Guarantee Treaties with the United States and several European countries (including the Netherlands) at about the same time, and provided other facilitating guarantees (see Oei, 1969, p. 38).

The statement by Professor Sadli, a senior official and Minister for much of the New Order period, is indicative of the government's initial approach. With little room to manoeuvre, and even less bureaucratic experience in regulating foreign investment, the new posture was very much an open-door policy.[1] The new very liberal era lasted about five years. Beginning in the early 1970s, the government began to adopt a more restrictive approach, as the economy recovered and as nationalist sentiment reasserted itself. For much of the New Order period, foreign investment has been tolerated rather than actively encouraged. It is therefore not without coincidence that the most liberal policies toward the entry of foreign firms have been introduced in the late 1960s and mid-1980s, when the economic situation was the most difficult.

The purpose of this chapter is to provide an overview of foreign investment since 1966, as a prelude to a more detailed examination of manufacturing in following chapters. Several issues warrant attention in this overview. The first is the government's policy towards foreign investment, including the specific measures adopted in the more regulated environment after 1970. An assessment of these measures is important in order to understand trends in foreign investment and the response of foreign firms. Apart from anything else, there has not been a review of the course of foreign investment policies since 1966 to the author's knowledge, with the partial exception of Sumantoro (1984). Secondly, there is an examination of foreign investment flows in total, and a comparison of these flows with other aggregate indicators, such as total capital imports and gross domestic investment. Thirdly, it is useful to compare foreign investment and domestic investment, at least that which occurs under the auspices of the BKPM. The relative importance of the two magnitudes is a contentious issue in Indonesia, since 'foreign domination' is a charge levelled by many critics of the New Order regime. Finally, it will be useful to assess Indonesia's experience since 1966 in the international context through a broad comparison with its neighbouring ASEAN countries, and other large developing countries which are also oil exporters.

It is necessary, at the outset, to emphasize that the data on foreign investment in Indonesia—and many other countries—are rather poor. The limitations are referred to below and examined in more detail in the Appendix. As a rule of thumb, all figures should be treated as approximate.

Foreign Investment Policies[2]

Foreign investment regulations in Indonesia are based on the Foreign Investment Law No. 1/1967 and subsequent modifications. The regulations apply to all firms with less than 100 per cent domestic equity operating in industries under the jurisdiction of the BKPM and its predecessor, the Technical Team for Foreign Investment (*Panitia Teknis Penanaman Modal*, PTPM).

The major industries excluded from BKPM coverage are oil and gas and related products, and several services, most important of which are banking and insurance. Firms wholly owned by Indonesian nationals are regulated by the Domestic Investment Law No. 6/1968 and subsequent amendments, or by the licensing legislation introduced by the Colonial government (the BRO, *Bedrijfs Reglementeerings Ordannantie*, of 1934). Domestic firms seeking financial incentives—such as they now exist—must be licensed by the BKPM. In practice, the distinction between foreign (PMA, *Penanaman Modal Asing*) and domestic (PMDN, *Penanaman Modal Dalam Negeri*) firms is not always great. Both groups have obtained capital from overseas; the difference is that for PMA firms, at least, some of this capital has taken the form of equity investments.

The new Law[3] offered a surprisingly wide range of financial incentives for a country in which foreign capital was being expropriated less than three years earlier. Most incentives took the form of a reduction or elimination of taxes. The most important were: a basic tax holiday of two years for all investments in (liberally defined) 'priority' areas, and longer periods in certain circumstances;[4] exemption from payment of import duties and sales taxes on initial machinery and equipment; a guarantee that profits and capital could be repatriated; loss carry-forward provisions; and an accelerated depreciation allowance. There were initially no restrictions on foreign equity, and very few on the employment of foreign personnel. Special provisions applied to foreign enterprises restored to their original owners.

More important than the new provisions, however, were the regulatory regime under which they were implemented and the underlying bureaucratic politics in Jakarta. The Technical Team, as its later name suggested, played an essentially co-ordinating role. The real power, in many cases, effectively resided with the departments in whose jurisdiction a proposed project fell. Applicants were first required to obtain the approval of the relevant department, which evaluated the proposal in conjunction with the Technical Team. The application was then forwarded to the President, who was empowered to give approval on the advice of a Ministerial Advisory Board. Final sanction was then provided by the relevant Minister.

We shall examine in Chapter 8 the operation of the system in more detail. But it is worth emphasizing three aspects at this stage. The first has been the complexity of the investment regulatory regime from the outset. By 1969, two years after the promulgation of the Law, approvals were reportedly taking six to nine months. The licensing requirements were onerous, and the commercial environment—including taxation regulations, labour laws, and land titles—was (and still is) extremely uncertain.[5] The second point was that, although the Technical Team could offer financial incentives, the departments made the policies and largely determined the priority areas. Moreover, it was (and generally still is) the departments which had control over trade policy, especially quotas and licences. Thirdly, there was little economic rationale in selecting priority areas. Most decisions appear to have been based on 'back-of-the-envelope' calculations comparing domestic production capacity and demand, or on lobbying by producer groups. All these features have been present, to a greater or lesser extent, throughout the New Order period.

In spite of these difficulties, the Technical Team did 'bag contracts' in the early years. In 1967, it approved 22 projects, of which five were new approvals of returned enterprises and seven were fully foreign owned. By the end of the decade, there had been 177 approvals, ten of which were returned enterprises and thirty-seven 100 per cent foreign-owned projects. It is interesting to note that, while the absence of exclusive foreign ownership provisions has been criticized by foreign firms in recent years, in the period when foreign investors did have such an option the majority chose a joint venture.

Minor administrative changes were introduced in 1970 through Law No. 11/1970, and in 1973 Presidential Decrees (*Keputusan Presiden*, KP) 20 and 21 formally established the BKPM. The BKPM performed the same function as the Technical Team, and its authority was extended to include all foreign investments except those in oil and gas, banking and insurance. More important than the administrative changes, however, was the adoption of more restrictive policies. These first became evident in the early 1970s when certain fields were closed off to new foreign investments (for example, new weaving mills located on Java and selling locally). But the big push for greater controls came after the violent protests which accompanied the visit of Japanese Prime Minister Tanaka in January 1974.

The government's response to these protests came in a strongly worded statement by the President on 22 January, which outlined the principles governing all new foreign investments. These included that: all new investments were to be joint ventures; Indonesian equity should be increased to 51 per cent within a 'certain period' (subsequently ten years was mentioned); the list of industries closed to foreign investments was to be extended; tax incentives were to be reduced; and the number of foreign personnel was to be restricted. Corresponding to these changes were new measures affecting domestic investors, principally that *pribumi* firms were to be given preferential access to state bank loans.

The new principles were never fully implemented—the ten-year majority deadline has already passed, for example—but they dominated the foreign investment climate for the next few years. So much so that, combined with the Pertamina crisis in 1975/6, the interest of foreign investors waned considerably. In response, the government actually implemented the new regulations less vigorously, rather than scrapping them altogether, and it also introduced new administrative reforms.

These latter took two forms, both introduced in 1977. First, the bases for the BKPM's decisions on investment applications became more transparent. In February, it issued its Investment Priority List (*Daftar Skala Prioritas*, DSP) for the first time. This might appear to have been a minor change, but it was very significant. Previously, the priorities were not publicly available, and so intending investors often had little idea of which areas the government was promoting. The first DSP was extraordinarily detailed, listing 831 activities, divided into four categories—open with full incentives, open with some incentives, open without incentives, and closed. New DSP have been issued at irregular intervals since 1977. The second, in February 1978, expanded the number of activities to 1,095 and increased those closed to foreign firms.

Under the second reform, of October 1977, administrative procedures were simplified and centralized. Henceforth, the BKPM was to offer a 'one-stop-service'. Foreign investors were, with minor exceptions, able to deal exclusively with the BKPM, which was empowered to act on matters previously the province of the ten relevant departments. At the same time, it was stated that the approval period was to be reduced from up to fourteen months to a maximum of fourteen weeks.

The cycle of harsher measures followed by more liberal policies has continued in the second decade of the New Order. Shortly after the 1977 measures, Indonesia received another massive revenue windfall from the second round of oil price increases, and foreign investment requirements were tightened. The new measures were hastened—indirectly through the oil price rises—by the push for 'industrial deepening' in *Repelita III* and *Repelita IV*. Economic growth accelerated, prompting renewed interest by foreign investors, and the government could afford to be more selective.

The introduction in 1982 of the Export Certificate (*Sertifikat Ekspor*, SE) scheme, which provided generous rebates on some inputs, also began to attract a few export-oriented investment proposals. From 1980, more areas were closed to foreign investors. In the 1981 DSP, certain areas were to be reserved exclusively for co-operatives. The chairman of the BKPM declared 1982 to be '*tahun komponen*' (the year of components), consistent with the promotion of backward integration.

This brings us finally to the investment packages of 1985 and 1986, in which the pendulum has swung back to a more liberal approach. In 1984, investment applications and approvals nosedived for three main reasons: the general economic slump, increasingly restrictive foreign labour regulations, and the abolition of tax holidays on new investments as part of the 1984 tax package (which included the introduction of a value added tax in the following year). The measures of April 1985 concerned mainly administrative procedures. New projects could be considered immediately for Presidential approval (previously there had been an intermediate step—'temporary approval') and administrative requirements were simplified.[6] The maximum period for BKPM approval was also reduced, from twelve to six weeks.

The 6 May package of 1986 introduced more fundamental changes, perhaps the most far-reaching since the original Law of 1967. These included:

1. PMA firms with 75 per cent Indonesian equity (or 51 per cent if a public company) would receive equal treatment with PMDN firms with regard to domestic distribution rights[7] and access to state banks.

2. All sectors would be open to foreign firms which exported at least 85 per cent of their production (previously the requirement was 100 per cent).

3. Reinvestment of profits of PMA companies in their own activities or in PMDN firms would be permitted if the sector is open to investment.

4. Domestic equity requirements are being liberalized, including a provision that the initial 20 per cent could be paid in instalments over the first five years. In some cases (for example, high risk projects), the initial local equity could be as low as 5 per cent.

5. Foreign firms can be licensed for an additional 30 years, subject to certain conditions. This replaced the earlier regulation that all licences were valid only until 1997.

6. The minimum investment requirement of $1 million can be relaxed for some activities, such as consultancies.

It is, of course, too early to predict the effects of the new measures, and in any case the domestic market is rendered increasingly unattractive to new investors because of the current economic recession. But other recent policy changes have induced the first real beginnings of multinational export-oriented operations. Moreover, the current BKPM Chairman, Ginandjar Kartasasmita, is widely regarded as being politically more powerful than some of his predecessors.

It is clear from this discussion that, while foreign investment policies in the New Order have been far more liberal than those which existed before 1966, it would be a mistake to characterize them as an 'open-door' posture.

The government has sought to balance its own ideological views, nationalist sentiment, and political lobbying on the one hand, against economic conditions on the other.[8] The pendulum has swung quite sharply from liberalism to control and back again over the last two decades. An understanding of the policy environment is essential to a thorough analysis of the pattern of foreign investment in this and following chapters, and to a critique of these policies in Chapter 8. Let us now look more closely at the broad trends in foreign investment.

Foreign Investment in Aggregate

For statistical purposes we shall adopt the definition of foreign investment given in the IMF *Balance of Payments Manual* (fourth edition), which is also used by Bank Indonesia. The definition is: 'Direct investment refers to investment that is made to acquire a lasting interest in an enterprise operating in an economy other than that of the investor, the investor's purpose being to have an effective voice in the management of the enterprise.' The operative words are 'lasting interest', that is, investment undertaken with a view to acquiring control. Excluded in this definition are portfolio investment—which in any case is very small in Indonesia—and loan capital, which has entered Indonesia in large quantities since 1966.

There are formidable data constraints to a thorough analysis of foreign investment in Indonesia. It is important to refer briefly to these at the outset to avoid any confusion; the Appendix examines the limitations in more detail. In this and the following chapters we will be dealing with four separate sets of data; a rough comparison of some of the magnitudes is given in Table A.1.

1. *Total foreign investment inflows*. These purportedly refer to *all* direct foreign investments, and are derived from balance of payment data. Estimates are available from Bank Indonesia (BI), the OECD and the IMF, but they differ substantially, especially in the case of the OECD. The IMF data are used here since they correspond closely to those of BI, and since their use facilitates international comparisons.

2. *BKPM data*. These are a minefield for the unwary. Because they are relatively accessible they have been widely quoted, but uncritical use can—and has—generated quite misleading results. There are three main deficiencies in the BKPM data.

a. First, the sector coverage is incomplete. The data exclude the huge petroleum sector, together with banking and insurance.

b. Secondly, the BKPM figures generally refer to *approved* (or intended) investment, as indicated in the firms' applications. *Actual* investment is a good deal less (see Table 3.3 below) for several reasons: there is always a lag between approval and implementation; some approved projects never get off the ground;[9] and the actual investments of some firms do not necessarily match their original commitments. The absence of regular BKPM data on foreign investment is not so serious, because BI compiles a comprehensive monthly bulletin. But there are major problems in the case of BKPM domestic investment, since there are no accurate estimates of the actual totals.

c. Thirdly, the approved data refer to gross investment. They include the equity contribution of both the foreign and domestic partner, and loan capital. Consequently, the BKPM data substantially overstate the equity contribution of foreign investors. Table 3.3 provides some indication of the magnitude of the overstatement.

The country shares in the BKPM data also need to be interpreted carefully. For one thing, the share of the group 'more than one country' is often large, and no indication is given of its composition in the published data. For another, the distinction between foreign and domestic investment is somewhat fuzzy. This is so primarily because the Chinese business community in Indonesia is closely linked to the vast Chinese business network in North-East and South-East Asia. As noted, domestic firms have borrowed extensively overseas. It is quite plausible that some of these funds, from predominantly Chinese countries (Singapore, Hong Kong, and Taiwan), could have in reality been equity capital, although it has not been recorded as such. One reason for capital entering in this form is that foreign investment from these countries has occasionally been discouraged in deference to domestic Indonesian political sensitivities (see Wells, 1983) Conversely, it is also likely that some Indonesian capital has been channelled through these Chinese countries to take advantage of incentives offered by the BKPM to foreign investors (Thee, 1984a, p. 96), or possibly to secure the greater political and legal protection which foreign status is thought to confer. It is not known how these two effects balance out.

3. *BI data*. Bank Indonesia compiles monthly reports on actual and approved foreign investment, disaggregated by source country, (Indonesian) region, and industry sector. These are the best source of foreign investment data in Indonesia, and they are used in several tables below. However, the BI data still suffer from two of the BKPM's shortcomings. These are the limited sector coverage and the difficulty in interpreting the country shares.

4. *BPS data*. Unpublished data from the *Statistik Industri* series indicate ownership shares for value added and employment. These were discussed in Chapter 2; see also the Appendix.

How important have capital inflows in general, and foreign investment in particular, been since 1966? Indonesia has been a significant capital importer throughout the period, reflecting its large current account deficits. Net inflows (that is, net of outflows) have risen from less than $300 million annually in the late 1960s to over $3 billion in recent years (see Table 3.1). In only one year was there a net outflow, following the crisis in Pertamina, in the mid-1970s.[10] Foreign investment has accounted for a little over 10 per cent of net inflows, but in some years it has contributed almost one-third of the total. Initially, direct investment was quite slow to respond to the New Order's policies, and there was even some repatriation of capital. Since 1970, however, these investments have averaged over $200 million annually, apart from the slump in 1973 and 1974. In the early 1980s, their share of total inflows declined, mainly because foreign investments have been overshadowed by borrowings to finance the very large current account deficits, but in 1985 the share rose again as borrowings declined. In real terms, direct investments peaked with the very large inflows in the mid-1970s (final column, Table 3.1).

Despite their limitations, the BKPM approvals data are of some interest, first because they provide a breakdown for foreign and domestic firms in all BKPM sectors and in manufacturing, and secondly because they are at least a broad indication of the investment climate in Indonesia (see Table 3.2). For reasons outlined above, BKPM foreign investment approvals (see Table 3.2, second column) are much greater than the actual net inflows (see Table 3.1, second column) and even the trends differ substantially. The one feature they have in common, however, is the gradual increase beginning in the late 1960s and the huge inflows to the mid-1970s. This comparison is a little more plausible if the approvals data are 'lagged' by a year or so, to allow for implementation. Not surprisingly, foreign and domestic investment approvals diverge considerably in both totals and trends, although the trends are more similar in the case of manufacturing investments.

TABLE 3.1

Indonesia: Net Capital Inflows, 1968–1985 ($ million)

	Nominal		Direct Investment as Percentage of Total	Real Direct Investment[b] (1975 Prices)
	Direct Investment	Total[a]		
1985	271	1,902	14.2	143
1984	227	3,410	6.6	121
1983	289	6,041	4.8	157
1982	226	5,607	4.0	124
1981	122	1,878	6.5	69
1980	184	1,329	13.8	115
1979	226	868	26.0	164
1978	279	1,708	16.3	229
1977	235	1,101	21.3	207
1976	344	1,717	20.0	323
1975	476	−846	c	476
1974	−49	405	c	−55
1973	15	738	2.0	20
1972	207	655	31.6	302
1971	139	437	31.8	210
1970	83	293	28.3	130
1969	32	273	11.7	52
1968	−2	214	c	3

Source: IMF (annual, monthly), various issues.

[a] Includes long- and short-term capital inflows to public and private sectors; excludes errors and omissions, which are large in some years.

[b] Deflated using United States index of wholesale prices for industrial goods.

c = Negative.

TABLE 3.2

Approved Foreign and Domestic[a] Investments, 1967–1985

($ million or percentage)

	Total			Manufacturing		
	Foreign	Domestic	$\frac{Domestic}{Foreign} \times 100$	Foreign	Domestic	$\frac{Domestic}{Foreign} \times 100$
1985	859	2,833	330	687	1,124	164
1984	1,121	1,873	167	1,002	1,277	127
1983	2,882	7,707	267	2,615	4,172	160
1982	1,800	2,949	164	1,120	2,147	192
1981	1,092	2,676	245	835	484	58
1980	914	2,086	228	773	1,743	225
1979	1,320	1,242	94	1,158	931	80
1978	397	1,715	432	275	1,181	429
1977	328	1,386	422	327	945	289
1976	449	672	150	348	431	124
1975	1,757	593	34	1,160	470	41
1974	1,417	554	39	1,069	410	38
1973	655	1,465	224	472	829	176
1972	522	718	138	216	463	214
1971	426	939	220	249	483	194
1970	345	319	92	143	234	164
1969	682	101	15	75	58	77
1968	230	13	6	50	13	26
1967	125	—	—	28	—	—

Source: BKPM.

[a] Domestic investments have been converted to $ at the average exchange rate for each year.

How large is the overstatement in the BKPM data, which refer to approved, gross investments? Of the $15.4 billion approved up to 30 September 1985, only $3.5 billion (or 23 per cent) was the intended equity contribution of the foreign partners (see Table 3.3). Foreign loans actually contributed the major part, about two-thirds of the total (a similar proportion, also, for the period 1967–77). And of the $3.5 billion of intended investments, a little over half ($1.9 billion) had been realized. This illustrates the importance of interpreting the approval data with great care: the 'total approvals' figure (in this case $15.4 billion) is the most widely cited estimate of foreign investment, but the correct figure is in fact the realized foreign equity contribution.[11] Up to September 1985, this totalled $1.9 billion, or about 12 per cent of the first amount. It is true, of course, that the comparison is a little more complicated than this. Foreign partners have often 'lent' their Indonesian partners equity capital to comply with government ownership requirements, and foreign partners have also facilitated—directly or indirectly—much of the foreign loans. Moreover, some of the projects recently approved will later be realized. Nevertheless, the data clearly illustrate the fallacy of equating the 'total approved' and the 'realized foreign equity' figures.

TABLE 3.3

Sources of Finance for Foreign Investment, 1967–1985
($ million or percentage)

	Total	Foreign Equity	Indonesian Equity	Foreign Loans
(1) Approved Investments				
(a) Total, 30 September 1985	15,414	3,544	1,772	10,098
percentage of total	100	23	12	66
(b) Total, 31 December 1977	6,864	1,898	536	4,430
percentage of total	100	28	8	65

	Total	Foreign Equity	Foreign Loans
(2) Realized Investments			
(a) Total, 30 September 1985	6,071	1,904	4,166
percentage of total	100	31	69
(b) Total, 31 December 1977	2,639	984	1,655
percentage of total	100	37	63

Source: Bank Indonesia.
Note: In this and following tables '1985' refers to 'up to 30 September 1985' unless otherwise indicated.

Three sets of factors appear to explain the large annual fluctuations in actual and approved foreign investments. The first is, simply, the 'lumpiness' of certain large investments. For example, the huge Asahan hydroelectric and aluminium complex in North Sumatra accounts for the very large figure in 1975.[12] Real actual foreign investment (final column, Table 3.1) has subsequently been much smaller than this peak year.

The second factor is the state of the Indonesian and world economies. BKPM approvals declined substantially after the mid-1970s in part because of the slowdown in the OECD economies and the Indonesian government's tight fiscal management in response to the Pertamina crisis. Moreover, by this time many of the 'easy' opportunities for import substitution had disappeared, and Indonesia was not an attractive export base. Conversely, in the early 1980s, BKPM approvals rose sharply as the economy grew very rapidly and the push for backward integration commenced. More recently, approvals have declined again in the current economic recession. Surprisingly, the two rounds of oil price increases have had only an indirect effect on both total inflows (Table 3.1) and BKPM approvals (Table 3.2). In the case of total inflows, in which oil investments figure prominently, foreign investment was rather low in 1973–4 and 1979–80, presumably because of other, policy-related factors. BKPM approvals have risen following the oil price increases, mainly because of the effects of large windfall revenue gains, which accrued to and were 'recycled' by the government; there is also the special case of Asahan in 1975.

A third explanation for the fluctuations is that they are sensitive to changes in government policy towards foreign investment. The negative figure for actual foreign investment in 1974 was due in part to the restrictive policies announced at the beginning of that year. Similarly, the decline in 1977 was due in some measure to the forced renegotiation of production-sharing contracts with the foreign oil companies. BKPM approvals have also been affected by policy changes. The most noticeable is the huge increase in 1983, as investors sought approval under the old taxation regulations and before the abolition of many incentives in January 1984. Approvals also rose sharply in the early 1980s because new opportunities emerged in the government's push for heavy industries and also because of the plywood boom, following the progressive prohibition of log exports. Sluggish domestic approvals from 1974 to 1976 arose in part because of apprehension in the Chinese business community about implementation of the government's policies favouring *pribumi* firms. Conversely, a factor in the increase after 1976 was simpler and faster BKPM administrative procedures.

Changes in investment policies have affected not only the *total* level of foreign investment, but also the choice between equity and loan capital. The latter proposition is indicated by changes in debt–equity ratios of approved and realized investments over time. The ratio of foreign debt to foreign equity of both the approved and realized figures was a little over two for the period 1967 to 1985 (see Table 3.4).[13] For the first four years of the new regulations, 1967 to 1970, the debt–equity ratios were less than one for approved investments, whether or not Indonesian equity is included. Thereafter they rose quite sharply, to about 1.7 for most of the 1970s. The year 1975 was an exceptional one, dominated by the huge Asahan project, which had a much higher debt gearing ratio, through funds obtained from the consortium of Japanese interests.

It is likely that the debt–equity ratio rose after 1970 for three reasons. First, in response to increased pressure for greater local control, foreign

TABLE 3.4

Debt–Equity Ratio of Foreign Investments, 1967–1985

	Including Indonesian Equity	Excluding Indonesian Equity
(1) Approved Investments		
1967–1970	0.72	0.99
1971–1974	1.71	2.65
1975	3.29	4.49
1976–1979	1.71	2.76
1967–1977	1.82	2.33
1967–1985	1.90	2.85
(2) Realized Investments		
1967–1977	n.a.	1.68
1967–1985	n.a.	2.19

Sources: Bank Indonesia and BKPM.
n.a. = Not available.

partners acquiesced in a higher proportion of Indonesian capital in the total equity, but sought to preserve control through resort to greater foreign borrowings. Many of the foreign investors—especially Japanese—have facilitated these foreign loans through affiliated financial institutions. Secondly, in the early years of the New Order, foreign banks were understandably nervous at the prospect of a large exposure in Indonesia, and required reassurance from the foreign investors in the form of greater equity contributions. After 1970, as confidence in the new regime increased, this factor became less important. Thirdly, the rise in debt–equity ratios was proportionately greater if the Indonesian equity is excluded (see final column, Table 3.4), presumably indicating that in the 1970s more Indonesian equity capital was available for joint ventures than was the case in the late 1960s.

Foreign and Domestic Investments Compared

It is very difficult to obtain an accurate comparison of foreign and domestic investments using the BKPM data. Accurate estimates of realized domestic investment (PMDN firms) are not available. Moreover, the foreign investment data also include a good deal of domestic capital, since the Indonesian partners' shares are included in the total approvals. Conversely, domestically owned firms have borrowed extensively overseas. Finally, BKPM approval for domestic firms is required only if investors require the (until recently available) incentives. Much domestic investment in the 'factory' sector— let alone among the small and household industry sector—occurs under the BRO system. For these reasons, the comparison is more usefully undertaken using the BPS *Statistik Industri* data (see Chapter 5 and Tables 2.4–2.6).

Nevertheless, it is of some interest to relate overall magnitudes for PMA and PMDN firms as an indication of relative size and investor interest. The appropriate comparison is for approved totals given in Table 3.2, since it would be misleading to use the *realized* PMA and *approved* PMDN figures. BKPM approvals for foreign investment have generally been appreciably less than those for domestic investment (columns 2–4, Table 3.2). PMDN approvals were initially sluggish following the introduction of the 1968 Domestic Investment Law, but after 1970 domestic approvals were more than double the corresponding foreign figures in most years. Only in 1974 and 1975—the latter due to the 'Asahan bulge'—was the total for foreign firms much higher. The picture is broadly similar for manufacturing investments (columns 5–7, Table 3.2): that is, PMDN figures were higher than PMA in most years after 1970, except for the mid-1970s.

This pattern, of PMDN approvals exceeding those of PMA firms, may be reversed in the near future. This is not necessarily because foreign firms may become relatively more important—although the recent liberalizations could have this effect—but because of the abolition of the fiscal incentives package. Domestic firms are likely to start opting out of the BKPM system altogether—since BKPM approval confers little more advantage on firms than official sanction—and simply be licensed under the old BRO system. Foreign firms, of course, must still seek BKPM approval.

It seems reasonable to conclude that throughout the New Order foreign and domestic investments have been complementary rather than competitive. There is no evidence to support the contention that foreign investment has triggered a wholesale process of 'denationalization' which to some extent may have occurred in Latin American countries (see, for example, Newfarmer (ed.) (1985) and Evans (1971)). It is certainly true that the rapid infusion of new capital and technology into Indonesia has been disruptive, as is inevitable when a country's economic policies change suddenly. There has been some displacement of domestic firms using traditional technologies, as in the rice milling and weaving industries. But the displacement has occurred primarily because of the new technologies, rather than ownership *per se*; domestic firms have been adopting these new technologies just as much as foreign firms.

The interactions between foreign and domestic investments have been a good deal more complex than a simple statistical comparison reveals, for other reasons. There have been important changes in the domestic capitalist class since 1966, in part the result of foreign investments. Most noticeable, perhaps, has been the decline of traditional *santri* business groups, in industries such as textiles and *kretek* cigarettes. Much Chinese capital has also transferred from traditional commercial activities into modern manufacturing, and a large 'bureaucratic capitalist' class has emerged in the form of state enterprises and those dependent on the government patronage network.[14] Consequently, although the *composition* of domestic business groups has changed, their importance *vis-à-vis* foreign investors has not diminished.

The Regional Distribution of Foreign Investment

Critics of foreign investment in Indonesia frequently allege that such investment exacerbates regional inequalities, by locating in enclaves around major cities and resource projects. Such a concentration is, of course, to be expected because of the special characteristics of foreign investment which dictate such a location. It reflects as much as anything the industrial composition of foreign investment in the extractive sectors, and in more capital-intensive manufacturing activities which must establish near centres of physical and human infrastructure.

Does the regional pattern of foreign investment in Indonesia conform to this 'enclave' stereotype? In many respects the answer is yes. The exclusion of the huge oil and gas sectors from the BKPM data creates an immediate problem in addressing this question. These sectors are obviously region specific—mostly outside Java—and they account for a large share of foreign investment in Indonesia. To answer the question with reference only to the BKPM sectors is clearly inadequate, but that is all the data permit.

BKPM approved foreign investments have been located in just a few provinces. Jakarta, West Java (a good deal of which is located near Jakarta)[15] and North Sumatra (mainly Asahan) account for over 60 per cent of the total (see Table 3.5). The inclusion of another two provinces—Aceh and East Java—raises this to nearly three-quarters. The regional distribution of *realized* foreign investment in manufacturing is broadly similar.[16] West Java and North Sumatra each account for about one-quarter of the total. These two, plus Jakarta, have received over 70 per cent of all foreign investments since 1967. By contrast, Kalimantan, Sulawesi, and Eastern Indonesia have received only 11 per cent of PMA approvals—mostly timber in Kalimantan and the two large mining projects (Inco in Sulawesi

TABLE 3.5

Regional Distribution of Investment, 1967–1985[a] ($ million or percentage)

Region/ Province	Approvals, BKPM Sectors		Realized Foreign, Manufacturing		
	Foreign	Domestic	Total	Percentage of Total	Manufacturing as Percentage of All BKPM Sectors
Java	52	62	640	57	84
Jakarta	22	18	228	20	69
West Java	23	24	300	27	98
Central Java and Yogyakarta	2	10	38	3	94
East Java	6	11	74	7	93
Sumatra	27	18	339	30	80
North Sumatra	18	3	283	25	84
Aceh	5	4	33	3	93
South Sumatra	1	5	1	n	6
Other	3	6	22	2	61
Kalimantan	5	9	10	1	15
East Kalimantan	3	6	4	n	17
Other	2	3	5	n	37
Sulawesi	2	3	2	n	22
South Sulawesi	1	2	2	n	50
Other	1	1	n	n	28
Eastern Indonesia[b]	4	3	n	n	1
More than one province	10	5	131	12	22
Total Indonesia	100	100	1,123	100	59

Sources: BKPM and Bank Indonesia.
[a] Up to end of 1985 for approvals data, and to 30 September for realized data.
[b] Bali, Nusa Tenggara, Maluku, Irian Jaya.
n = Negligible (less than 1 per cent).

and Freeport in Irian Jaya)—and a miniscule 1 per cent of manufacturing investments. Some of the foreign investments located in more than one province may have been in the latter group of regions—an accurate break-down is not published—but the share is probably small. Thus, with a few important exceptions, most foreign investors have been attracted either to the large resource projects, or to the commercial industrial base of Jakarta, West Java and, to a lesser extent, East Java.

To examine the pattern in more detail, it is useful to take a closer look at realized foreign investments in manufacturing. First, how important has manufacturing been in the BKPM sectors? It has clearly been the major sector in aggregate, but its share of the total has varied considerably between regions (final column, Table 3.5). In the two more developed islands, Java and Sumatra, it has accounted for over 80 per cent of all BKPM investments. The share of manufacturing is less than this figure in only a few provinces: marginally lower in the case of Jakarta because services are relatively larger, and very small in South Sumatra where mining predominates. By contrast, as noted, manufacturing has been unimportant in the remaining regions, and resource-based projects have attracted most of the foreign capital.

The composition of foreign investment in manufacturing *within* each province varies between regions (see Figures 3.1 and 3.2). What little foreign investment has been attracted to regions outside Java and the more industrialized provinces of Sumatra has been mainly in the plywood indus-try. For Java and the rest of Sumatra, their more developed industrial base is clearly evident. Specific features of industrial development in these provinces are also important. Asahan accounts for most of the investment in North Sumatra, while the ASEAN industrial project (PT ASEAN Aceh Fertilizer) and related investments constitute most of the total for Aceh. In West Java, the traditional importance of textiles is evident; in Central Java, it is cement; and in East Java, breweries and cigarettes are very important.

As noted, this pattern of heavy regional concentration is not surprising. It is explained by the attributes and motives of foreign investors. It also reflects the nature of developments in Indonesia's modern manufacturing industry and in other sectors. Indeed, the regional distribution of domestic investment approvals in BKPM sectors is surprisingly similar to that of foreign investment. Putting aside the special case of North Sumatra, dominated by one large PMA project, there is little difference in the regional shares of BKPM approvals. Up to 1985, indeed, Java and Sumatra absorbed 80 per cent of both PMA and PMDN approvals (see Table 3.5).

While the concentration of foreign investment in just a few provinces is, understandably, a contentious political issue in Indonesia, the explanation for the pattern is fairly clear, especially in the case of 'footloose' industries. The latter investments tend to locate near their major markets—principally Java since few until recently have been export oriented—and supplies of labour and infrastructure. But the concentration has undoubtedly been exacerbated by government policies, notwithstanding the goal of regional dispersal. For one thing, the complex system of regulation and licensing

FIGURE 3.1

Foreign Investment in Manufacturing: Major Sectors by Region
(percentage of region total, three largest manufacturing industries)

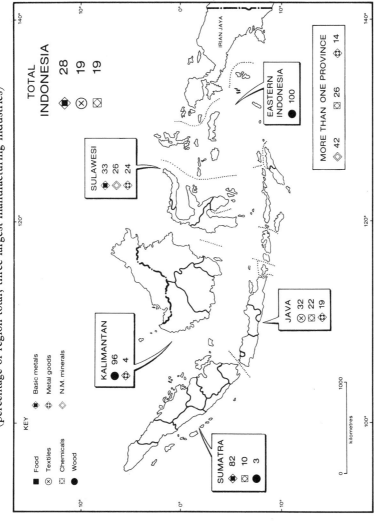

44

FIGURE 3.2

Foreign Investment in Manufacturing: Major Sectors by Province
(percentage of province total, three largest manufacturing industries)

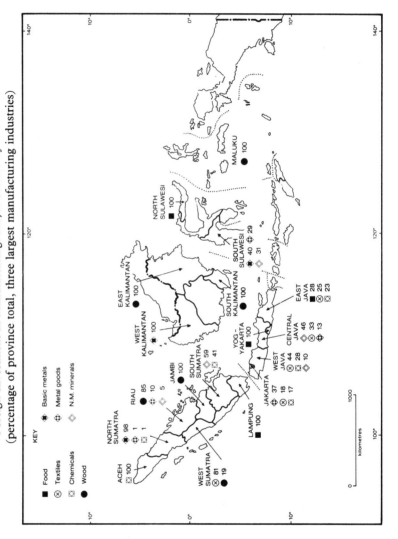

has encouraged firms to establish in close proximity to the centre of bureau-cratic power, Jakarta (see McCawley, 1983). For another, the 'cascading' structure of protection has promoted the development of consumer goods industries (appliances and automobiles), which in any case tend to be located near large markets (Azis, 1985). Consequently, the system of industrial intervention has biased development towards these Java-based industries, at the expense of the Outer Islands. Foreign firms, like their domestic counterparts, have simply responded to the existing price and bureaucratic 'signals'. We shall return to these questions later, in Chapter 8.

'New Forms' of Foreign Involvement

Some recent literature on foreign investment has suggested the emergence of 'new forms' of capital and technology transfer (see, for example, Oman, 1985). This is the argument that there has been a shift away from the 'old' package, in which foreign firms introduced both capital and technology in the context of exclusive—or majority—foreign ownership. The new arrangements have evolved, it is maintained, from host government press-ures, the increased importance of state enterprises in the 'commanding heights' of important developing countries, the preferences of multinational corporations for reduced equity exposure, and, at least until recently, the recycling of huge OPEC surpluses.

These new forms of foreign involvement are of considerable importance in Indonesia. There is hardly an enterprise in Indonesia's modern manu-facturing sector which does not have (or has not had in the past) some commercial tie-up with foreign firms, with the exception of traditional activities within the food and textiles industries. These commercial arrange-ments range from simple and informal links involving occasional advice on marketing and technology, to major licensing agreements in which the foreign licenser is largely responsible for much of the firm's operations. Many licensing agreements—probably the majority—take place on an 'arm's length' basis, in which the foreign supplier has no equity stake in the local firm.

There are some grounds for believing that these 'new forms' of involve-ment might be less attractive to foreign firms wishing to establish a presence in Indonesia. For one thing, licensing generally implies less control, as compared to equity investment, and there is still a limited supply of Indo-nesian entrepreneurs able to meet foreign licensers' standards in some areas. For another, the domestic legal environment is such that proprietory technology—to the extent it forms the basis of the foreign investor's com-petitive advantage—is very difficult to protect in Indonesia. Finally, repatriation of capital, which in other countries provides an incentive to license rather than invest, faces minimal restriction in Indonesia.[17]

Nevertheless, licensing is often the *only* means of entry for foreign firms, especially to the large state enterprise sector, and for industries which have been closed to foreign investment. Moreover, as noted, there are large movements of capital, personnel, and technology between Indonesia and the Chinese business community elsewhere in South-East Asia, and in these transactions the distinction between 'old' and 'new' is necessarily blurred.

It is virtually impossible to obtain any reliable estimates of the importance of these new forms to direct foreign investment in Indonesia. As we have seen (Table 3.1), direct investment has constituted only a small proportion of Indonesia's total capital imports. But it cannot be inferred from this that 'new forms' have been important, since the non-equity capital imports went to many other activities besides loans to manufacturing enterprises. In contrast to several neighbouring countries (for example, the Philippines and Malaysia), and to most of Latin America, Indonesia does not have a technology regulating and monitoring authority—although there are plans to establish such a body. Consequently, it is not possible to obtain estimates of licensing payments in total, let alone the division between 'arm's length' and equity investment arrangements.[18]

Some indirect estimates of Indonesia's technology imports can be obtained from data published in two of the major investing countries, Japan and the United States, on licensing payments to their firms. In the second half of the 1970s, for example, payments to United States manufacturing firms totalled between five and six million dollars annually. This may be compared to the total realized equity investments of United States firms in manufacturing of $51 million at the end of 1977 (the gross realized figure was $117 million). The payments to Japanese manufacturing firms were appreciably higher, ranging from ¥3.5 billion in 1978 to ¥7.6 billion in 1980[19] ($17 million and $33 million respectively at the prevailing exchange rates), as compared to a realized cumulative Japanese equity investment in manufacturing of $225 million in 1977. Nevertheless, these data do not say a great deal about possible new forms of involvement. Technology statistics are notoriously unreliable, not least because there are a variety of means by which foreign investors may appropriate their returns to superior technology. Moreover, the data above do not distinguish between 'arm's length' licensing agreements and those which are part of equity investments.

Another very approximate indication of the relative importance of direct foreign investments and other forms of technology inflows is the pattern of Indonesia's capital goods imports. Much of the foreign exchange component of direct foreign investment has taken the form of payment for imported capital equipment and machinery. The comparison indicates that realized foreign (equity) investments in manufacturing have been a very small proportion of capital goods imports (see Table 3.6). For the period as a whole, machinery imports were about fifteen times greater than realized foreign investment in manufacturing.[20] In the case of textiles, where a more direct comparison is feasible, the proportion of foreign investment to machinery imports is a little higher, but still only one-third for the years 1967–77 and one-seventh for the entire period. In other words, the data suggest that channels other than direct foreign investment have been much more important in the acquisition of production technology. Most capital goods imports have been through direct purchases overseas by domestic firms, or through licensing (non-equity) arrangements which include the supply of machinery.

TABLE 3.6

Foreign Investment in Manufacturing and Imports of
Capital Goods Compared ($ million)

	Cumulative Totals	
	1967–77	1967–85[a]
1. Capital goods imports		
711 Power machinery (non-electrical)	919	2,955
715 Metal working machinery	161	693
717 Textiles and leather machinery	612	1,558
718 Machines for special industries	960	3,464
719 Machines (non-electrical)	1,943	8,252
Total	4,596	16,922
2. Realized Manufacturing Investments[b]	563	1,124
of which textiles	209	218

Sources: Bank Indonesia; and International Economic Data Bank, Australian National University.
[a] Up to 30 September 1985 for investments, 1967–83 for imports.
[b] Foreign equity investment only.

These estimates, it needs to be emphasized, are extremely approximate. They overstate the importance of foreign investment as a means of technology acquisition, to the extent that these investments were used for purposes other than the import of machinery (for example, for other imports or for domestic currency purchases). Conversely, the importance of foreign investment as a source of technology is understated in the sense that the data refer to financial flows, rather than the (probably more significant) diffusion of production and managerial know-how. But the figures are at least indicative of broad magnitudes; clearly, much new technology has been introduced into Indonesian manufacturing through channels other than direct investment.[21]

Indonesia in International Perspective

Indonesia's open international capital market and relatively liberal foreign investment policies during the New Order period have attracted much critical comment both domestically and overseas. Where does Indonesia stand in international perspective? Has there been a flood of foreign capital compared to other countries, as some critics contend? The answer is that, by almost any indicator, Indonesia has been a surprisingly small recipient of direct foreign investment since the late 1960s, both in total and within the manufacturing sector.

Although cumulative foreign investment in Indonesia from 1970 to 1984 was very sizeable—about $3 billion—the total was quite small compared to other countries (see Table 3.7). During this period, two smaller ASEAN economies received much larger amounts: three times larger in the case of Malaysia, and over four times larger in Singapore. Only in the Philippines— with its more uncertain business climate and longer history of foreign

TABLE 3.7

Foreign Investment in Indonesia and Selected Developing Countries,
1970–1984 ($ million)

Country	Sub-periods			Total, 1970–84
	1970–4	1975–9	1980–4	
Indonesia	395	1,560	1,048	3,003
Other ASEAN				
Malaysia	1,051	2,128	5,898	9,077
Philippines	−2	541	179	718
Singapore	1,385	3,277	8,291	12,953
Thailand	416	369	1,370	2,155
Other oil exporters				
Mexico	2,066	3,957	7,216	13,239
Nigeria	1,426	1,715	883	4,024

Source: IMF (annual), various issues.

investment—was foreign investment much smaller. In two other large
'petroleum economies', Mexico and Nigeria, investment was also much
higher, especially in the former.

Indonesia's relatively modest foreign investment inflows are illustrated
more clearly by comparing them with other aggregate magnitudes. Whatever indicator is chosen, the relative inflows have been very small indeed
(see Table 3.8; see also Table A.4 which presents the data in a more disaggregated format). As noted above, equity investments have constituted a
little over one-tenth of Indonesia's capital imports, compared to three-

TABLE 3.8

Relative Importance of Foreign Investment in Indonesia and Selected
Developing Countries, 1970–1984

Country	Foreign Investment as Percentage of			
	Capital Inflows	GDP[a]	Gross Capital Formation[b]	Foreign Investment Per Capita[c] ($)
Indonesia	11.5	0.4	1.6	18.8
Other ASEAN				
Malaysia	48.0	3.8	13.1	597.2
Philippines	4.6	0.2	0.8	13.5
Singapore	74.6	10.5	26.5	5,140.1
Thailand	12.8	0.7	2.8	42.8
Other oil exporters				
Mexico	18.3	0.6	3.6	172.4
Nigeria	48.3	1.4	3.7	43.7

Source: IMF (annual, monthly), various issues.
[a] 1970–83 for Singapore.
[b] 1970–83 for Mexico and Singapore; 1970–82 for Nigeria.
[c] Foreign investment, 1970–84, divided by 1984 population.

quarters for Singapore, and almost half for Malaysia and Nigeria. As a percentage of both gross capital formation and GDP these investments have been tiny—less than 2 per cent in the case of the former—and below any other country except the Philippines. Finally, the stock of cumulative net investments per capita was just $19 by 1984, compared to over $5,000 in Singapore, $600 in Malaysia, and $170 in Mexico. Clearly, the assertion that Indonesia has been a very large recipient of foreign investment, *relative to the size of its economy*, is quite inaccurate.

Much the same picture emerges in the case of foreign investment in manufacturing. Recent comparative data for most countries are not readily available, but the current situation is unlikely to differ substantially from that in the late 1970s. By the end of 1977, according to official statistics, cumulative realized foreign (equity) investment in Indonesia was $560 million, less than that in most other countries, especially the Latin American countries and Singapore (see Table 3.9). Like the earlier data, these estimates probably overstate the relative importance of foreign investment in Indonesian manufacturing.[22] Indonesia is a more recent recipient of foreign investment than the other countries. The overstatement thus arises from book value estimates of Indonesia's newer investment, and the fact that data in most of the other countries refer only to inflows after the establishment of monitoring agencies.

A somewhat more reliable indicator of the relative importance of foreign investment in manufacturing is the share of foreign-owned firms of

TABLE 3.9

Stock of Foreign Investment in Manufacturing in Indonesia and Selected Developing Countries ($ million or percentage)

Country	Year	Stock of Foreign Investment	Stock as Percentage of Manufacturing Value Added
Indonesia[a]	1977	563 (1,549)	13 (35)
Other ASEAN			
Malaysia	1977	433	17
Philippines	1978	530	9
Singapore	1977	1,773	93
Thailand	1977	198	5
Other Asia			
India	1974	1,328	11
Korea	1978	737	6
Hong Kong	1978	434	12
Other			
Mexico	1976	3,868	19
Brazil	1978	10,594	23
Nigeria	1976	873	15

Sources: Manufacturing value added from World Bank (1984); foreign investment from UNCTC (1983b) for all countries except Indonesia. Indonesian estimates from Bank Indonesia.

[a] Data refer to realized foreign equity investment. Bracketed data refer to realized foreign equity plus loans.

TABLE 3.10

Share of Foreign Investment in Manufacturing in Indonesia
and Selected Developing Countries, 1970s
(percentage of total)

Country	Employment		Gross Value of Production	
Indonesia[a]	10	(1974)	21	(1974)
Other ASEAN				
Malaysia	34	(1978)	44	(1978)
Philippines	7	(1970)		n.a.
Singapore	58	(1978)	83	(1978)
Other Asia				
India[a]	13	(1977)	13	(1975)
Korea	10	(1978)	11	(1975)
Other				
Argentina	10–12	(1970)	31	(1972)
Brazil	30	(1977)	44	(1977)
Mexico	21	(1970)	39	(1970)

Sources: 1. UNCTC, 1983a, p. 136.
      2. Indonesia BPS.
[a] Firms employing 20 or more workers.

employment and production. Consistent with our main argument, foreign investment in Indonesian manufacturing is a good deal less important than in several other countries according to these measures (see Table 3.10). Though rather dated, the shares for Indonesia are less than those of the Latin American countries and at least two of its ASEAN neighbours, Singapore and Malaysia. Moreover, the Indonesian data refer only to firms employing 20 or more workers. If small and cottage firms were included, the output and (especially) employment shares would be much smaller. Details of the cut-off point for most of the other countries are not provided. But the definition of the 'organized sector' in Indonesian manufacturing statistics is somewhat more restrictive than in other countries (for example, Singapore excludes firms with fewer than ten workers, the Philippines until recently fewer than five workers), thus suggesting that the real share of foreign firms in Indonesia may be relatively smaller still.

1. The project referred to in the Sadli quotation was the huge Freeport Sulphur Inc. copper investment in Irian Jaya, the first really large approval under the new law.

2. Information in this section is from a variety of sources. In addition to the 'Survey of Recent Developments' in each *BIES*, these include *Kompas, Business News* (both Jakarta), *Far Eastern Economic Review*, and *Asian Wall Street Journal*. A useful, if rather formal, review of foreign investment policies in Indonesia and nineteen other (mainly developing) countries is provided in UNCTC (1983b).

3. Sumantoro (1984, Appendix) reproduces the 1967 Law and provides some discussion, much of it from a legal point of view. See also Gurney (1983).

4. Priority areas numbered about thirteen in the late 1960s, and included most broad sectors within the BKPM's coverage, in addition to general provisions, such as firms exporting over half their output. Longer tax holidays were available for firms investing outside Java, for those which 'increased exports or reduced imports' (in effect practically all firms if the output is not socially priced), and for those also investing in infrastructure or meeting other (unspecified) objectives.

5. For an early comment on these issues, see Clapham (1970) and the reply by Sadli (1970). See also Sadli (1972).

6. These requirements, taken individually, were fairly minor, but together they amounted to a significant simplification of procedures. They were also indicative of the complex requirements which existed up to 1985, and still exist. Among the conditions waived were evidence of a feasibility study, initial approval of plant layout, a pro forma invoice on machinery, a statement from the Indonesian Embassy of the foreign investor's country of origin, and evidence of the investor's land application permit. For further details, see *Simplification of Procedures and Investment Approvals* (BKPM, Jakarta, 1985).

7. Previously PMA firms could not engage in (domestic) retail trade.

8. A prominent Indonesian academic has characterized the equation as follows: '. . . the continuing pressures for further tightening of controls on the inflow of external capital have tended to be counter-balanced by the concern that Indonesia is becoming less attractive for foreign investment. . . .' (Kuntjoro-Jakti, 1985, p. 71)

9. In principle, approved projects which fail to commence subsequently appear as negative items in the approvals data, but this is often not the case. The BKPM occasionally attempts to update its records. For example, during 1985, Indonesian newspapers carried prominent advertisements listing firms which were to contact the BKPM confirming their status. It might be noted that one effect of the revisions to *approved* data is that approved investments *for a given year* may vary enormously over time (that is, an estimate of approved investment for the year 1975 made in 1976 is likely to differ from that made in 1980).

10. For a detailed examination of the capital account of Indonesia's balance of payments up to 1976, see Rosendale (1978, pp. 81 ff. and 292 ff.). To the author's knowledge, this study is the only comprehensive analysis of the country's balance of payments in the Independence era.

11. Unfortunately, accurate estimates of the realized Indonesian equity investment in PMA firms are not available.

12. Asahan accounted for almost 90 per cent of the 1975 approvals figure, and indeed about 10 per cent of total approvals in the entire New Order period. For a fascinating and informative account of this huge investment, by a former Minister of Industry and Chairman of the BKPM who has been closely associated with it, see Soehoed (1983).

13. The ratios refer to *foreign* debt to equity since, until the 1986 policy package, PMA firms were technically not allowed to borrow from domestic banks. In practice, it is likely that some firms did borrow domestically, especially from the state banks, which offered negative real interest rates for much of the 1970s. However, since these loans were illegal there are obviously no data available.

14. See Robison (1986, chaps. 7–10) for a detailed discussion of domestic business groups in the period after 1970.

15. Over the period 1967–86, 45 per cent of approved foreign investment in West Java was located in Botabek, the region consisting of the three *kabupaten* adjacent to Jakarta together with the city of Bogor. A further 38 per cent was in the Banten region, most of it at the Cilegon complex west of Jakarta (Hardjono and Hill, 1986).

16. Note that the realized foreign investment data in Table 3.5 refer to foreign investors' equity investments.

17. Hasan (1981, pp. 65 ff.) elaborates on some of these points.

18. The only restriction on licensing arrangements is an indirect financial one in that, for taxation deduction purposes, firms may claim royalties up to a maximum of 2 per cent of ex-factory sales.

19. These data are from various issues of Japan, Office of the Prime Minister (annual) and the United States Department of Commerce. The Japanese statistics refer specifically to payments for technology exports, whereas the US data are for 'royalties and fees'. But the definitions are broadly comparable.

20. Note also the understatement arising from different time periods.

21. See also Langhammer (forthcoming) for an analysis of the capital imports/foreign investment nexus from a somewhat different perspective, namely the effects of foreign investment in Indonesia on imports from source countries.

22. As is frequently the case, the data source for the other countries (UNCTC, 1983b) uses the misleading BKPM figures.

4 The Major Foreign Investors

. . . the cost-benefit impact on host countries [of direct foreign investment]
is not so much a function of the national characteristics of transnationals but
of host countries' domestic policies. (Dorrance and Hughes, 1984, p. 3.)

THE most important determinant of the benefits and costs of foreign investment to the host country is the latter's policy environment. Multinational
corporations introduce a package of production, management, and marketing technology. The principal issue for the host country is to maximize its
share of rents accruing to these factors, consistent with its broad development objectives.

Nevertheless, the sources of foreign investment are not without significance, for at least two reasons. The first is that most countries seek to avoid
undue reliance on one country, or a very small number, for foreign investment. This is not only in deference to political sensitivities, nationalist
sentiment, or even fear of foreign manipulation. There are also important
economic reasons. A diversity of foreign investment sources expands information flows for technology and overseas markets, and therefore en-
hances the bargaining power of host governments and firms. The second
reason is that there is now increased interest in alleged differences in the
behaviour of foreign investors from different countries. These include
factors such as firms' propensity to export, to enter into joint ventures, and
to transfer and modify technology. This is a relatively recent subject of
investigation, mainly because substantial capital exporters among the
market economies consisted before 1970 almost exclusively of the United
States and a small number of European countries.

Both of these reasons are of relevance to Indonesia, and it is thus useful
to examine the composition of foreign investment by country of origin. As
to the first issue—concentration of investment sources—there has been a
flood of Japanese investment and technology into Indonesian manufacturing,
and American companies have been active in the petroleum sector. The
presence—many would argue 'over-presence'—of these investors has
been a sensitive political issue throughout the New Order period. Secondly,
the range of foreign investors in some Indonesian industries permits a
comparison of behaviour patterns. Several studies have attempted such
comparisons, and it is useful to look at their results in the light of the general
literature on the subject.

Foreign Investment by Country of Origin

Who are the major foreign investors? Despite the attention given to foreign investment in Indonesia, there have been very few serious attempts to ascertain the composition of *all* foreign investment by country of origin.[1] The most easily accessible data relate to BKPM approvals, and these have been used uncritically to reach the conclusion that Japan has been the dominant investor in Indonesia since 1966. While this is correct for the manufacturing sector, which accounts for the majority of the BKPM approvals, the conclusion is quite erroneous for all sectors. This is because, as noted already, the petroleum sector—excluded from the BKPM data—accounts for most of the foreign investment in the New Order, and the United States has been the major investor in oil.

Our primary focus in this chapter is on manufacturing. But it will be useful, initially, to look at the country shares for Indonesia as a whole, and then the BKPM sectors, before narrowing our focus.

Companies from Japan and the United States have been by far the largest investors in Indonesia since 1966. Over the period 1967–84, the two accounted for almost 80 per cent of gross realized investments in all sectors (see Table 4.1).[2] Their share has actually increased over time—up to 1977 they totalled 73 per cent—mainly owing to the surge in American oil investment since the late 1970s. There is surprisingly high sectoral specialization by each of the two countries, such that in many cases they are hardly competing directly. Japan dominates the BKPM sectors, accounting for almost 70 per cent of realized investments. By contrast, American investments in these sectors have been comparatively small—less than 10 per cent up to 1977, and just 5 per cent for the period as a whole. In fact, American investments through the BKPM have been a good deal less than those from both European and Asian developing countries, and only a little more than the 'other' category (comprising mainly Australia, Canada, and Liberia).

The inclusion of oil changes the picture dramatically. American companies have on average accounted for almost 80 per cent of the total, while Japan has had a very small presence, smaller even than some European countries. Putting the two series together provides an estimate of source country shares for Indonesia as a whole (final two columns, Table 4.1). Since realized investments in oil are much larger (about two and a half times for the whole period), the country shares in this sector have a major bearing on the final outcome. Thus America, with only 5 per cent of the BKPM total, has almost 60 per cent for all sectors; the latter share for Japan falls sharply because of its unimportance in oil.

More detailed information on foreign investment by source country is available only for the BKPM sectors. This is not a serious limitation for our study since the major focus is manufacturing, which has accounted for well over half the BKPM approved and realized investments.[3] The BKPM and Bank Indonesia data provide estimates of approved (or 'planned') and realized investments, disaggregated into equity and loan financing. As a first step, it is useful to compare these totals for the major investing countries, including separately the category 'more than one country' (see Table 4.2).

TABLE 4.1

Realized Foreign Investment by Country in All Sectors, 1967–1985

($ million or percentage)

Country/Region	BKPM Sectors[a]		Petroleum[b]		Total	
	Value	Per Cent	Value	Per Cent	Value	Per Cent
(1) 1967–1984[c]						
Japan	4,128	68	457	3	4,585	21
United States	304	5	12,314	78	12,618	58
Europe	546	9	2,302	15	2,848	13
Other Asia[d]	911	15	205	1	1,116	5
Other[d]	182	3	476	3	658	3
Total	6,071	100	15,754	100	21,825	100
(2) 1967–1977						
Japan	1,448	55	100	3	1,548	25
United States	243	9	2,697	78	2,940	48
Europe	258	10	504	15	762	13
Other Asia[d]	551	21	45	1	596	10
Other[d]	139	5	,115	3	254	4
Total	2,639	100	3,461	100	6,100	100

Sources: Bank Indonesia and United States Embassy (annual), various issues.

[a] Some figures do not add owing to rounding. Investments from more than one country have been allocated in accordance with single country shares. The data include foreign equity and loans.

[b] Investment includes exploration, development and capital production expenditures by foreign oil companies. The country shares are based on those given in Pangestu (1985, Appendix 1, p. 2).

[c] Up to September 1985 in the case of BKPM sectors.

[d] For country composition, see listings and notes in Table 4.2.

This generates a very large set of observations. To simplify the analysis, it is useful to address three main questions.

First, what is the pattern of investment approvals (columns 1–4)? It is clear that most investors planned to finance a large proportion of their projects using foreign loans. For almost all countries, this source was to have contributed about two-thirds. By contrast, the share of Indonesian equity was very small: a little over 10 per cent of the total and only half that of foreign equity. In the typical joint venture operation, Indonesian partners have played a very small role in terms of equity contribution; this extends to other facets of firms' operations, as we shall see later (Chapter 7). The means of finance (equity versus loan capital) are broadly comparable across countries, except for the much smaller Indonesian equity share (and larger foreign equity share) for investments from more than one country. There is no obvious explanation for the difference.[4]

The second question relates to realized investment (columns 5–7). No information on realized Indonesian equity investment is available for PMA firms, so the figures refer only to foreign equity and debt. Broadly the

TABLE 4.2

Planned and Realized Foreign Investment by Country in BKPM Sectors, 1967–1985[a] ($ million, ratio, or percentage)

Country/Region	Planned Investment				Realized Investment			Realized as Percentage of Planned $\frac{(5)}{(3+4)}$	Realized Debt/Equity Ratio (7)/(6)	Country/Region Total Realized as Percentage of Total
	Total	Equity		Foreign Debt	Total	Foreign Equity	Foreign Debt			
		Indonesian	Foreign							
	(1)	(2)	(3)	(4)	(5)	(6)	(7)	(8)	(9)	(10)
1. Japan	4,903	509	940	3,454	2,857	649	2,208	65	3.40	47
2. United States	1,381	194	291	897	206	89	117	17	1.31	3
3. Europe	2,802	478	659	1,667	377	193	183	16	0.95	6
Netherlands	499	55	198	246	138	56	82	31	1.46	2
United Kingdom	346	67	123	156	59	35	24	21	0.69	1
West Germany	472	82	112	278	59	29	30	15	1.03	1
Belgium	954	197	124	634	44	33	11	6	0.33	1
Switzerland	322	38	60	225	32	23	9	11	0.39	1
France	72	19	15	37	18	7	11	35	1.57	n
Norway	25	2	6	17	15	3	12	65	4.00	n
Other[b]	112	18	21	74	12	7	4	13	0.57	n

4. Other Asia	2,191	299	504	1,387	628	244	381	33	1.56	10
Hong Kong	1,390	184	318	888	497	173	323	41	1.87	8
South Korea	197	32	39	126	63	24	38	38	1.58	1
Singapore	149	25	40	84	33	22	12	27	0.55	1
Philippines	58	8	19	31	13	11	1	26	0.09	n
Other[c]	397	50	88	258	22	14	7	6	0.50	n
5. Other	487	40	79	369	132	33	100	29	3.33	2
Australia	322	18	47	256	106	25	80	35	3.20	2
Liberia	20	1	4	15	17	3	14	89	4.67	n
Other[d]	145	21	28	98	9	5	6	7	1.20	n
6. More than one country	3,648	254	1,070	2,324	1,871	696	1,176	55	1.69	31
Total	15,414	1,772	3,544	10,098	6,070	1,904	4,166	44	2.19	100

Source: Bank Indonesia.

[a] Up to 30 September 1985.

[b] Includes Denmark, Italy, Lichtenstein, Spain, Sweden.

[c] Includes Brunei, India, Malaysia, Taiwan, Thailand.

[d] Includes Canada, New Zealand, Panama, Bahamas.

n = Negligible (less than 1 per cent).

Totals do not add owing to rounding.

same conclusions as for the first question hold, namely of Japanese dominance, and much greater reliance on foreign debt than foreign equity.

Thirdly, how does the pattern of investment vary among the major investing countries and regions? Over the period 1967–85, Japan accounted for almost one-half of the total, and the multi-country group almost one-third (column 10). No other country or region contributed more than 10 per cent (recall that these figures, unlike those in the 'BKPM' part of Table 4.1, treat the multi-country group separately). In terms of regional shares, developing Asian countries have been more important than the combined total of both Europe and the United States. Looking just at the single-country shares, Hong Kong has been by far the largest investor after Japan, followed by the United States, the Netherlands,[5] and Australia. No other country has contributed much more than 1 per cent of the total.

The country shares of realized and approved investments differ significantly, as indicated by variations in the percentage of realized to approved investments (column 8). Japan has by far the highest percentage of realized investments of any major investor, in large measure owing to the implementation of the huge Asahan project. The figures for both Europe and America are appreciably lower, partly because some very large projects have been approved but not implemented (note especially the very low percentage for Belgium), and partly because it is thought that some realized investments, which have subsequently been bought out by local firms or closed down, have not been excluded from the approved data. There is no reason for believing that inherent 'behavioural' factors explain the difference between countries; rather, they seem to be the result of particular circumstances and investment projects.

There are equally large variations in (realized) debt–equity ratios (column 9). Once again the higher figure for Japan may be attributed in large part to the much higher gearing ratio in the Asahan project. The overall figure, of a little over two, is not high by international standards, but it needs to be remembered that the data exclude Indonesian equity and local capital market borrowings (which occurred even though the latter have been technically illegal until recently).

In addition to the general limitations of the BKPM and Bank Indonesia data, two specific qualifications should be attached to these country shares. The first is that, not surprisingly, source country and Indonesian statistics do not necessarily correspond, owing to differences in definitions and concepts. Exact estimates at the same point in time are not easy to obtain, but broadly comparable magnitudes are available. For example, United States investment in Indonesian manufacturing at the end of 1983 was reported as being $144 million (Bureau of Economic Analysis, 1985, Table 10). By contrast, Bank Indonesia data indicate realized equity investments by American companies in manufacturing at 30 September 1985 were $54 million (although the realized equity and loans figure ($143 million) was almost the same as the American estimate). Another example is given by Thee (1981), who pointed to the large discrepancy between Indian investments as reported by the BKPM and that from Indian sources. One explanation for the difference was the treatment of investments by investors of Indian origin residing permanently in Indonesia.

The second qualification is that some of the investment is undertaken by subsidiaries of multinational corporations. The BKPM usually records the source country as being that of the subsidiary's location whereas, from the point of view of control, the head office country might be more appropriate. For example, a substantial proportion of Hong Kong investment is, in reality, investment by British companies based in that colony. It is likely that Japanese companies, with the benefit of proximity (compared to European and American firms), do not employ such a 'two-stage' strategy for investment in Indonesia. But several large Japanese firms (for example, the textile company Toray) have large investments in Hong Kong companies, which in turn have extensive investments in South-East Asia. Consequently, the two-stage thesis cannot be completely discarded for Japan.[6]

Let us examine, finally, the pattern of investment within manufacturing by country of origin. The shares of the major countries and regions are broadly similar to those for all BKPM sectors (first two columns of Table 4.1), except that Japanese dominance is even more pronounced (see Table 4.3). Up to September 1985, Japanese companies accounted for an extraordinarily high proportion of investments—almost 80 per cent—if loan and equity capital are both included, and if the distribution of multi-country investments corresponds to that of single countries; the figure is still two-thirds if only equity investments are included.[7] The share of Japanese companies has also been rising over time: for the period 1978 to 1985, their share of total realized investments increased to a remarkable 89 per cent.[8] Moreover, even these figures to some extent understate the Japanese commercial presence, since Japanese companies play a key licensing role in industries such as automobiles in which new foreign investments are prohibited. Clearly it is not inaccurate to characterize foreign investment

TABLE 4.3

Foreign Manufacturing Investment by Country/Region, 1967–1985[a]
(percentage of total, realized)

Country/Region	Total, 1967–85		Sub-periods			
			1967–77		1978–85	
Japan	65	(79)	52	(63)	79	(89)
United States	6	(4)	11	(9)	1	(1)
Europe	15	(7)	15	(9)	14	(6)
Other Asia	12	(8)	18	(14)	6	(4)
Other	2	(2)	3	(5)	n	(n)
	100	(100)	100	(100)	100	(100)

Source: Bank Indonesia.
[a] Data refer to foreign equity investments; bracketed data refer to foreign equity plus foreign loans. Investments from more than one country have been allocated in accordance with single country shares.
n = Negligible (less than 1 per cent).

in Indonesian manufacturing since 1966 as basically Japanese investment. To the author's knowledge, no such similar country concentration exists in any of the other major developing market economies in Asia, with the possible exception of United States investment in the Philippines prior to the mid-1970s. The Japanese presence in Indonesian manufacturing parallels—and perhaps exceeds—that of the United States in parts of Latin America, in terms of country shares.

Investments from other countries, by comparison, pale into insignificance for the period as a whole. In the first decade after the introduction of the PMA law, there was a greater diversity of investing countries and shares, and the percentage of equity investments from both European and developing Asian countries was quite substantial. However, these percentages fell—sharply in the case of the latter—after 1977, and American investments have never been important in aggregate. Putting aside Japan and the multi-country group, Hong Kong investors have been the most important. The only European country to register over 2 per cent of investment by either measure was the Netherlands (see Table A.5).

Is the high share of Japanese investments explained by concentration in one or two very large sectors, or does it reflect dominance across all industries? The answer is a little of both. Japan's pre-eminent position is due mainly to its huge investments in basic metals (much of it in Asahan), the industry with the largest stock of foreign investment (see Table 4.4). It has also been by far the largest foreign investor in textiles, non-metallic minerals (mainly glass and cement), and metal goods. In fact, with the exception of wood and paper products, there is hardly an industry in which Japanese companies have *not* been one of the two major investors (by either or both measures of realized investment). Among the other investors, Hong Kong is the only country which features prominently in several sectors. But the sectors in which it is the largest investor—food, wood, and paper—have generally not been among the largest recipients of foreign investment.

Another way of looking at the country and industry breakdown is to determine the three largest areas of manufacturing investments of the major investors (see Table 4.5). This reveals that in spite of Japan's huge investments in the basic metals industry, its companies have no greater sectoral specialization than those from other countries. In the early years of the New Order, much Japanese capital was invested in the textiles industry. But Japanese companies followed—or perhaps led—Indonesia's industrial diversification into intermediate and capital goods industries. The pattern of the other sizeable foreign investors is fairly clear. Hong Kong companies have been attracted mainly to consumer goods (textiles especially in the early years) and resource-based industries. On the other hand, most of the American and European investments have been in chemicals and metal goods.

We shall examine the pattern of manufacturing investments from the various source countries shortly, but already it is fairly clear from Tables 4.4 and 4.5. In resource-based processing industries—especially wood and paper products—resource-poor Asian countries figure prominently. Japan and the three North-East Asian NICs have invested as a means of securing

TABLE 4.4

Foreign Manufacturing Investment by Country and Sector, 1967–1985 (percentage of sector total, realized)

Sector		Sector's Share of Investments	Three Largest Investors		
			(1)	(2)	(3)
Food	(1)	5	Belgium (25)	Hong Kong (19)	Japan (13)
	(2)	4	Hong Kong (39)	Japan (17)	Netherlands (13)
Textiles	(1)	19	Japan (77)	Hong Kong (18)	United Kingdom (2)
	(2)	18	Japan (84)	Hong Kong (11)	Liberia (3)
Wood	(1)	2	Hong Kong (55)	South Korea (17)	Japan (15)
	(2)	1	Hong Kong (38)	South Korea (34)	Japan (20)
Paper	(1)	2	Hong Kong (40)	Taiwan (26)	Japan (18)
	(2)	1	Norway (31)	Taiwan (30)	Hong Kong (24)
Chemicals	(1)	19	United States (22)	Netherlands (21)	Japan (17)
	(2)	14	Japan (29)	United States (22)	Netherlands (9)
Non-metallic Minerals	(1)	12	Japan (74)	United States (10)	Australia (9)
	(2)	13	Japan (84)	Australia (8)	United States (5)
Basic metals	(1)	28	Japan (97)	West Germany (1)	Canada (1)
	(2)	40	Japan (99)		
Metal goods	(1)	13	Japan (60)	West Germany (12)	United States (9)
	(2)	9	Japan (65)	United States (8)	West Germany (8)
Other	(1)	(n)	Thailand (35)	Japan (32)	West Germany (15)
	(2)	(n)	Japan (38)	West Germany (25)	Thailand (19)

Source: Bank Indonesia.

Note: (1) and (2) for each sector refer to equity and equity plus loans, respectively. Multi-country investments have been excluded. n = Negligible (less than 1 per cent).

TABLE 4.5

The Five Largest Investors in Manufacturing: Sectoral Composition,
1967–1985 (percentage of country total, realized)

Country		*(1)*		*(2)*		*(3)*	
				Three Largest Sectors			
Japan	(1)	basic metals	(50)	textiles	(24)	metal goods	(13)
	(2)	basic metals	(59)	textiles	(18)	metal goods	(9)
Hong Kong	(1)	textiles	(43)	wood	(15)	food	(14)
	(2)	textiles	(35)	food	(28)	chemicals	(17)
United States	(1)	chemicals	(64)	metal goods	(20)	non-metallic minerals	(9)
	(2)	chemicals	(59)	metal goods	(29)	non-metallic minerals	(8)
Netherlands	(1)	chemicals	(68)	food	(14)	metal goods	(11)
	(2)	chemicals	(48)	food	(25)	metal goods	(21)
West Germany	(1)	metal goods	(42)	chemicals	(37)	basic metals	(13)
	(2)	metal goods	(51)	chemicals	(34)	food	(7)
More than one	(1)	non-metallic minerals	(41)	chemicals	(27)	textiles	(17)
	(2)	non-metallic minerals	(38)	chemicals	(31)	textiles	(21)

Source: Bank Indonesia.
Note: (1) and (2) for each country refer to equity, and equity plus loans respectively.

access to Indonesia's natural resources, particularly (as in the case of plywood) when the Indonesian government has prohibited their export in unprocessed form. Japan and, to a lesser extent, Hong Kong have dominated the textiles industry. This is not surprising: they both have large established export industries which, to penetrate Indonesia's trade barriers, required a local presence. Moreover, the Indonesian expansion coincided with Japanese companies going offshore in any case, as the country lost its comparative advantage in the labour-intensive end of the industry.

The case of basic metals, and Japan's dominance of the industry, has already been referred to. Japan's importance in metal goods is explained by the large and increasing acceptance of a wide range of Japanese appliances, automobiles, and other metal products by Indonesian consumers, together with high import barriers in some instances. In chemicals, international brand name products from the United States and Europe explain Japan's lower share, but it is still the largest country in terms of total realized investments.

Differences among Foreign Investors

We emphasized at the beginning of this chapter that host country policies are a more important determinant of the benefits of foreign investment to the local economy than the country composition of this investment. Moreover, Japanese companies so dominate foreign investment in Indonesian manufacturing that there is little point in conducting very detailed intercountry comparisons. Nevertheless, the general literature on this subject is now quite extensive, and several analyses for Indonesia make a useful contribution to it. We focus on two comparisons: the United States and Japan, and developed and developing countries.

There is no need to repeat here the arguments concerning alleged differences between American and Japanese foreign investments. The purportedly 'unique' characteristics of Japanese investments, it is argued by some (for example, Ozawa (1979) and Yoshihara (1978)), require a reformulation of the monopolistic theory of foreign investment, based on the North American and European experience, which derive from the work of Hymer (1976). According to this view, the traditional theory is deficient because much Japanese investment occurs in relatively labour-intensive industries in which the technology gap—from which the competitive advantages of foreign firms are believed to derive—is minimal. Kojima (1978) is one of the originators of alternative theories for Japanese investment. He argues that Japanese investment, in declining (in Japan), relatively labour-intensive industries, is predominantly trade creating. By contrast, he maintains, United States investments tend to occur in technologically advanced industries which are mainly domestic-market oriented; consequently they are anti-trade creating.

The data for Indonesia, though poor, provide little support for the Kojima hypothesis.[9] The evidence suggests that Japanese investors neither *intend* to be more export oriented than those from the United States nor are they *actually* more so. A large survey (more than 500 firms) of developed

TABLE 4.6

Motives Underlying Foreign Investment in ASEAN and Indonesia (primary and secondary sectors only)

Motive	ASEAN, by Investing Country/Region						Indonesia	
	United States	Japan	Europe	Australia	Total	(Percentage of Total)	No.	(Per Cent)
Securing, maintaining, or developing an overseas market	144	70	37	39	290	(52.3)	28	(50.9)
Securing, maintaining, or developing raw material supplies	45	37	21	—	103	(18.6)	25	(45.5)
Competitive forces necessitating low-cost bases	60	16	14	3	93	(16.8)	2	(3.6)
Securing, maintaining or developing a regional base	25	2	11	—	38	(6.8)	0	
Complementation of activities	3	2	2	—	7	(1.3)	0	
Others	18	4	2	—	24	(4.3)	0	
Total	295	131	87	42	555	(100)	55	(100)

Source: Allen, 1979, pp. 68–9.

country investors in ASEAN, conducted in the late 1970s by Allen (1979), revealed a strong preference for sales in host country markets as a motive underlying Japanese investment in ASEAN (see Table 4.6). Resource security was an important motive, accounting for about 28 per cent of Japanese investments (almost double the American figure of 15 per cent). Among the other motives, which presumably refer mainly to manufacturing, Japan had the highest proportion for local market sales (53 per cent compared to 49 per cent for the United States) and the lowest for exports (12 per cent compared to 20 per cent). A comparable breakdown is not provided for Indonesia, but it is likely that the first two motives are the major ones for Japanese firms.

The survey data for motives are confirmed by data relating to the actual sales orientation of Japanese and American firms in Indonesia and elsewhere (see Tables 4.7 and 4.8). For Asia and the Pacific (excluding Japan and Oceania), United States investments appear to be more local-market oriented than those from Japan (79 per cent of sales, compared to 72 and 67 per cent for Japan depending on the year chosen). However, the coverage of the region differs somewhat, and in every case for which a direct comparison is available, Japanese firms have a higher percentage of domestic sales. In Indonesia they are virtually entirely oriented towards the domestic market (96 per cent versus 59 per cent for United States firms), confirming also that the bulk of foreign investment in the Indonesian manufacturing sector has been import substituting in nature. (More recent United States data are available, but for many countries, Indonesia included, they are affected by non-disclosure requirements.) In other countries, the proportion devoted to domestic sales is higher for Japanese than American firms—three times in Malaysia, nine times in Singapore and more than half as much again in Korea and Thailand.

TABLE 4.7

Sales Destination of United States Direct Foreign Investment in Manufacturing, 1977 (percentage of sales)

| Country/Region | Local Market | Export Markets | | | |
		Total	United States	Other Countries	Total
Asia and Pacific[a]	79	21	7	14	100
Indonesia	59	41	2	39	100
India	97	3	n	3	100
Malaysia	24	76	46	31	100
Philippines	74	26	14	11	100
Singapore	7	93	62	31	100
Korea	32	68	37	32	100
Taiwan	29	71	57	15	100
Latin America	90	10	4	6	100

Source: United States Department of Commerce, 1981.

[a] Excludes Japan and refers to 1975.

n = Negligible (less than 1 per cent).

TABLE 4.8

Sales Destination of Japanese Direct Foreign Investment in Asian
Manufacturing, 1970s (percentage of sales)

| Country | Year | Local Market | Export Markets | | | Total |
			Total	Japan	Other Countries	
All Asia	1979	67	33	10	23	100
	1973	72	28	4	24	100
Indonesia	1973	96	4	4	n	100
Hong Kong	1973	29	70	n	70	100
Korea	1973	52	48	34	13	100
Malaysia	1973	87	13	8	5	100
Singapore	1973	63	37	5	32	100
Taiwan	1973	47	54	44	10	100
Thailand	1979	91	9	3	6	100
	1973	94	6	1	6	100

Sources: 1. Japan, MITI (annual) for All Asia, 1979.
   2. Chinwanno and Tambunlertchai (1983) for Thailand, 1979.
   3. Sakurai (1982) for all 1973 data.
n = Negligible (less than 1 per cent).

Additional data, derived from investment approvals by the BKPM,
support this conclusion. According to estimates prepared by Hasan (1981)
up to 1977, intended exports by Japanese firms were a smaller proportion
than for American firms (see Table 4.9). The data are rather dated, and
qualitative evidence suggests that Japanese firms have increased exports in
response to changes in the host countries' trade regimes. But the hypothesis
that Japanese firms are more outward oriented receives little support in a

TABLE 4.9

Distribution of Manufacturing Subsidiaries by Export Orientation and
Home Country, 1967–1977 (percentage of all subsidiaries)

| Home Country | Exports as Percentage of Total Sales | | | All Subsidiaries |
	≤ 30 Per Cent	31–70 Per Cent	> 70 Per Cent	
Hong Kong	88	2	10	100
ASEAN	91	0	9	100
Other developing countries	92	8	0	100
Japan	84	2	14	100
USA	76	7	17	100
Other developed countries	82	8	11	100
Multi-country	92	5	3	100

Source: Hasan, 1981, p. 56.

direct statistical sense. Nor do Japanese firms in Indonesia appear to accord closely with the model developed by Kojima.

Do Japanese firms differ from American firms in other respects? The literature on Japanese firms suggests that, relative to other developed country investors, they tend to locate in labour-intensive, 'mature' industries and are more willing to accept joint venture (including minority equity) arrangements. Indonesia is a good test of the latter assertion since, initially, the government adopted a liberal policy towards foreign investment with minimal controls on foreign equity shares. Once more, the Indonesian data provide little support for the Japanese stereotype. Of the 505 approvals in the first decade (1967–76) for which data were available, more than 90 per cent had majority foreign equity (see Table 4.10). The differences between the United States and Japan are not significant, however; in fact, in a marginally higher percentage of cases United States investors had a minor equity share (11 per cent compared to 9 per cent for Japan).

Data on foreign and local equity shares for approved manufacturing investments up to September 1985 do show a somewhat different picture (see Table A.6). Among the major investors, Japanese partners' equity shares were generally lower than those from most of the other major countries, both in aggregate and for direct comparisons within industries. Indeed, the Japanese shares were generally lower than those for the 'small' investing countries, Hong Kong and Australia. These data do need to be interpreted carefully, however, as they are particularly sensitive to the year in which the approvals were granted. Because Japan has been an especially dominant investor after 1974 (when local equity shares became an important issue), the lower shares could be attributable as much to this factor as to the country characteristics.

Nor do other characteristics of Japanese and United States investments appear to accord with those suggested in the Japanese literature. As already noted, Japanese investment in the labour-intensive textiles industry has been extensive, whereas United States investments have been negligible (see Table 4.4). Nevertheless, for manufacturing as a whole, Japan's actual investments are not more labour intensive than those from the United States, nor do they appear to be located in more labour-intensive industries.

TABLE 4.10

Foreign Ownership Shares of Five Major Investing Countries, 1967–1976

Share of Foreign Partner	Total, Five Countries	Japan	Hong Kong	USA	Singapore	Netherlands
< 30 per cent	1	0	0	2	5	2
30 – < 50 per cent	8	9	5	9	19	2
50 – < 80 per cent	70	82	68	52	55	78
≥ 80 per cent	20	9	27	37	21	18
All firms	100	100	100	100	100	100
Number of investments	(505)	(199)	(117)	(98)	(42)	(49)

Source: Siahaan, Thee et al., 1978, p. 47.

Indeed, the actual data, reported by Wells and Warren (1979) for the period 1967–75, suggest the reverse has been the case, probably in large measure because of the Asahan project (see Table 4.11). Compared to United States firms, Japanese firms appear to be larger and to have higher capital–labour ratios, whether measured in terms of total fixed assets or machinery[10] (the latter, in particular, are significantly higher). In one area of operations, the data do support the findings of the general literature—concerning the Japanese proclivity for a higher number of expatriate personnel compared to American firms—but the difference is hardly significant.

The Indonesian data also shed some light on the characteristics of foreign investors from other developing countries, as compared to those from developed countries. The recent literature on this subject (Lall et al. (1983) and Wells (1983)) has drawn attention to some of the features of these investments, which appear to resemble those of Japanese investments in the 1960s. Developing country investors, it is argued, tend to locate in more labour-intensive industries, to adopt more labour-intensive technologies, to be more inward oriented, and to be slower to transfer technology.

The Indonesian data support many of these arguments. Up to 1975, developing country investors were less capital intensive than developed country investors, both with respect to total fixed assets and machinery (see Table 4.11, columns 2 and 3). They were also smaller, in some but not all cases (column 4). Subsequently, Hasan (1981) extended the comparison up to 1977 and for each major industry group. He found capital–labour ratios of developing country firms to be about one-half those of developed countries for manufacturing as a whole (see Table 4.12). This was also the case for most industries, the differences being particularly large (more than three times) for textiles, non-metallic minerals, and basic iron and steel. The only exception to this conclusion was the heterogeneous food, beverages, and tobacco group; disaggregated data, which would be necessary to explain the difference, are not available.

Other differences between the two groups of investors are also important. Wells and Warren (1979) found that developing country investors in Indonesia tend to locate in industries characterized by lower research and development and advertising expenditure compared to developed country investors. This provides some support for the view that the former group of firms tend to rely less on product differentiation and advanced technology as a basis for competition.[11] Developing country investors also tend to be even more domestic-market oriented than other investors (see Table 4.9). In fact, for approvals up to 1977, developed country investors planned to export 17 per cent of their sales, as compared to 11 per cent for developing countries (Hasan, 1981, p. 55). Even Hong Kong investors—for which one motive for investing in Indonesia is apparently 'quota hopping' (Chen, 1983a, 1983b)—had little intention to export.[12] These differences reflect the importance of one 'firm-specific' advantage which firms from developed countries possess but which those from developing countries cannot easily replicate—knowledge of and access to a larger (and generally more open) market. Perhaps surprisingly, Hong Kong investors tend to have higher equity shares than investors from other countries, notably Japan (see

TABLE 4.11

Capital Intensity and Employment of Foreign Manufacturing Projects by Country of Origin, 1967–1975

	Number of Projects	Average Capital-Labour Ratio ($'000)	Average Machinery Investment per Worker ($'000)	Average Total Investment per Project ($'000)	Average Number of Expatriates per Project	Expatriates as Percentage of Total Employment (Median)
Chinese[a]	48	8	4	2,772	14	5
Other South-East Asia	10	8	2	960	12	8
Other developing countries	6	10	5	3,935	20	6
Japan	80	19	8	5,687	11	5
United States	50	17	5	2,403	5	4
United Kingdom	n.a.	20	5	1,189	6	6
Other industrialized countries	92	13	7	2,063	7	4

Source: Wells and Warren, 1979, Tables 2, 6–9.
[a] Refers to Hong Kong, Singapore and Taiwan.
n.a. = Not available.

TABLE 4.12

Capital–Labour Ratios of Developed (DC) and Developing Country (LDC)
Manufacturing Subsidiaries, 1967–1977 ($'000 per worker)

	Fixed Assets		Machinery	
ISIC Industry	DC	LDC	DC	LDC
31 Food, beverages and tobacco	11.3	15.7	6.6	11.1
32 Textiles	20.5	6.2	16.6	5.1
33 Wood and wood products	21.1	9.4	12.0	7.0
34 Paper and printing	17.8	17.9	12.6	13.2
35 Chemicals	20.9	10.5	11.4	6.3
36 Non-metallic minerals	34.9	7.4	17.7	5.0
37 Basic iron and steel	37.4	5.4	21.6	4.1
38 Metal products	16.6	7.3	9.6	4.5
39 Miscellaneous	8.5	—	2.9	—
Total	18.5	8.9	11.1	6.1

Source: Hasan, 1981, pp. 50–1.

Tables 4.10 and A.6). This might be explained by the fact that a considerable proportion of Hong Kong investment entered Indonesia when the foreign investment laws were more liberal.

The Indonesian data thus throw considerable light on differences among foreign investors in manufacturing. The distinctive features of developing country investments are confirmed. By contrast, however, Japan–United States differences do not appear to be significant. The diversity of foreign investors in Indonesia—the heavy reliance on Japan notwithstanding—suggests that there is considerable scope for countries like Indonesia to 'shop around' in the international markets for technology, capital, and management in many industries.

Nevertheless, differences among foreign investors—and the importance of the issue—should not be exaggerated. The data base is not strong, and the (Indonesian) policy environment is a major determinant of investors' behaviour. It matters little, for example, that developed country investors are somewhat more export oriented when foreign investors are, as a whole, overwhelmingly oriented towards the domestic market. The fundamental solution, if foreign investors are to be more outward looking, is reform of Indonesia's trade regime rather than the selection of investors from certain countries.

The Characteristics of Major Investors: Towards an Explanation

What factors account for the pattern of foreign investment in Indonesia by country of origin? In the case of merchandise trade flows, there is a well-developed body of theory, based on the Heckscher–Ohlin–Samuelson factor proportions theorem, and subsequent extensions of it, which attempts to explain trade patterns. But theory provides a lot less guidance in the case of investment patterns. International differences in relative resource endowments—the basis for trade between countries—do not in themselves induce investment flows. Indeed, in many cases international investment is a substitute for trade, when the erection of trade barriers in the host country dictates that investment (or licensing) is the only effective means of market access. The absence of a general theory of patterns of foreign investment among countries suggests that a more profitable approach to explaining the country composition in the case of Indonesia is to look at the record of the major investing countries, in light of the factors which are generally regarded as significant in the decision to invest overseas. These factors include tariff policy, historical (colonial) ties, relative distance, the resource endowments of the source and host countries, and the product cycle (see Caves, 1982, pp. 56–64 for an elaboration). Proximity, in particular, appears to be an important factor for all but the very large investing countries, and for the same reasons that relative distance matters more in the case of services trade than it does in merchandise trade. In the words of Caves (1982, p. 64): 'Casual evidence . . . confirms the general impression that the bulk of their [source countries'] foreign investments go where the transactional and information-cost disadvantages are least.'[13]

What are the global investment patterns of the major foreign investing countries in Indonesia? The United States, until recently the world's largest capital exporter, has invested mainly in developed countries. In 1983, about 75 per cent of its investments were in these countries; for manufacturing investments, developed countries accounted for an even higher share—80 per cent.[14] Among developing countries, Latin America has been the largest recipient (58 per cent). But the share of developing Asian and Pacific countries (26 per cent) has been growing and, within this group, Indonesia is the second largest destination (6 per cent of all developing countries), marginally less than Hong Kong. As we have seen, most American investment in Indonesia is in the oil sector. Manufacturing investments in Indonesia account for just 5 per cent of the American total in that country. By contrast, the share of manufacturing in total American investments in all other developing Asian and Pacific countries was 27 per cent; for Latin America it was 50 per cent.

American investment in Indonesia is therefore somewhat atypical, and theorizing regarding the pattern of and motives for this investment has to be modified accordingly. In particular, the proposition that American manufacturing firms go abroad to capitalize on firm-specific advantages, such as superior technology or established international brand names (see, for example, Sekiguchi and Krause, 1980), is not so relevant to Indonesia since manufacturing investments are so small. Rather, it is Indonesia's oil and gas resources, and American expertise in this sector, which explain most of the American investment.[15]

Since Japanese investment is a large part of the story of foreign investment in Indonesian manufacturing after 1966, it is worth looking at that country's investment patterns in a little more detail. The remarkable intensity of Japanese investment in Indonesia is explained both by the factors which led to the rapid emergence of Japan as a major foreign investor, and by specific developments in Indonesia. Until its recent push into North

America and Europe, the geographic pattern of Japanese investments differed significantly from that of the United States in two important respects. First, over half (55 per cent) of its investments were in developing countries for the period 1951–82. Secondly, there was a much higher geographic concentration in Asia, and ASEAN in particular. Up to 1982, ASEAN accounted for one-fifth of all Japanese investments, Indonesia alone contributing two-thirds of this total.[16]

The factors explaining the rapid growth of Japanese foreign investment from the late 1960s have been well documented elsewhere.[17] Two were particularly important for Indonesia. First, rapidly rising real wages in Japan rendered many labour-intensive industries uncompetitive, and foreign investment was seen as a means of utilizing accumulated managerial and technical expertise in these industries. For example, Japanese investments have been particularly large in the Indonesian textiles industry, where, in addition, output was rising very quickly in response to the accumulated demand backlog in the 1960s and to rapid economic growth. Secondly, the Japanese government increasingly came to see foreign investment as an important means of fulfilling the country's supply security objectives, a factor which explains several large Japanese investments in resource-based projects.

Perhaps even more important in explaining the upsurge were a number of general factors. One was the remarkable coincidence of investment regimes in both countries changing more or less simultaneously. Something of a 'gold rush' mentality developed among foreign investors towards Indonesia from the late 1960s, and this occurred precisely as Japanese companies were eagerly seeking out overseas investment opportunities. A second factor was the key role Indonesia occupied in Japan's commercial and strategic policies towards the region. Indonesia was—and is—the dominant power in ASEAN, in Japan's view, and the strong economic complementarity between the two countries—particularly in the resource trade—reinforced Japan's interest. Consequently, a range of measures (aid,[18] trade, and political initiatives) spurred Japanese investments, and built on the contacts developed during the Old Order period. Perhaps the only puzzling feature of Japanese investment in Indonesia is the tiny proportion in the oil sector, in view of Japan's leading position as an oil importer. The explanation appears to be, simply, the superiority of American technology and commercial experience in the industry. Looking to the future, it is quite likely that both the magnitude of new Japanese investment in Indonesia and its share (the share of Japan in inflows and the share of Indonesia in outflows) may decline because Indonesia is currently an unattractive investment environment, and because Japanese companies have recently been directing increased investment to Europe and North America (see Kinoshita, 1986, pp. 46–9).

Little need be said about the pattern of investment from the other countries, since by comparison the totals are much smaller and the investments much less intensively studied. Hong Kong investments resemble the early pattern of Japanese investments in some respects (see Chen (1983a, 1983b)). Most Hong Kong companies going abroad have ventured little further than South-East Asia and, more recently, China. They have invested in industries in which they developed production and managerial technology, especially in those labour-intensive activities in which Hong Kong is losing its comparative advantage (for example, weaving and garments). Other investments have been in industries, such as plywood, where Hong Kong companies can exploit their knowledge of international marketing channels. These investments have, of course, been greatly facilitated by the extensive Chinese business network in the region. This factor, together with immediate proximity and historical ties, also explains much of the Singapore investment.

Dutch investments, though small in aggregate, are also explained by historical ties. Indonesian–Dutch relations have generally been close during the New Order, despite the record before 1966. Although much of the 'denationalized' Dutch capital did not return after 1966, there was sufficient residual knowledge and interest in the Indonesian economy to attract some Dutch investors. Some of these firms were re-established under the Foreign Investment Law of 1967, which provided additional incentives for firms—nationalized during the Old Order—resumed by their former owners.

Investments from Australia also reflect the effects of proximity and changes in the policy environment. Australian firms have traditionally been quite significant investors in the South Pacific (particularly in New Zealand and Papua New Guinea). The removal of restrictions on outward investment and increased interest in the ASEAN countries in the early 1970s led to increased investments. ASEAN's share of Australian direct investment rose quite sharply, from 3 per cent in 1970 to about 11 per cent in 1975, and it remained at about this share until the general downturn in foreign investor interest in Indonesia in the mid-1980s. Indonesia had also been the largest recipient (or second largest, to Singapore) of Australian investment in ASEAN. A small survey of firms in Indonesia confirmed impressionist evidence that most Australian companies are engaged in manufacturing for the domestic market; mining investments have also been significant.[19]

Is it possible to classify the various factors affecting the patterns of investment between countries more systematically? One approach is to adapt the analysis of trade intensities to investment flows.[20] The trade intensity index provides a useful means of gauging the relative importance—and determinants—of bilateral trade flows. The index measures the share of one country's trade with another country as a proportion of the latter's share of world trade. Formally, the index I_{ij} is given by

$$\frac{X_{ij}}{X_i} \bigg/ \frac{M_j}{M_w - M_i} \cdot 100$$

where X_{ij} = exports of country i to country j
X_i = total exports of country i
M_j = imports of country j
M_w = total world imports
M_i = total imports of country i

This approach to the analysis of trade flows has recently been modified to permit further examination of foreign investment in ASEAN by Pangestu (1980, 1985). These pioneering studies—the first of their kind to the author's knowledge—provide a useful framework in which to explain investment patterns, and it is therefore useful to briefly report her main results.

She develops an index of the intensity of direct investment in country j from country i, defined (using her symbols) as:

$$D_{ji} = \frac{I_{ji}}{I_j} \bigg/ \frac{O_l}{O_i} \cdot 100$$

where I_{ji} = direct investment in country j by country i
I_j = total direct investment in j
O_l = total direct investment from (developed) source countries to developing countries
O_i = total direct investment from country i to developing countries

Thus an index of 100 indicates that the share of direct investment by country i in country j out of i's total investment outflows is equal to the share of i's outflows in total investments in developing countries. An index of 200 indicates that the former share is double that of country i's outflows in total investment in developing countries. In other words, indices in excess of 100 illustrate shares which are higher than would be expected on the basis of the investing country's share of all outflows to developing countries.

Following the trade intensity approach, she decomposes the investment intensity index into two measures, a complementarity index and a country bias index.[21] The first refers to factors which contribute to complementarity in investment structure by industry for the two countries, that is, to the correspondence between the industry composition of the source country's investment outflows and of the host country's investment inflows. These factors include relative resource endowments and the bases for competitive advantages of foreign investors on the one hand, and policies which seek to affect the level and composition of investments, on the other hand. The second index, that of country bias, refers to factors which affect resistance to investment flows, given the composition of investment in the two countries. These factors include relative proximity, political and economic associations, and information flows.

What do the indices, as calculated by Pangestu, reveal about the pattern of foreign investment in Indonesia in particular and ASEAN more generally? Broadly, they provide empirical verification for the observations in the last section. Looking first at investment in all sectors, the investment intensity index of the major investors varies enormously for Indonesia and the other ASEAN countries (see Table 4.13, where the intensity index is given by I). That for Japan is consistently over 200, in the case of Indonesia (and the other ASEAN countries in most years), indicating that Japanese investment has been more than double the amount which would be expected on the basis of its share of investment in developing countries. By contrast,

TABLE 4.13

Intensity, Complementarity, and Country Bias in Foreign Investment in Indonesia and ASEAN

Investing Country	Year[a]	Indonesia			Other ASEAN (I^b only)			
		I^b	C^b	B^b	Malaysia	Philippines	Singapore	Thailand
Japan	1971	287	127	226	217	77	104	533
	1974	241	210	115	128	247	115	225
	1976	446	178	251	225	392	298	293
	1980	277	153	181	326	156	234	446
United States	1971	70	118	59	51	103	60	79
	1974	53	99	53	29	56	60	52
	1976	45	89	51	22	38	36	49
	1980	76	95	80	13	98	41	40
Australia	1971	171	144	119	32	—	103	—
	1974	239	78	306	104	157	116	40
	1976	136	104	131	321	664	212	48
United Kingdom	1971	13	102	13	167	24	118	18
	1974	16	141	11	167	114	152	65
	1976	10	162	6	176	81	123	79
West Germany	1971	12	35	34	3	21	14	7
	1974	30	64	47	2	3	42	7
	1976	30	80	37	9	5	12	18
Hong Kong	1976	731	257	284	1,019	74	1,559	1,041

Sources: Pangestu, 1980, Table 5, and 1985, Table 10.

[a] In most cases three-year averages.

[b] I, C, B indicate intensity, complementarity, and country bias indices respectively.

the index is much lower for all American investment in Indonesia and ASEAN. For Indonesia, it peaked at 76 in 1980, reflecting the upsurge in (mainly American) oil investments at that time. The index for American investments in the other ASEAN countries is also below 100, the notable exception being the Philippines where historically strong ties explain the higher figure.

Consequently, Japanese investment in Indonesia—and the rest of ASEAN—is large not only because Japan is a sizeable foreign investor, but also because of its heavy regional concentration in South-East Asia. Aggregate United States investments in Indonesia and ASEAN are also large, but their size primarily reflects the country's global importance as a foreign investor. Adjusting for investment shares, American investments in the region are actually *less* than what would be expected on the basis of its total investments in developing countries.

Decomposing the intensity index into complementarity (C) and country bias (B) indices, presented only for Indonesia in Table 4.13, provides further insights. There has been a reasonable correspondence between the industry composition of American investment outflows and Indonesian inflows, indicated by the fact that the complementarity index is close to 100 for most of the period. This is almost entirely due to large American investments in Indonesia's oil industry. In 1980, for example, the complementarity index (of 95) consisted mainly of petroleum (see Table 4.14). Manufacturing, services, and other sectors contributed very little. Country bias in American investment has generally been low. In other words, the resistances to investment flows—distance, fairly weak political association, information flows, and so on—explain the low intensity index for American investment over most of the period.

TABLE 4.14

Complementarity in United States and Japanese Investment
in Indonesia, 1980

Sector	United States	Japan
Mining and petroleum	84	121
Manufacturing	9	31
Food	1	n
Textiles	2	14
Wood and paper	n	n
Chemicals	2	4
Metal products	4	11
Electrical products	0	0
Machinery and transport	0	0
Other	1	1
Services	2	1
Other	n	n
Total	95	153

Source: Pangestu, 1985, Table 12.
n = Negligible (less than 1 per cent).

The pattern of Japanese investment in Indonesia is quite different. Both the complementarity and the country bias indices were greater than 100 throughout the period (see Table 4.13). Thus, not only was there a close correspondence in the composition of investment flows between the two countries, but resistances to Japanese investments were low. As noted above, close political ties and the importance of proximity in Japan's initial investment outflows explain these low resistances. The main sectors contributing to high complementarity were mining and manufacturing (see Table 4.14).[22]

Some interesting patterns are evident also in investment by other countries in Indonesia (Table 4.13). The first is the very low investment intensity indices for the two European investors up to the mid-1970s.[23] In the case of the United Kingdom, especially, the complementarity index is quite high. But for both, the country bias index is extremely low, indicating the absence of special circumstances (past political associations, distance) contributing to reduced resistances. Investments by these countries in Indonesia are therefore a reflection primarily of their global importance as foreign investors. By contrast, the intensity indices for two smaller regional investors, Australia and Hong Kong, were much higher (exceptionally so in the case of Hong Kong). As would be expected, country bias is very strong; so also is complementarity in most cases.

1. The only writer who has made a serious effort to include oil is Pangestu (1980, 1985). For some partial attempts, see Thee (1984a) and Hill (1984).

2. Three qualifications to this statement are necessary. First, data on investments in financial services are not available. However, these investments are unlikely to have been large (Thee (1984a, p. 92) suggests a cumulative figure of $100–200 million), and so their exclusion does not alter the picture greatly. The second, more important qualification is that investments from more than one country have been allocated to single countries according to each of the latter's shares. The Appendix discusses this limitation in more detail. Thirdly, the country shares of petroleum investment are assumed to be constant throughout the period, using the breakdown which has been obtained for just some of the years. The shares are a reasonably accurate approximation, and it is well known that American companies have dominated the petroleum industry throughout the New Order.

3. In most years, manufacturing has constituted about twice the combined total for agriculture, mining (non-oil), and services. The exceptions have been years in which large mining projects have been approved or have commenced (see Table 5.1).

4. It is possible that, since there are by definition several foreign investors in these projects, the foreign firms have already secured sufficient risk diversification. For single country investors, the diversification strategy has entailed greater resort to foreign loans, as indicated by the generally higher debt to (foreign) equity ratios for both approved and realized investments, especially for Japanese firms. Such an explanation remains at best speculative, however.

5. In passing it should be noted that the Netherlands has not played as important a role in Indonesia's trade and investment as have the other ex-colonial powers of South-East Asia, the United States (in the Philippines) and the United Kingdom (in Malaysia and Singapore), in their former colonies. One reason for the difference is simply that the Netherlands is a much smaller commercial power than the other two countries. In addition, the events surrounding the achievement of independence in Indonesia, the sensitivity of public opinion towards any vestige of colonialism, and the bitter experience for the Dutch in 1957–8 are important explanatory factors.

6. I am grateful to Yoshihara Kunio for raising this point in correspondence.

7. Shares according to both equity and total investments are presented in Table 4.3 and the next three tables. On *a priori* grounds, there is little to choose between the two as a measure of the relative importance of foreign investors. The total figure is, perhaps, a better indication of the magnitude of a country's investment presence in Indonesia, since the foreign partner generally arranges (and guarantees) overseas loans, and controls their disbursement. The equity figures, on the other hand, are a better guide to the direct financial commitment of foreign investors.

8. Note that the investment totals and shares for the years 1978–85 are calculated as the difference between the cumulative totals for the periods up to the end of 1977 and 30 September 1985.

9. See also Thee (1984a) for a careful rebuttal of Kojima's thesis, and Heimenz (1987) for an interesting comparison of the pattern of West German, Japanese, and United States investments in ASEAN manufacturing. Heimenz verifies the important point that, whatever the differences originally observed, these have converged as technology differences within the three investing countries have become less pronounced over time.

10. Lecraw (1983) reports the results of a survey of 153 subsidiaries of foreign firms in ASEAN manufacturing in 1978–9 which do not confirm these conclusions. United States investments, for example, were substantially larger than those from Japan. (US firms also located in more concentrated industries, and in those in which research and development and advertising expenditures were higher.) However, he provides no breakdown for each of the ASEAN countries, so the study does not necessarily conflict with the data presented in the text and in Table 4.11.

11. This finding was confirmed in the ASEAN study by Lecraw (1983).

12. More recent data suggest that the market orientation of developing country investors may be changing. In his examination of the Jakarta export processing zone, Warr (1983) found that all fifteen of the firms with foreign equity were from developing Asian countries, although there was, indirectly, United States and European ownership.

13. Another related query concerns the size of aggregate investment flows to countries. Young (1978) addressed this question for several South-East Asian countries, and sought an answer with reference to a range of explanatory variables. He concluded that profitability, relative wage rates, and tariff protection were the most important. However, there were shortcomings in the measures adopted, and his results should at best be regarded as illustrative.

14. Data in this paragraph relate to 1983 and are taken from the Bureau of Economic Analysis (1985).

15. It might also be noted that Indonesia's unattractiveness as a base for manufactured exports has resulted in very small American investments of the 'product cycle' variety, that is, of the labour-intensive stages of 'mature' industries being pushed offshore, in search of low labour costs, for re-export to America. This is illustrated in United States imports of semiconductors under Tariff Items 806.30 and 807.00, which provide liberal market entry conditions for offshore assembly and processing of components manufactured in the United States, and which are often facilitated by American investment abroad. By 1983, imports under Items 806/807 had totalled $3.4 billion. For the above Tariff Items, neighbouring Malaysia and the Philippines accounted for 31 and 18 per cent of the total respectively, while Indonesia's share was just 2 per cent (see Grunwald and Flamm, 1985, pp. 68–85).

16. The figures in this paragraph are drawn from Tsao Yuan (1986, Table 3.12), who cites the Ministry of Finance, *Private Sector Overseas Investment*, Tokyo.

17. See, for example, Yoshihara (1978), Sekiguchi (1979), and Ozawa (1979).

18. Writing on Japanese aid policy, Rix (1980, pp. 234–41) refers to the 'special relationship' between Indonesia and Japan. He notes (p. 236) that in aid projects, as a consequence, 'economic feasibility was easily subordinated to political necessity'. In these and other ways the facilitating 'spill-over' effects on investment have probably been very substantial, although they are not easy to quantify.

19. See Bureau of Industry Economics (1983), and Hill (1986) for studies of Australian investment in ASEAN.

20. For a synthesis and exposition of the index, and its decomposition, see Drysdale and Garnaut (1982).

21. The product of the complementarity and country bias indices is equal to the intensity index. Pangestu provides proof of this proposition, following that derived by Drysdale and Garnaut (1982). The proof is set out in all three references.

22. The high figure for mining and petroleum in Table 4.14 is puzzling, in view of the small Japanese investments in petroleum. The explanation, presumably, is substantial (non-oil) mining investments—principally gas—and the possibility that some Japanese investments in metal-based manufacturing activities may have been mis-classified in the Japanese statistics.

23. The estimates are now rather dated, but there is no reason to presume that the same pattern would not hold for more recent years.

5 Foreign Investment in Manufacturing

We can characterize the Indonesian industrial structure as 'upstream socialism, downstream capitalism'. (Thee and Yoshihara, 1987, p. 343.)

PREVIOUS chapters have examined the importance of foreign investment in Indonesia in aggregate and in terms of investment patterns of the major investors. This chapter will focus more closely on the manufacturing sector. Specifically, we address two main questions. First, what has been the composition of foreign investment within manufacturing? Which sectors have been the major recipients? We can answer this question with reference to the realized Bank Indonesia data, although the level of aggregation (2-digit ISIC) is too high to permit detailed analysis. Secondly, how significant is foreign investment in manufacturing, and what factors explain inter-industry variations in foreign ownership shares? The *Statistik Industri* data provide a comprehensive picture of ownership shares, disaggregated to 5-digit ISIC industry groups, thereby enabling a far more detailed examination of ownership shares. The second question is the more important of the two. Aggregate magnitudes of foreign investment by themselves provide little indication of the importance of foreign investors in manufacturing. To obtain a complete picture we need to look at the other two actors—domestic investors and the state.

Two points need to be stressed at the outset. First, as previous chapters have emphasized, reference only to foreign investment misses a major part of the activities of foreign firms in Indonesia. Many of these firms have sought entry to the domestic market through licensing arrangements rather than through investments, whether because of government regulations (that is, foreign investors are prohibited or discouraged) or for commercial reasons. Secondly, it is important to take account of the role of the state as an investor. State enterprises dominate several industries—petroleum refining, fertilizer, steel—which in other countries tend to be the preserve of foreign firms. We shall return to both these points later in the chapter.

How important has manufacturing been in total foreign investment? In the BKPM sectors, two-thirds of the realized investments up to 1985 were in manufacturing (see Table 5.1). But, in aggregate, manufacturing has been greatly overshadowed by the petroleum sector. Over the period 1967–85, petroleum has received over 70 per cent of the total, and manufacturing almost 20 per cent. Investments in agriculture and services have

TABLE 5.1

Sectoral Composition of Realized Foreign Investment, 1967–1985
($ million)

Sector	1967–1977		1967–1985[a]	
	Value	Per Cent	Value	Per Cent
Agriculture, forestry and fisheries	310	5	271	1
Mining and petroleum	3,975	65	17,002	78
(Petroleum)	(3,453)	(57)	(15,767)	(72)
Manufacturing	1,549	25	4,084	19
Services	259	4	482	2
Total	6,095	100	21,839	100
Manufacturing as percentage of all BKPM sectors		59		67

Sources: Bank Indonesia and United States Embassy (annual).
[a] To 31 December 1984 for petroleum, and to 30 September 1985 for all other sectors.

been very small, partly because of government restrictions on the entry of foreign capital.[1]

The disaggregated Bank Indonesia data for the BKPM sectors provide a more detailed picture of manufacturing and other non-oil foreign investments (see Table 5.2). They illustrate once again the huge difference between total approvals and realized equity investments. For manufacturing, the former total $11.5 billion up to 1985 (column 1), while the latter are only about one-tenth of this figure (column 6). The main reason for the difference is that only 40 per cent of the approved investments in manufacturing have been realized (column 8). Manufacturing differs little from the other sectors in this respect. The principal exception is the much higher approvals percentage for (non-oil) mining, presumably because two very large mining projects—Freeport in Irian Jaya and Inco in Sulawesi— commenced operation shortly after approval.

The other reason for the large difference between total approvals and realized equity investments is the inclusion of foreign loans in the former figure. In manufacturing, with two minor exceptions (paper and other industries), loans have been a more important source of capital than foreign equity (compare columns 6 and 7, and 3 and 4). Consequently, the debt– equity ratio for realized manufacturing has been substantial (2.6—see column 9), and higher than that of the other sectors. This may at first sight appear surprising. Mining is usually regarded as a more risky activity, and therefore foreign investors might have been expected to 'gear up' in an effort to spread the risks. The reasons for the higher ratio for manufacturing are actually twofold. First, relatively more of the manufacturing investments took place after the introduction of more restrictive policies on foreign ownership. 'Gearing up' for foreign firms was a means of preserving control in the face of enforced lower (foreign) equity shares. As we have

TABLE 5.2

Planned and Realized Foreign Investment in BKPM Sectors, 1967–1985[a] ($ million, ratio, or percentage)

Sector	Planned Investment				Realized Investment			Realized as Percentage of Planned $\frac{(5)}{(3+4)}$ (8)	Realized Debt/ Equity Ratio (7)/(6) (9)	Sector Total Realized as Percentage of Total (10)
	Total (1)	Equity		Foreign Debt (4)	Total (5)	Foreign Equity (6)	Foreign Debt (7)			
		Indonesian (2)	Foreign (3)							
1. Agriculture, forestry and fisheries	694	118	232	344	271	146	125	47	0.86	4
2. Mining (non-oil)	1,709	15	682	1,013	1,234	493	741	73	1.50	20
3. Services	1,495	208	297	990	481	142	339	37	2.39	8
4. Manufacturing	11,518	1,431	2,332	7,752	4,083	1,124	2,963	40	2.64	67
Food	410	65	144	200	144	61	84	42	1.38	2
Textiles	1,410	119	376	914	723	218	506	56	2.32	12
Wood	168	27	27	113	54	21	34	39	1.62	1
Paper	500	68	100	331	36	18	18	8	1.00	1
Chemicals	2,173	291	567	1,314	589	211	379	31	1.80	10
Non-metallic minerals	779	97	155	527	529	135	394	78	2.92	9
Basic metals	3,593	421	463	2,710	1,618	311	1,307	51	4.20	27
Metal goods	2,472	337	496	1,640	385	146	239	18	1.64	6
Other	13	6	4	3	5	3	2	71	0.67	n
Total	15,414	1,772	3,544	10,098	6,070	1,904	4,166	44	2.19	100

Source: Bank Indonesia.

[a] Up to 30 September 1985.

n = Negligible (less than 1 per cent).

seen, by contrast, the first mining company 'virtually wrote its own ticket' (see Chapter 3, introductory quote). The second reason for the higher ratio is simply the huge Asahan project, which includes a large consortium of Japanese financiers. Its debt–equity ratio was over 4, and it pulls up the manufacturing average. The ratios for most of the other manufacturing industries were less than 2, and broadly comparable to the average for the other non-oil sectors.

The Composition of Foreign Investment in Manufacturing

Of the nine major industry groups, three—basic metals, chemicals, and textiles—have received the largest foreign investments (see Table 5.3). For the period 1967–85, they accounted for about 70 per cent of realized investments in manufacturing, depending on which definition of foreign investment is adopted. There have also been quite large inflows into the metal goods and non-metallic minerals industries. The remaining four industries—food, wood, paper, and other—have received less than 10 per cent of the total.

There have been significant changes in the composition of realized investments since 1967. During the first decade of the New Order, textiles alone received more than one-third of the total—higher still in the very early years—but its share declined markedly thereafter. In fact, the share of light industry (that is, food and textiles, ISIC 31–32), which accounted for almost half the total in the first decade, fell sharply to about 5 per cent after 1977.

' The heavy concentration in textiles may, at first, appear puzzling. Compared to much of manufacturing, textiles is a labour-intensive industry

TABLE 5.3

Foreign Manufacturing Investment by Sector, 1967–1985[a]
(percentage of total, realized)

Sector	Total Period 1967–85		Sub-periods 1967–77		1978–85	
Food	5	(4)	11	(6)	n	(2)
Textiles	19	(18)	37	(39)	2	(4)
Wood	2	(1)	1	(1)	3	(1)
Paper	2	(1)	1	(1)	2	(1)
Chemicals	19	(14)	19	(15)	18	(14)
Non-metallic minerals	12	(13)	11	(20)	13	(9)
Basic metals	28	(40)	7	(7)	48	(59)
Metal goods	13	(9)	12	(10)	14	(9)
Other	n	(n)	n	(n)	n	(n)
	100	(100)	100	(100)	100	(100)

Source: Bank Indonesia.

[a] Data refer to foreign equity investments; bracketed data refer to foreign equity plus foreign loans.

n = Negligible (less than 1 per cent).

employing 'mature' technologies. Consequently, foreign investors might not be expected to have a substantial competitive advantage over domestic investors. Moreover, until recently, the Indonesian industry attracted very little export-oriented foreign investment relocating from high wage countries or, to avoid quotas, from the more advanced developing countries.

The explanation for the initial heavy concentration of foreign investment in textiles lies in the policy liberalizations after 1966. The new policies led to extraordinarily rapid output growth and structural change in the industry. Both factors attracted foreign investors. Textile output more than quadrupled in the decade 1968–78, for several reasons. On the demand side, increased economic growth and the backlog in consumer demand (production in the first half of the 1960s actually declined) were the main factors. On the supply side, the removal of foreign exchange restrictions meant that firms were able to obtain inputs which had previously been in scarce supply.[2] At this time of rapid output growth, new technologies proliferated quickly, in the form of more mechanized weaving equipment and new production processes. Both developments attracted substantial foreign investment. Extremely rapid market growth and liberal entry controls were a major stimulus. Moreover, foreign firms tended to locate especially in the new, more mechanized sectors of the industry.

All this came to a halt in the mid-1970s. By then the domestic demand backlog had been met and the 'easy phase' of import substitution had been completed. In addition, exports remained negligible. Consequently, foreign investment approvals declined sharply, exacerbated—but not fundamentally caused—by the increasingly restrictive investment guidelines.[3] Just as the declining share of foreign investment in textiles may be attributed to the general slow-down in that industry, so the push for import substitution in intermediate and capital goods industries has resulted, more recently, in increased foreign investment in these sectors. Basic metals (mainly Asahan) received only 7 per cent of the total up to 1977, but they accounted for half of all investments in the second period. Investments in chemicals and metal goods also rose appreciably, although the increase is not reflected in higher shares (as shown in Table 5.3) because they were 'squeezed' by the huge figure for basic metals. Consequently, the changing industry composition of foreign investments is a good indication of both new directions in the manufacturing sector and the government's industry priorities.

Inter-industry Variations in Foreign Investment Shares

The data on foreign investment flows, as noted, give little indication of the relative importance of foreign investment in each industry. In which industries are foreign-owned firms most significant? Are variations in foreign ownership shares explainable in terms of the industrial organization theory of foreign investment? The theory does go some way to explain these variations in Indonesia, but specific institutional and policy factors are also very important.

We can address these questions by referring to the *Statistik Industri* series. The BKPM data, it needs to be emphasized, are of little use because there are no accurate *realized* PMDN data, because they refer only to 2-digit ISIC groups, and because they exclude much domestic investment. We have seen already (Table 2.4) that, while exclusively foreign-owned firms are unimportant in Indonesia (only 1.5 per cent of value added), joint ventures involving foreign and domestic firms are quite significant. In 1983, these joint ventures contributed about 26 per cent of manufacturing output. To simplify the analysis, the shares of the seven ownership groups were consolidated into four categories in Chapter 2. The results suggest that the share of foreign firms in manufacturing output in 1983 was 23 per cent, little changed from the 1975 figure of 21 per cent. (In addition, the share of government–foreign joint ventures rose from 2 to 5 per cent.)

It needs to be emphasized again that the ownership data in the *Statistik Industri* series are very approximate. In many nominally domestic-owned industries, foreign firms play a crucial role through licensing and other commercial arrangements. Conversely, the exclusion of firms—almost entirely domestic private—employing fewer than 20 workers understates the share of domestic ownership, although this matters less if we are concerned only with the 'factory sector'. Finally, the share of state enterprises is greatly understated by the exclusion of the petroleum sector and several large state-owned firms from the data. Despite these limitations, the data are the best available; used carefully they shed much light on developments in the manufacturing sector.

In 1983, foreign firms constituted a majority in very few of the major industry groups, but they were important in several (see Table 2.6). One such industry was beverages (ISIC 313), because of their dominance of the brewery industry (ISIC 31330). These firms were also important in the 'other chemicals' group, especially pharmaceuticals, detergents, and cosmetics. A surprising instance of high foreign ownership was footwear. This is explained by the presence of the huge Bata plant, which produces three-quarters of the industry's value added. Most of the other cases in which foreign firms have above average presence were capital and intermediate goods industries. The latter include sheet glass (ISIC 3622, 100 per cent of the total), and tyres and tubes (ISIC 35510, 56 per cent). Foreign firms have also been playing an increasingly important role in the newly developing basic metals industry. In addition, they are of some significance in assembling and machine goods industries, including electrical appliances (ISIC 3833, over half the total). These industries encompass a diverse range of industry characteristics, which we will examine in more detail shortly.

The industries in which foreign firms are of little or no importance are of equal interest. Textiles (especially weaving), discussed above, is a notable example. Despite the large foreign investments, domestic private firms produce more than five times that of foreign firms. Another is garments, an increasingly export-oriented industry, in which the role of foreign firms is negligible (at least in production). In a range of other industries—including tobacco, wood products, furniture, printing, and some non-metallic industries—foreign firms play a very small role in aggregate. Indeed, in most 'traditional' industries, where domestic firms are better established and the usual advantages of foreign firms (superior technology, brand names and so on) are less important, foreign ownership is not significant.

How does Indonesia compare with other developing countries in the pattern of foreign ownership within manufacturing? We have already seen that foreign investment in Indonesian manufacturing is comparatively modest. This is confirmed by a comparison with, for example, ownership shares for Brazilian industry, although in the case of Korea, also, foreign ownership is not large (see Table 5.4).[4] The relative importance of foreign investment in the three countries' industries varies substantially, as would be expected given differences in resource endowments, stages of industrialization, and the policy environment. In fact, the variations between countries are so great that few, if any, general patterns emerge. The share of foreign firms in Korea is very large only in the case of petroleum refining; yet it is very low for this industry in Brazil and Indonesia (although exact estimates are not available), in both cases because of the presence of state enterprises. Foreign firms figure prominently in industrial chemicals in both Korea and Brazil, but they play a very small role in the Indonesian industry, again mainly because of state ownership (in the fertilizer industry).

Nevertheless, some general patterns are evident. In the 'traditional' industries mentioned above, foreign firms do not play a significant role in any of the countries, for reasons already discussed.[5] On the other hand, foreign firms have above average shares in industries in which they can exploit their competitive advantages over domestic competitors. These industries include mainly the machine and capital goods sectors—electrical and non-electrical machinery, and transport equipment. They are also relatively more important in technology-intensive intermediate goods industries, such as glass products, and industries in which international brand names assume some significance. These include beverages, tobacco, and other chemicals for one or more of the countries.

Explaining Inter-industry Variations

What explains these inter-industry variations in the shares of foreign firms? The absence of a general pattern for the three countries immediately suggests that there is no universally applicable theory. In attempting to explain the results we need to resort both to the theory of industrial organization, and to specific country factors, including especially the policy environment. We consider the former first.

The theory and determinants of foreign investment are not well understood, and not surprisingly empirical investigations of a range of possible explanatory variables have generally met with little success. Moreover, what little work has been completed refers mainly to developed countries, and there are reasons why the same pattern may not apply in the case of developing countries. According to the theory of direct foreign investment, foreign firms will be more important in industries in which these firms have greater competitive advantages over domestic firms. There are intrinsic costs of 'being foreign' in a less familiar overseas commercial environment, and foreign investors require firm-specific advantages in order to overcome these costs.

TABLE 5.4

Shares of Foreign Firms in Manufacturing, Indonesia, Brazil, and Korea[a]
(percentage of total for each industry)

Industry	Indonesia (1983)	Brazil (1977)	Korea (1979)
311 Food manufacturing	16	} 0–52	} 6
312 Food manufacturing	24		
313 Beverages	51	23	1
314 Tobacco	10	99	2
321 Textiles	27	37	10
322 Garments	3	5	7
323 Leather products	0	39	2
324 Footwear	76	26	6
331 Wood and wood products	19	11	(n)
332 Furniture	12	24	(n)
341 Paper and paper products	24	20	8
342 Printing and publishing	2	3	3
351 Industrial chemicals	18	57	48
352 Other chemicals	61	51–82	10
353 Petroleum products	n.a.	9	92
355 Rubber products	22	62	2
356 Plastic products	29	42	10
361 Pottery	47	11	15
362 Glass	70	69	31
363 Cement	11	41	0
364 Structural clay products	0	n.a.	0
369 Other non-metallic minerals	0	25	2
371 Iron and steel	8	4	3
372 Non-ferrous metals	n.a.	38	17
381 Fabricated metal products	37	n.a.	8
382 Machinery (excluding electrical)	32	51	19
383 Electrical machinery	54	74–86	34
384 Transport equipment	23	57–100	14
385 Professional and scientific equipment	0	15	15
390 Other	58	13	11
All industries	23	33	13

Sources: 1. Indonesia, BPS.
2. Brazil, information kindly supplied by Dr Peter Cory.
3. Korea, Mining and Manufacturing Census, Economic Planning Board (information kindly supplied by Dr E. Y. Park).

[a] Value added for Indonesia and Korea, fixed assets for Brazil. Indonesian data refer to firms employing twenty or more workers.

n.a. = Not available.

n = Negligible (less than 1 per cent).

These advantages broadly take three forms. The first is technological superiority, based on access to firm-specific production or management technology, and on a capacity to develop and adapt new technologies. Secondly, there are marketing advantages. These derive from possession of international brand names, and other 'product differentiation' advantages. Another example concerns knowledge of international marketing channels and access to large developed country markets, both of which are relevant to export-oriented investments by foreign firms. Finally, there are advantages which derive from scale, including access to international capital markets on more favourable conditions, and capacity for risk diversification, and the economies of operating and co-ordinating multi-plant operations, frequently in more than one country.

The empirical challenge has been to identify variables which accurately capture these factors. Studies have usually included a range of explanatory variables: research and development expenditures and advertising have been found to be good proxies for technology and product differentiation in some studies (Caves, 1974); skills have been approximated by occupational categories and relative wage levels; and scale by average plant size or engineering estimates of minimum efficient scale. As would be expected, the variables which are thought to explain foreign investment shares are also important in the industrial organization literature on barriers to entry as determinants of market structure. Consequently, foreign investment and seller concentration are often positively related, even though the direction of causality is not immediately obvious. In the case of developing countries, moreover, empirical analysis is rendered much more difficult by the poorer data base, and the selection of appropriate variables.[6]

The second set of factors determining foreign investment shares relates to the policy environment in the host country. In Indonesia, three factors in particular warrant attention. The first is the presence of state enterprises. The other two affect the choice between foreign investment and other methods of market entry, namely (non-equity) licensing and exporting from the home or subsidiary bases.

The importance of state enterprises in Indonesia has already been referred to (Chapter 2). Although domestic private firms are more important in aggregate, state enterprises play a crucial role in several scale- and capital-intensive industries, including petroleum refining, fertilizer, cement, and iron and steel. In the absence of state intervention, these are industries in which foreign firms usually feature prominently, because industry characteristics are closely associated with the competitive advantages of foreign investors. In the case of Indonesia, therefore, testing the theory of foreign investment without allowing for the presence of state enterprise would be quite misleading.

The significance of the trade regime in determining the mode of entry of foreign firms requires little elaboration. The four major studies of protection policy in Indonesia since 1970[7] have produced somewhat different sets of estimates of effective protection for manufacturing industries. But they are in agreement on important issues. One is the enormous range of effective rates between industries, ranging from negative to several hundred per cent. There is also some evidence to suggest a 'cascading' structure of protection, with low rates for capital and machine goods, higher rates for intermediate goods, and rates which are higher still for consumer goods (especially consumer durables). Although it is difficult to quantify the effects of a highly differentiated protection structure with any precision, it is clear that trade policy has had important implications for foreign investment patterns. The initial heavy concentration of foreign investment in consumer goods is explained partly by this cascading structure. More recently, the push for industrial deepening, promoted by 'made-to-measure' protection, has attracted investors into the newer industries. In some industries—especially consumer durables—barriers have been prohibitive, forcing interested foreign firms to either invest or seek a local licensee.

This final means of market entry—licensing—has been adopted by firms in some cases in preference to direct investment, and in others because BKPM regulations have precluded or discouraged a foreign equity presence. It is worth looking at the nature of foreign involvement in selected industries, both to gauge the importance of licensing and to support our earlier argument that foreign equity shares greatly understate the importance of foreign firms in manufacturing. We cannot hope to cover all industries; this is necessarily a very selective review.[8]

The *brewery* industry is dominated by three large firms, all with foreign connections. The largest is PT Multi Bintang Indonesia, which produces Bintang beer in association with the Dutch firm, Heineken. It has a little under 60 per cent of the market. The other two firms are also joint ventures: PT San Miguel, a joint venture between the West Java provincial government and the Hong Kong subsidiary of the Philippine parent company, has almost 40 per cent of the market; a joint venture with Dutch interests, producing the Anker brand, makes up the rest.

In *tyres and tubes*, foreign firms are also significant. The oldest company is Goodyear, first established in 1935, and then as a PMA company (PT Goodyear Indonesia) in 1969. Other large multinationals, notably Bridgestone, are present. In 1984, these two companies had over half the production capacity of motor vehicle tyres (3.5 million units out of a total of 6.4 million). A government firm, PT Intirub, had about one-quarter. It was noted earlier that the share of foreign firms in tyre production declined from 1975 to 1983. One reason was simply a switch from sole to joint ownership. Another was that the market for motor cycle (and even bicycle) tyres has been growing quickly; in these cases, brand names and technology are less important, and local firms play a larger role. In 1984, the country's first tyre-cord plant was established. It is locally owned but has a technical assistance agreement with Goodyear.

In the *glass* industry, foreign companies are very important, especially in certain product lines. In the case of flat glass, a 50 : 50 joint venture between Asahi Glass of Japan and a local company, Roda Mas (PT Asahimas Flat Glass Company), had a virtual monopoly of the industry for over a decade, until a rival emerged in 1984. An American joint venture (PT Supreme Indo American Ceramics) has cornered the market for heat-proof glasswares. A joint venture with the Australian company, Australian Consolidated Industries (PT Kangar), is a major producer of glass bottles.

The *aluminium* industry is also dominated by multinationals. The Asahan project, PT Indonesia Asahan Aluminium, is of course the largest. The investment has totalled $2.1 billion, including the hydroelectric project; the Indonesian government has a 25 per cent equity stake in the company, while the remainder is held by the Nippon Asahan Aluminium Company, a consortium of Japanese companies. From 1982 to 1985, 90 per cent of the firm's output was exported. The American aluminium company, Alcan, also has a presence in Indonesia.

In the *steel* industry, state and foreign firms are especially important. The controversial PT Krakatau Steel Company, producing hot rolled steel at its plant in Cilegon (West Java), began commercial production in 1983. PT Cold Rolling Mill Indonesia, a joint venture between the Liem Sioe Liong group and Belgian interests, is also in the process of plant construction and expansion. In metal goods and steel products, there are estimated to be over 20 joint ventures with Japanese companies.

In the *chemicals* industries, foreign firms are also important. The government held a near monopoly of the fertilizer industry until 1984, when the $410 million plant of PT Aceh ASEAN Fertilizer was opened. The plant was built with Japanese funds, and 40 per cent of the shares are held by the other ASEAN countries. It is Indonesia's first AIJV (ASEAN Industrial Joint Venture) project. In pesticides and industrial chemicals, a very large number of internationally known companies have either investments or licensing agreements in Indonesia. The American companies include Du Pont, Dow Chemical, and Union Carbide, while the European companies include Bayer, Hoechst, ICI, Blue Circle, Ciba Geigy, and Roche. In pharmaceuticals, there are over ten American companies with investments in Indonesia. Not surprisingly, foreign firms dominate many of the chemicals industries.

In several industries, foreign companies are heavily specialized in the skill- and technology-intensive subsectors. *Textiles* is a notable example. In the labour-intensive garments industry, foreign investors play a minimal role. In weaving, although they are more important, domestic firms dominate the industry. In spinning, several joint ventures have been established, mainly from Japan and Hong Kong, and they account for about 30 per cent of the industry's spindles; state enterprises have about 20 per cent. In the industry's most capital-intensive stage, synthetic fibre production, foreign firms have been dominant until recently. In 1982, for example, the country's first rayon fibre plant was established, a joint venture between Hong Kong interests (45 per cent of the equity) and a Taiwan firm (25 per cent).

In other industries, foreign investors have little direct investment but they play a crucial role in supplying technology. Perhaps the best known example is IPTN (Industri Pesawat Terbang Nusantara, formerly Nurtanio), the company set up at the instigation of the Minister for Research and Technology, Dr Habibie. IPTN's growth has been spectacular. Formally incorporated in Bandung, in 1976, with a work-force of 500, it now employs over 10,000, many of them skilled technicians. Initially it assembled helicopters and fixed-wing aircrafts under licence from West German and Spanish companies. In 1979, it announced the establishment of a 50 : 50

joint venture with the Spanish company, CASA, to jointly manufacture short take-off, 35-seater aircraft; the first one was produced in 1983. Other agreements have been signed with foreign companies, both for Nusantara and for a range of other ambitious projects with which the Minister is associated. In these cases, direct foreign investment is relatively small, but foreign technology is extremely important.

There are other industries heavily reliant on foreign technology but in which foreign equity investments are unimportant. The *motor vehicle* industry consists entirely of international brand name products made (until recently with little local content) under licence from foreign companies. But foreign-owned firms accounted for only about 20 per cent of the industry's value added in 1983. The *motor cycle* industry is another example, with an even lower foreign equity share (6 per cent, ISIC 38449). All the firms produce under licence from foreign (mostly Japanese) companies. Only one (Vespa) has foreign equity, it being established before the government closed the industry to further foreign investment (see Witoelar, 1983, pp. 38ff.). In the case of *electrical appliances*, the share of foreign firms is much higher (50 per cent in 1983), largely because the industry was closed off to foreign investors much later than the other two.

In these and many other industries, the involvement of foreign firms is greatly understated by the data on equity shares. Licensing and other agreements are very significant in domestically owned firms. The equity share is misleading because the government has reserved some activities for state enterprises (such as IPTN); in others the BKPM has closed the industry to new PMA ventures (as in most appliances); while in some, foreign firms have preferred licensing to direct investment.

The preceding survey has focused on industries in which foreign firms are known to be important. Nevertheless, it would be misleading to assume that *all* industries are dominated by foreign firms. Quite the opposite. Many of the largest, and fastest growing industries, are in domestic hands. The *kretek* cigarette industry, by far the largest 5-digit industry, is exclusively domestic, and it is growing much faster than the 'white' cigarette industry. Even in the latter industry, although foreign firms are more important, there are several large domestic producers, located in North Sumatra. Another rapidly expanding industry, plywood, is predominantly domestically owned. In 1983, for example, there were about 83 PMDN companies, which produced 5.1 million cubic metres of plywood; the production of the fifteen PMA companies was only one million. In the capital-intensive segments of the textiles industry—synthetic fibres and spinning—foreign firms in the early years of the New Order were particularly significant, but since the late 1970s most of the large new investments have been by private companies. And in the traditionally important weaving industry, and the rapidly expanding garments sector, the role of foreign firms is comparatively small. Even in bottled drinks—in many countries a preserve of international brand names—the local *teh botol* (literally, bottled tea) is reported to be out-selling the international giants.

The theory of foreign investment is thus consistent with Indonesia's experience in the sense that foreign investments and other forms of foreign involvement are concentrated in industries in which these firms have specific advantages, which they choose to exploit through investment or, if forced, through licensing. Do the Indonesian data support the theory more formally? The earlier discussion suggests immediately a number of pitfalls. Data on some of the explanatory variables are not available, nor is it clear in any case whether Indonesian data should be used (for example, in the case of research and development expenditure). Indonesia's period of modern industrialization is still fairly short, so there are problems of dynamic 'leads and lags' in any analysis. Finally, the effects of the regulatory regime—especially but not only the closure of some industries to new PMA investments—are almost impossible to capture.

Rather than attempt any rigorous econometric testing of the theory, it may be useful to simply examine the characteristics of industries in which there is substantial foreign equity investment, relative to those of manufacturing as a whole. Several of the characteristics usually associated with foreign investors have been assembled, although data on some others (research and development, and advertising expenditures) are not available in Indonesia (see Table 5.5). The industries chosen are those in which 'foreign' firms (broadly defined) accounted for over half the output in 1983. The shares have been provided at the more meaningful 5-digit level of disaggregation where available.

What consistent patterns, if any, emerge from the data? First, state enterprises (column 3) are generally unimportant, except for a few industries, such as iron and steel, basic chemicals, and 'other tobacco products'. The low correlation might appear surprising because the factors which attract foreign investors (for example, advanced technology) not infrequently induce state investments. This is the explanation in most of the industries for which a correlation is present. In other cases, extensive state investment has virtually precluded foreign investors, either directly or because these investors are wary of the industry regulation which is often associated with state enterprises (for example, price control and privileged access to credit).

Secondly, there is no general pattern in the size or growth of the industries with substantial foreign investments. Although this group of industries includes several very large ones,[9] there are also many which are insignificant (column 4). In fact, what is surprising is that only two of the industries in which foreign investors have played a dominant role could be described as 'large' (greater than 2 per cent of manufacturing value added), and in one of these—basic metals—the state has been the driving force. Similarly, large foreign equity shares are associated about equally with industries growing at both above and below the average for manufacturing as a whole (column 7). No clear correlation emerges, although most of the industries with higher equity shares in Table 5.5 grew faster than the average.

A somewhat stronger association is present for value added and employment costs per worker. These may be regarded as proxies for (physical and human) capital intensity and skill intensity respectively (see Lary, 1968). Over three-quarters of the industries had above average value added per worker, and in half these cases the industries were more than double the

TABLE 5.5

Correlates of Foreign Investment Shares in Indonesian Manufacturing*

| Industry | Share of Industry Value Added | | | Industry Value Added as Percentage of Total Industries, 1983 | Value Added per Employee as Percentage of Ratio for All Industries, 1983 | Employment Costs per Employee as Percentage of Ratio for All Industries, 1983 | Annual Growth of Value Added, 1975–83, as Percentage of All Industries | Four-Firm Concentration Ratio | | Effective Rate of Protection | |
| | Foreign Firms | | State Firms | | | | | | | | |
	1983[a] (1)	1975[a] (2)	1983[b] (3)	(4)	(5)	(6)	(7)	1975 (8)	1982 (9)	1975 (10)	1984 (11)
36220 Sheet glass	100	99	0	0.8	513	378	240	100	100	–IVA	387
35231 Soap and detergent	92	54	0	1.4	243	205	140	89	95	–IVA	n.a.
31121 Dairy products	91	86	8	1.5	719	330	125	100	72	221	28
35140 Mosquito coils	77	0	0	0.9	220	210	249	83	88	n.a.	n.a.
324 Footwear	76	85	7	0.6	109	141	50	94	71	n.a.	n.a.
35290 Other chemicals	73(+9)	52(+15)	n	0.4	178	199	112	56	68	411	26
38311 Storage batteries	70	44	1	0.2	158	133	114	92	90	116	51
31430 White cigarettes	69	82	0	3.5	615	211	52	78	87	4	n.a.

TABLE 5.5 (continued)

Industry	Share of Industry Value Added			Industry Value Added as Percentage of Total Industries, 1983 (4)	Value Added per Employee as Percentage of Ratio for All Industries, 1983 (5)	Employment Costs per Employee as Percentage of Ratio for All Industries, 1983 (6)	Annual Growth of Valued Added, 1975–83, as Percentage of All Industries (7)	Four-Firm Concentration Ratio		Effective Rate of Protection	
	Foreign Firms		State Firms								
	1983ᵃ (1)	1975ᵃ (2)	1983ᵇ (3)					1975 (8)	1982 (9)	1975 (10)	1984 (11)
35233 Cosmetics, toothpaste	65	38	0	0.6	118	207	131	67	63	315	317
38320 Radio, TV, etc.	63(+1)	29(+5)	1	1.9	136	120	93	86	69	210	n.a.
31330 Breweries	60(+40)	43	0	1.9	1,187	389	96	100	89	117	91
35510 Tyres and tubes	56	55	13	1.0	95	182	64	94	81	4,315	167
38112 Cutlery, nails, etc.	56	51	0	0.3	80	110	89	72	47	36	12
38140 Metal containers	55(+18)	62(+10)	1	0.8	102	138	141	75	72	17	34

34120	Paper cartons	55	37	1	0.1	52	123	3	95	82	87	160
38330	Electrical equipment	54(+8)	33(+27)	6	1.5	115	150	137	65	54	10	64
38460	Motor vehicle parts	53	8	0	0.4	74	122	106	69	64	n.a.	n.a.
371	Basic metals	8(+47) 16		36	5.2	450	195	270	82	78	18	57

Sources: All data from *Statistik Industri*, various issues, including unpublished data; except last columns, which are from World Bank (unpublished study) and Parker (1985).

Notes:

* Industries in which shares of foreign firms in industry value added was at least 50 per cent in 1983.

[a] Figures in parentheses refer to government–foreign and government–foreign–private joint venture shares.

[b] Refers to state enterprises plus government–private joint ventures. IVA indicates negative international value added.

There are, in addition, several very small industries (less than 0.1 per cent of value added) in which the share of foreign firms exceeds 50 per cent. In 1983 these were (foreign shares in parentheses): other textiles (66 per cent), mattresses (75 per cent), other tobacco products (77 per cent), and musical instruments (98 per cent).

manufacturing average (column 5). An even stronger correlation exists between equity shares and employment costs, with none of the industries being below the average (column 6). These figures need to be interpreted carefully, since part of the reason for the higher employment costs may be the presence of foreign investors *per se*, independent of the association between equity shares and industry characteristics (see Manning, 1979).

Fourthly, as would be expected, high foreign investment shares are associated with high levels of seller concentration (columns 8 and 9). Indonesian manufacturing as a whole is characterized by very high levels of seller concentration (see Hill, 1987), and this seems to be especially so in industries in which there is substantial foreign investment: in about half the industries listed, four-firm concentration ratios exceeded 80 per cent. The link between these two variables is only poorly understood at a theoretical level. A plausible explanation, developed by Lall (1979) in the case of Malaysia, is that the entry of foreign firms into an industry may initially *lower* concentration, since there are more firms (and putting aside displacement effects). Subsequently, however, foreign investment may result in higher concentration, to the extent that these firms erect increased barriers to potential new entrants. In Indonesia's case, some of the industries which attracted foreign investment in the early years of the New Order barely existed, so there was no question of foreign firms reducing concentration levels.

In assessing the impact of foreign investment on industry structure, concentration matters a lot less than the trade and regulatory regime, with the exception of non- or minimally-traded goods. In Indonesia, it is the coincidence of high concentration *and* high effective protection which confers monopoly power on foreign investors in Indonesia. The effective rates of protection, calculated for 1975 and 1984 (columns 10 and 11), are little more than rough orders of magnitude. But estimates for both years suggest that there are wide variations in effective rates between industries, and that most of the industries in which there is considerable foreign investment have above average protection.

Economic theory provides few clues as to the links between the trade regime and foreign investment. But a high correlation is consistent with the political economy literature, especially that relating to 'rent-seeking' societies (Krueger, 1974). Foreign investors seek to maximize the return on their investments. Since, until very recently, the overwhelming majority of foreign investments were import substituting, both protection and the licensing system played an important role in reducing competitive pressures. It is widely believed that the entry of many foreign investors into Indonesia has been conditional on government-sanctioned protection both from foreign competition (through tariffs and other barriers) and domestic competition (through licensing). Moreover, foreign investors in Indonesia frequently select their domestic partners on the basis of the latter's political leverage rather than their commercial or technical expertise (Weinstein, 1976a and 1976b), which would have the effect of reinforcing the political economy hypothesis. It is possible, of course, that the direction of causality is in the opposite direction; that is, that the presence of high import barriers attracts foreign investors. While this is often the case, for reasons discussed above, the fact that so much of Indonesia's protection is 'made-to-measure' suggests many of the barriers have been erected in response to lobbying by foreign (and domestic) investors.

This cursory examination of some of the variables usually associated with foreign investment confirms our earlier suggestions. Although, as expected, there is a positive association between equity shares and industry characteristics, the overall relationship is not strong, mainly because it is difficult to quantify variables on both sides of the equation.

These measurement and data problems are illustrated in the careful study by Hasan (1981), the only empirical investigation of the determinants of foreign investment in Indonesian manufacturing of which the author is aware. Hasan's emphasis was somewhat different from the discussion so far, but his poor results are indicative of the pitfalls present. The dependent variable in his formulation was $A/(A+B)$ where:

A = total domestic sales of all foreign firms in Indonesia for a given industry; and

B = total imports into Indonesia in the corresponding industry.

He was thus concerned with the determinants of the relative profitability of two entry modes for foreign firms into the Indonesian market, namely production in Indonesia compared to exporting from the head office or a subsidiary.[10]

He identified a number of independent variables for which he was able to develop suitable proxies. These included trade barriers, relative production costs, relative wage levels, relative resource costs, cost effects of operating in the small local (Indonesian) market, and the threat of oligopolistic competition from other multinational companies. The results were very disappointing. At an aggregate level (that is, for all manufacturing), the results were extremely poor. Regardless of the functional form or specification, the best R^2 in twelve industries was only 0.12, and the signs were not always as expected (Hasan, 1981, pp. 102–4). Improved—though hardly satisfactory—results were obtained when the analysis was conducted at a more disaggregated level of industrial classification. Significantly, consistently the most important predictor of foreign investment as a mode of entry was trade barriers, confirming the arguments above.

1. Recall that foreign investments in banking and insurance are not included in Table 5.1. Their exclusion does not alter the picture greatly, however.

2. Rough estimates prepared by Palmer (1972) suggest that for most of the period 1960–8 actual production was less than half the 'potential' level. Moreover, the latter was based on a very conservative definition of one shift per day.

3. The large foreign investments in textiles led many observers to conclude, erroneously, that foreign investors dominate the industry. Weinstein (1976b, p. 383), for example, reflects this view, asserting that 'Japanese firms have acquired a position of overwhelming influence in Indonesia's textile industry'. While it is true that foreign-owned firms have been significant among the very large integrated mills and in the capital-intensive stages (especially in synthetic fibres), there is little basis for the view that these firms dominate the industry. As we shall see

shortly, domestically owned firms employ most of the textiles work-force and produce more than half the output.

4. Note that in Table 5.4 the Brazilian data refer to fixed assets, whereas those for Indonesia and Korea refer to value added. This is not a serious shortcoming, however, since shares for the two variables—where they are both available—tend to be highly correlated. The same is not the case for employment shares, however; the greater capital intensity of foreign firms results in a substantial understatement of their size if measured only by employment.

5. There are a few exceptions to this conclusion, which are explained by particular circumstances. One is the high share for footwear in Indonesia, due to the presence of the large Bata factory.

6. For example, in case of advantages based on technology and product differentiation, it is not clear whether the data on industry characteristics should be based on those of the source country (where they have generally been developed) or the host country. Caves (1974) is the most widely cited study of foreign investment shares in developed countries. The only rigorous study for developing countries is that by Lall and Mohammad (1983) on India.

7. These studies are Parker (1985), Pangestu and Boediono (1986), Pitt (1981), and the unpublished World Bank report for the year 1975.

8. Information in the following paragraphs has been obtained from newspaper, magazine, and other sources. Detailed footnotes are not provided. The acronym PT before a company stands for *perseroan terbatas*, or limited liability. After this section was written the paper by Thee and Yoshihara (1987) appeared. They provide a most informative analysis of ownership levels and trends, preferring a firm-based approach to one relying on the industrial statistics.

9. Recall that there are 119 5-digit industry classifications, so any industry with a share in excess of 1 per cent of MVA is 'above average' in size.

10. He excluded the third option, licensing, on the grounds of both data limitations and the argument that several features of the Indonesian commercial environment render such an entry mode unattractive.

6 Factor Proportions and Ownership

> This issue [choice of technology] has been extensively investigated, perhaps because the thought of capital and labor optimally combined can drive economists to ecstasies that other humans find baffling. (Caves, 1982, p. 267).

MUCH of the popular criticism of multinational corporations in Indonesia and elsewhere focuses on technology choice. One assertion is that foreign firms contribute little to employment creation,[1] because they allegedly employ highly capital-intensive production technologies. Another is that foreign firms exacerbate problems of unemployment and underemployment, because they displace labour-intensive (and domestically owned) firms in traditional industries. A more general criticism is that the higher capital intensity of foreign firms is symptomatic of their inefficient use of domestic resources, including excessively import-intensive operations and the production of 'inappropriate' products.

The higher capital intensity of foreign firms, of course, indicates nothing about the social optimality of technology selection; it could equally be that the more labour-intensive technologies of domestic firms are sub-optimal. But, in any case, the debate over multinationals and factor proportions in Indonesia has been conducted largely in an empirical vacuum. The few studies conducted to date, useful as they are, mainly refer to the first half of the 1970s, when the manufacturing sector was still quite small. Moreover, in a period of infancy and rapid growth, a 'snap-shot' picture of factor proportions may obscure the fundamental preferences of different groups of firms. The unpublished *Statistik Industri* series provides the first opportunity to investigate factor proportions and ownership, using disaggregated and recent secondary data.

Much of the literature—especially the popular literature—on multinationals and technology choice is confusing, and so it will be useful at the outset to make some general observations on the issue. The first is that technology comparisons among different groups of firms have to be undertaken with great care. To assert simply that foreign firms are more capital intensive than domestic firms may be quite misleading. Quite apart from the social optimality of technology choice, there are actually three questions involved in the comparison. The greater capital intensity of foreign firms could be because they are located in more capital-intensive industries; or because, within the same 'industries' as domestic firms, they specialize in the production of goods for which the efficient production technology is more capital intensive; or because these firms employ more capital-intensive technologies for the same industries *and* goods. The first two outcomes are to be expected. Given the competitive advantages of foreign firms, it would be surprising if they did not behave in this manner. It is the third question which is most significant, and provides the only basis for allegations that multinationals adopt excessively capital-intensive technologies.

A second general observation is that, while the creation of productive employment opportunities in developing countries is crucial, the importance of the 'employment argument' as a criticism of multinationals is greatly overstated, for two reasons. The first is that, save for exceptional circumstances, multinationals in the industrial sector will have only a negligible *direct* impact on incremental employment and labour absorption. Manufacturing in middle-income developing countries typically employs no more than 20 per cent of work-force, and the vast majority of the manufacturing work-force is engaged in small and cottage industry. In other words, employment by foreign firms is only a small fraction of the total in the factory sector, itself an even smaller percentage of the manufacturing sector and a tiny percentage of the total work-force.

Some of these propositions can be illustrated with reference to the Indonesian work-force data. According to the 1980 Population Census, the manufacturing work-force in that year was 4.7 million, a figure broadly consistent with the 1979 Industrial Survey, which recorded 4.5 million (see Table 6.1). Of the 1979 total, 870,000—less than 20 per cent—were engaged in the factory sector, in firms employing 20 or more workers.

TABLE 6.1

Employment in Manufacturing

1. By Ownership, Large and Medium Firms

	1983	Per Cent	Increment, 1975–83	Per Cent
Government[a]	157,965	14	38,802	9
Private	828,696	74	308,544	73
Foreign	118,072	11	65,521	16
Government (joint ventures)[b]	14,897	1	8,519	2
Total	1,119,630	100	421,386	100

2. By Firm Size ('000)

		Sub-total	Total
1980	Population Census (Series S)		4,680
1979	Industry Survey		4,502
	Large & medium firms	870	
	Small firms	837	
	Cottage industries	2,795	

Sources: 1. BPS, *Statistik Industri*, unpublished data.
      2. Jones (1987).
[a] Includes government–private joint ventures.
[b] Includes government–foreign joint ventures, and combinations of all three groups.

And, within the factory sector, the great majority worked in privately owned (domestic) firms: in 1983, these firms employed three-quarters of the total, and a similar proportion of the increment to employment from 1975 to 1983. Although the employment share of foreign firms has been rising, as indicated by the higher incremental percentage, these firms only accounted for a little over one-tenth of factory sector employment in 1983.

The other reason why the importance of the employment argument has been overstated is that the primary reason for a host country inviting the entry of foreign investors is in order to extract some of the rents accruing to these firms' highly productive technology and marketing resources. However, these skills do not generally extend to special knowledge of labour-intensive technology. And nor should they. If multinationals were to enter traditional, labour-intensive, and village-based industries, there would most likely be a much greater displacement of indigenous entrepreneurship, and a much sharper 'social interface' between foreign and domestic interests than would be politically or socially acceptable.

A final general observation is that the main determinant of firms' technology choice is the policy environment in the host country, rather than the nationality of investors. Numerous case studies, to be referred to shortly, emphasize the key role of government-induced factor price distortions *and* a permissive product market (which does not compel firms to seek cost-minimizing, often more labour-intensive technologies) in explaining inappropriate technology selection. Both these factors are amenable to policy reform. The prescription for governments concerned about technology choice is therefore to reform the commercial environment rather than to focus on a particular group of investors.

The major part of this chapter examines differences in factor proportions among the major investors in Indonesia, followed by a discussion of the reasons for these differences. First, however, we review the handful of studies on technology choice and ownership in Indonesian manufacturing, and the very large literature on the subject in other developing countries.

Choice of Technique Studies

Indonesia

There have been just three empirical investigations of factor proportions and ownership in Indonesian manufacturing, all referring to the 1970s. The studies draw on different data sets, to some extent address different questions and, perhaps not surprisingly, reach somewhat different conclusions. Balasubramanyam (1984) utilized the 1974/5 Industry Census, adopting as an indicator of physical capital intensity the ratio of non-wage value added to wage value added. Regardless of the measure, he found foreign firms to be considerably more capital intensive than government firms, who in turn exhibited greater capital intensity than domestic private (hereafter referred to as private) firms.[2] He also found, unexpectedly, that the higher capital intensity of foreign firms was due entirely to the adoption of more capital-intensive technologies *within* the same industries. The other possible explanation—foreign firms locating predominantly in more capital-intensive industries—exerted a negative influence.

The author was careful to explain the limitations of the data base for the study. There were three in particular. First, the comparison was conducted at the 3-digit level of industrial classification, which is too aggregated for detailed comparisons. This is especially the case in Indonesia because, within broad industry groupings, there is considerable specialization according to ownership and factor intensity.[3] Secondly, it is not clear how the joint venture groupings were classified. As we have seen, these firms are significant in many industries, and it is not appropriate to allocate the totals equally between the joint venture partners. Finally, value added is not always the best indicator of factor proportions, for reasons to be discussed shortly. In our examination of factor proportions, the first two difficulties have been resolved, and the data are more recent, but we are still forced to rely on the value added measure.

The other two studies of factor proportions and ownership have relied on survey data. Wells (1973) examined technology choice in 43 firms covering six (mainly) consumer goods industries in the early 1970s.[4] Defining factor intensities by essentially a 'process description approach', supplemented by estimates of capital–labour ratios, he found that foreign firms generally, though not always, employed more capital-intensive technologies.

Wells was immediately sceptical of three common explanations for higher capital intensity. These were that it was too expensive for foreign firms to develop more labour-intensive technologies, that the selection of capital-intensive technologies was dictated by product specifications and requirements, and that intermediate technologies waste raw materials. He maintained that the different factor prices faced by the three major groups of investors (foreign, government, and private) explained part of the differences. But, in addition, he was more persuaded by his well-known thesis concerning 'engineering man'. His argument was that managers had a preference for more sophisticated and automated technology, and that such a preference was more likely to be manifested when firms were not subjected to the rigours of competition. It was the tendency for foreign firms to be located in less competitive industries which he saw as the major explanatory variable: 'The capital-intensive techniques were generally associated with foreign investors. However, they seem to be more closely associated with investors who had some monopolistic position. Foreigners happened to be in such a position more frequently than domestic investors.' (Wells, 1973, p. 337.)

The second survey, conducted by Soediyono et al. (1984), concluded that there was no systematic difference in factor proportions between foreign and domestic firms. This conclusion was based on a survey of 47 firms in three industries in the late 1970s. The results, summarized in Table 6.2, are somewhat ambiguous because the authors adopted three measures of capital intensity, and the conclusion is sensitive to the selection of the measure. In only one industry—pharmaceuticals—were foreign firms unambiguously more capital intensive, although even here the differences were statistically significant for only two of the measures. In the electronics

TABLE 6.2

Capital Intensity of Foreign and Domestic Firms in Three Industries

	Electronics and Electrical Appliances				Pharmaceuticals				Textiles			
	Number of Firms	Labour Cost per Rp 1,000 Output	Electricity Consumption per Worker (kwh)	Value Added per Worker (Rp)	Number of Firms	Labour Cost per Rp 1,000	Electricity Consumption per Worker (kwh)	Value Added per Worker (Rp)	Number of Firms	Labour Cost per Rp 1,000 Output	Electricity Consumption per Worker (kwh)	Value Added per Worker (Rp)
Domestic	8	76	4,509	1,821	7	252	1,906	4,456	8	90	4,795	3,067
Foreign	8	65	3,057	7,340[a]	8	208	9,453[a]	4,806[a]	8	113	10,379	2,726

Source: Soediyono et al., 1984, Tables 5.1A–5.3C.
[a] t-statistic significant at 5 per cent level.

and textiles industries, no clear conclusions emerge: foreign firms are more capital intensive according to one measure, but less so for another. Two of these measures—per capita value added and electricity consumption (as a proxy for physical capital)—are widely used. However, the third—labour costs per Rp 1,000 output—may be misleading as an indication of (physical) capital intensity, since it also incorporates the effects of higher skill intensity. An additional qualitative variable, assessing the type of equipment and processes in use, may have strengthened the authors' conclusions.

Other Developing Countries

The literature on multinationals and factor proportions is so vast, and the disagreements often so substantial, that it is difficult to summarize briefly these studies.[5] At the risk of great over-simplification, the majority of studies do suggest that foreign ownership exerts an independent (and positive) influence on capital intensity. But factors other than ownership are significant, and some studies have concluded that domestic firms are more capital intensive. We begin with a review of the majority of studies which have relied on secondary data (such as industrial censuses), followed by an examination of the studies using primary (firm survey) data. Our references to the case studies are, inevitably, highly selective.

Most studies of the larger Latin American countries using secondary data have found that foreign firms adopt more capital-intensive technologies. Willmore (1986) examined 282 matched pairs of firms in Brazilian manufacturing at the 4-digit ISIC level, using taxation returns for 1978. He found foreign firms to be more capital intensive—using a variety of measures of capital—and more skill intensive; these conclusions also held for major industry groups. Morley and Smith (1977) reached a similar conclusion, using 1969 census data for nineteen 4-digit industry groups. The authors' conclusions were more robust since they excluded government firms and, where possible, adjusted for scale differences. A particularly detailed study of 150 foreign and domestic firms in Brazil's electrical industry, using census data for 1972 and 1974, was undertaken by Newfarmer and Marsh (1981). They concluded that foreign firms were considerably more capital intensive, a result which generally applied after standardizing for other (non-ownership) variables. Blomstrom (1983), who had access to a rich Mexican census data set (230 4-digit industries) for 1970, came to the same conclusion, although the differences were often not statistically significant. A smaller study of 33 matched pairs in Costa Rican manufacturing, for 1971, found 'non-resident' firms were more capital intensive, but also with poor levels of significance (Willmore, 1976).

The results from studies of African manufacturing are not so clear-cut, probably because most industrial sectors are smaller and less developed. Ahiakpor (1986) distinguished between government, foreign, and private (domestic) firms, in a study of 297 enterprises across eleven industry groups at (generally) the 4-digit ISIC level for Ghana in 1970. His main conclusion was that the capital intensity of government firms exceeded that of foreign firms, which in turn exceeded that of their private counterparts. Forsyth and Solomon (1977), employing a comparable data set for the same country, reached a similar conclusion for foreign and private firms. They identified another intermediate group in terms of capital intensity, the 'resident expatriate' firms. Perkins (1983) also highlighted the role of government firms in Tanzania, emphasizing their low levels of efficiency. Several other studies (for example, Biersteker (1978) on Nigeria, and Gershenberg and Ryan (1978) on Uganda) generally produced inconclusive results. An interesting and thorough study by Pack (1976), of 42 Kenyan firms, actually found that domestic firms were generally more capital intensive, primarily because they lacked 'the managerial adaptive ability in searching for appropriate techniques'.

Studies of Asian manufacturing have also produced conflicting results. Agarwal (1976), examining 34 3-digit industries in India, found foreign firms were generally more capital intensive according to several measures. But Leipziger (1976), using aggregated and composite data to compare United States and local firms in India in 1964/5, found the reverse. Ranis and Schive (1985) cite conflicting census and survey data for 1966, 1971, and 1976 in the case of Taiwan manufacturing, some at a fairly high level of aggregation.

Authors using primary data, mainly from surveys of Asian manufacturing, have generally produced mixed or inconclusive results. A large study by Chen (1983c), of 369 firms across four industries in Hong Kong in 1979, found no clear pattern. In three of the four cases, foreign firms were less capital intensive, but in two of these the differences were insignificant. Riedel (1975) conducted an even larger survey of 445 firms in Taiwan in 1973. In four out of the six industries examined, there were differences, the most common pattern being the lower capital intensity of foreign firms. Chung and Lee (1980) investigated seventeen matched pairs of firms in Korean manufacturing for 1974, finding, in general, no clear pattern of differences. An earlier Korean study by Cohen (1973), for 1970, also produced mixed results. Mason (1973) analysed nine matching pairs in the Philippines and five in Mexico, using 1968 data. While concluding that the foreign firms were generally more capital intensive, differences were often insignificant.

These studies, though generating mixed and often seemingly contradictory results, do point to a number of conclusions. Of particular interest are the consistent findings from the three North-East Asian NICs—Korea, Taiwan, and Hong Kong—that differences among ownership groups are not marked. There are at least two plausible reasons for this result. One is the presence of a strong domestic entrepreneurial class, so that differences between domestic and foreign firms, in terms of knowledge of and access to production technologies, are not great. The second reason is that the economic environment is less distorted by government intervention, and firms are generally oriented to export markets where competitive pressures (including the pressure to adopt cost-minimizing technologies) are greater.

These studies also underline the importance of suitable definitions of ownership. In many countries, more elaborate classifications than the simple foreign–domestic dichotomy are required. The state is a significant investor in some countries, as is an intermediate 'local expatriate' group which is strictly neither foreign nor domestic. In other instances, foreign firms may exert an influence independent of equity investment through, for example, licensing arrangements; conversely, firms nominally owned by foreigners (through portfolio investments) may effectively be controlled by local managers.

The results of recent studies are probably more reliable. For one thing, the secondary data base in most countries has improved considerably in the last twenty years or so. For another, the enterprise population has expanded, permitting larger and more detailed studies. Statistical and measurement techniques have also been refined as the literature has expanded.

It is not immediately obvious which data source is superior. Secondary data sources provide a larger basis for comparison, but the findings depend crucially on the quality of the data (and studies based on, for example, taxation returns need to be interpreted with great caution). Firm surveys provide a more intimate and comprehensive picture of technology selection. But they are obviously extremely tedious, and the samples are small.

The mechanics of the comparisons are crucial. As noted, aggregated industry groupings may produce misleading results because they could conceal intra-industry specialization in the location of different ownership groups. It is also important, where possible, to standardize for the effects of other determinants of factor proportions, most importantly scale of operations. Similarly, differences may arise in particular stages of the production process such as, for example, the 'core' production technology or peripheral activities (packaging, materials handling, and so on). Survey data are usually necessary to detect these differences; some studies have suggested that differences between foreign and domestic firms arise primarily because the latter adopt more labour-intensive technology for the peripheral production stages.

Another difficulty is in obtaining an unambiguous measure of capital intensity. The two most common indicators—value added and capital per worker—have defects. Value added reflects not only factor intensities but also productive efficiency and market power (through product differentiation and protected market positions). These latter factors may especially be associated with foreign firms. Estimates of capital stock are notoriously unreliable, both because book value figures (the most common indicator available) are unsatisfactory in an inflationary environment, and because the capital data generally include not only machinery (the relevant variable) but also buildings and land. To the extent that foreign firms locate more frequently on expensive real estate, the total capital stock figures will be inflated. Some surveys employ a 'process description approach' to distinguish technologies. Such an option is not available for the majority of studies relying on secondary data; even for the surveys, accurate characterization of production processes is difficult.

Finally, most of the studies are concerned only with measuring the differences among ownership groups, rather than with the reasons for these differences. We take up this issue in the final section of this chapter.

Factor Proportions in Indonesian Manufacturing

The Data

To address the issue of factor proportions and ownership, we ideally require a full industrial census supplemented by interviews to obtain insights into the firm-level decision-making process. Unfortunately, such information is never available, so we have to resort to 'second best' data sources. The unpublished SI data provide value added (at factor cost) and employment at the 5-digit ISIC level (containing 119 industry groups) for seven ownership groups for the years 1975 and 1983. The strengths and weaknesses of the data will be apparent from the preceding discussion. The positive features of the data include:

1. There are observations for two years, so trends over time can be detected. The data are also reasonably up to date.

2. The quality of the data is relatively good.

3. The data are at a sufficiently high level of disaggregation.

4. The enterprise population is comprehensive, including not only state enterprises but also separate identification of joint ventures.

There are also several weaknesses in the data base:

1. There are no estimates of capital stock. This is perhaps not as serious a limitation as is commonly assumed, for reasons already indicated. Most studies of factor proportions which have access to both capital stock and value added data have concluded that the two measures produce consistent results. Nevertheless, while value added is generally a superior indicator of factor intensity to capital stock (Lary, 1968), the former is not an unambiguous indicator of factor proportions, especially as the Indonesian data do not include non-wage value added (a frequently used proxy for physical capital intensity).

2. There is no information on the distribution of firms within industries and ownership groups, so it is not possible to attach confidence limits to direct comparisons among groups at the 5-digit level. Nevertheless, the fact that the data are available at a high level of disaggregation renders this shortcoming less serious.

3. It is not possible to allow specifically for scale, a factor which generally exerts an independent influence on capital intensity. Fortunately, the data relate only to firms employing twenty or more workers, so the large 'tail' of small and cottage industry is excluded. Further, in the following analysis, industries with very large differences in *average* firm size will be excluded, to test whether the scale factor substantially alters the results.

4. The ownership categories are not always an accurate indication of effective control. This is especially so in the case of private firms with foreign licensing arrangements, for reasons already discussed. The appropriate approach to resolving this shortcoming will be to examine particular industries in which the problem is likely to be present.

Results

The differences in value per employee among the ownership groups are very large (see Table 6.3). In 1983, the figure for government–foreign joint ventures was over five times that of private firms. The range in 1975 was even greater, that of foreign to private being over seven times. There are also similarities in the rankings over time. Private firms have by far the lowest average in both years, although the differences are narrowing over time. Government–private joint ventures are the second lowest on both occasions, differing little from the private firms. The figure for government firms, although a good deal higher, is third lowest in both years. By contrast, it is the remaining joint ventures—and the purely foreign firms in 1975—which are appreciably higher.

To make comparisons more manageable, we adopt consolidated groups where a single ownership classification appears to be a reasonably accurate description of effective control. Foreign and private–foreign firms are grouped together since most of the latter (at least as far as technology selection is concerned) are effectively in foreign hands. The wholly foreign-owned firms were in any case few in number by 1983, because of the ban on such investments after 1974. The greatly reduced importance of these firms is explained by the prohibition, and the move towards joint venture status by the largest (and more visible) of these firms. The very small government–private group is combined with government firms since the majority of the latter is under effective state control. A separate category of

TABLE 6.3

Value Added per Worker by Ownership (Rp '000, or index)

	1983		1975	
	Value	Index, Private = 100	Value	Index, Private = 100
(1) All groups				
Government	3,943	144	1,333	232
Private	2,740	100	575	100
Foreign	4,948	181	4,179	727
Government–Private	3,236	118	715	124
Government–Foreign	14,254	520	2,445	425
Private–Foreign	7,957	290	1,622	282
Government–Private–Foreign	11,625	424	1,532	266
(2) Consolidated groups				
Government	3,881	142	1,288	224
Private	2,740	100	575	100
Foreign	7,641	279	2,318	403
Government (joint ventures)	13,707	500	2,252	392
Total	3,565	130	843	147

Source: BPS, *Statistik Industri*, unpublished data.

Note: In part (2) of the table 'Government' includes Government–Private, 'Foreign' includes Private–Foreign, and 'Government (joint ventures)' includes remaining joint ventures.

'government joint ventures' with foreign firms (and some private interests) is maintained since these enterprises do not fit into either of the first two categories. Value added per worker for the four consolidated groups is shown in the second part of Table 6.3. Private firms still have by far the lowest ratio.

Differences among firms within major industry groups (3-digit ISIC) are equally large, in both years (see Tables 6.4 and 6.5). There is also a good deal of variation across industries within each ownership category. These variations are especially pronounced within the two groups including state investments, reflecting the 'bunching' of large government-funded projects. For example, in eight of the 26 government–private comparisons

TABLE 6.4

Value Added per Worker by Ownership and Major Industry Group, 1983
(Rp '000)

	Industry	Government	Private	Foreign	Government (JV)
311	Food manufacturing	2,543	2,369	24,831	—
312	Food manufacturing	2,574	1,355	5,071	—
313	Beverages	2,179	3,163	24,095	36,688
314	Tobacco products	272	5,516	43,869	8,600
321	Textiles	1,534	1,317	3,150	932
322	Garments	2,536	1,550	1,033	—
323	Leather products	7,049	2,704	—	—
324	Footwear	6,235	971	12,359	—
331	Wood products	2,706	2,434	4,819	710
332	Furniture	594	1,002	2,686	—
341	Paper products	1,607	1,703	3,918	—
342	Printing and publishing	2,664	1,923	2,397	6,796
351	Basic chemicals	13,719	2,438	13,900	29,028
352	Other chemicals	3,257	1,867	11,031	2,697
355	Rubber products	1,922	3,309	5,984	—
356	Plastic products	—	1,074	4,438	—
361	Ceramics	509	855	4,185	—
362	Glass products	2,897	2,109	13,219	—
363	Cement	10,031	2,446	9,272	23,371
364	Structural clay products	984	562	—	—
369	Other non-metallic minerals	662	2,299	—	—
371	Basic metals	18,966	4,050	8,058	42,046
381	Fabricated metal products	2,762	2,460	6,853	9,397
382	Non-electrical machinery	4,069	2,390	9,760	5,719
383	Electrical machinery	3,655	2,678	7,964	4,858
384	Transport equipment	2,123	6,029	6,333	—
385	Professional and scientific equipment	—	1,062	—	—
390	Other manufactures	715	674	3,654	—

Source: As for Table 6.3.

TABLE 6.5

Value Added per Worker by Ownership and Major Industry Group, 1975
(Rp '000)

	Industry	Government	Private	Foreign	Government (JV)
311	Food manufacturing	1,034	612	512	—
312	Food manufacturing	535	283	733	1,504
313	Beverages	379	2,448	3,720	6,456
314	Tobacco products	656	750	9,040	2,724
321	Textiles	575	326	1,176	933
322	Garments	100	242	96	—
323	Leather products	269	579	104	—
324	Footwear	—	365	4,969	—
331	Wood products	424	488	1,154	—
332	Furniture	264	314	205	—
341	Paper products	1,080	1,100	2,076	—
342	Printing and publishing	1,279	603	1,852	4,095
351	Basic chemicals	5,520	459	1,697	2,320
352	Other chemicals	500	583	2,313	4,356
355	Rubber products	2,554	314	2,763	—
356	Plastic products	39	432	551	—
361	Ceramics	261	209	719	—
362	Glass products	1,085	338	947	—
363	Cement	4,145	320	3,162	1,283
364	Structural clay products	118	122	140	—
369	Other non-metallic minerals	213	311	—	—
371	Basic metals	501	1,114	1,417	—
381	Fabricated metal products	1,468	544	1,746	2,021
382	Non-electrical machinery	1,920	416	1,362	1,104
383	Electrical machinery	2,030	1,595	1,615	1,924
384	Transport equipment	1,061	1,946	1,404	—
385	Professional and scientific equipment	—	671	—	—
390	Other manufactures	2,590	274	187	—

Source: As for Table 6.3.

in 1983 the latter firms have a higher ratio. But the government firms'
average is pulled up by very high figures in three capital-intensive industries—basic chemicals (fertilizer), cement, and basic metals (steel). This
immediately suggests the differences between the two groups arise primarily
from the government firms' disproportionate location in capital-intensive
industries, a point to which we return shortly. Similarly, the government
joint ventures, which are represented in only about half the major industry
groups, have a much higher average than foreign firms because of a few
particularly high ratios. By contrast, in the case of the foreign–private
comparison, the former are consistently higher in virtually all industries—
23 out of 24 in 1983 and 20 out of 26 in 1975.

TABLE 6.6

Summary t-Statistics, Value Added per Worker

	5-digit		3-digit	
Comparison	*Observations*	*Significance*[a]	*Observations*	*Significance*[a]
(1) 1983				
Government (JV)–Foreign	15	—	12	—
Government (JV)–Private	16	***	12	***
Government (JV)–				
Government	15	***	12	***
Foreign–Private	45	***	23	**
Foreign–Government	45	***	23	**
Government–Private	71	—	26	**
(2) 1975				
Foreign–Government (JV)	10	—	10	*
Foreign–Government	49	***	25	**
Foreign–Private	48	***	25	**
Government (JV)–Private	12	**	11	***
Government (JV)–				
Government	10	—	10	—
Government–Private	68	—	26	**

[a] The following symbols are used: ** Significant at 5 per cent.
— Not significant at 10 per cent.   *** Significant at 1 per cent.
* Significant at 10 per cent.

Are the differences in the average ratios for each ownership group statistically significant? Do the variations arise primarily because of the selection of different technologies within industries, or are they due to the inter-industry composition of the groups? And are there special features of the comparisons at a disaggregated level which deserve comment? The remainder of this section addresses these questions, with primary reference to the 5-digit data.

Most of the differences between the four major ownership groups are statistically significant in the case of the disaggregated data (see Table 6.6). In 1983, four of the differences are significant at 1 per cent. In the two comparisons where this does not apply, it is either because the differences are not on the whole great (as in the government–private pair), or because of this explanation combined with a small number of observations (for the government joint venture–foreign pair). Broadly similar conclusions apply for the 1975 comparisons. Conducting the same comparisons within major industry groups—such as the 'old' and 'new' industries classification employed and elaborated on below—supports these conclusions, although some of the populations are too small to support statistical testing. The last two columns provide the same information, but at the aggregated (3-digit) industrial classification. Here also the conclusions are comparable. However, lower levels of significance are observed in some cases because of the smaller number of pairs, and the results are less reliable because the comparison does not necessarily involve similar industrial groupings.

The decomposition approach is a useful method of explaining these differences, and it is surprising it has not been used more widely in the literature.[6] The approach is as follows:

$$\text{Let } A = \left(\frac{V}{L}\right)x - \left(\frac{V}{L}\right)y$$

where $\dfrac{V}{L}$ is average value added per worker, and

x and y are ownership groups.

$$\text{Then } A = \Sigma\left(\frac{V}{L}\right)x \quad \left(\frac{L}{\Sigma L}\right)x - \Sigma\left(\frac{V}{L}\right)y \quad \left(\frac{L}{\Sigma L}\right)y,$$

summed across all industries.
It can be shown that

$$A = \tfrac{1}{2}\Sigma\left[\left(\frac{L}{\Sigma L}\right)x + \left(\frac{L}{\Sigma L}\right)y\right]\left[\left(\frac{V}{L}\right)x - \left(\frac{V}{L}\right)y\right]$$
$$+ \tfrac{1}{2}\Sigma\left[\left(\frac{V}{L}\right)x + \left(\frac{V}{L}\right)y\right]\left[\left(\frac{L}{\Sigma L}\right)x - \left(\frac{L}{\Sigma L}\right)y\right]$$

It will be apparent that the first term refers to the difference due to value added per worker within the same industry (since the $\left(\frac{V}{L}\right)$s are subtracted), while the second term refers to the difference due to the composition of the two groups across industries (since the $\left(\frac{L}{\Sigma L}\right)$s are subtracted).

The results of the decomposition analysis for each ownership group, using the disaggregated data, indicate that the relative importance of the two explanatory factors differ among ownership groups (see Table 6.7). For firms in which the government has an equity interest, the location in more capital-intensive industries generally explains these firms' higher value added per worker. The higher ratio for government joint ventures compared to foreign firms is explained by the former's industrial location in 1983, the main factor also in the comparison with private and government firms. In the government–private comparison it is also the overwhelming explanation. In fact, the first factor exhibits a *negative* influence, indicating that in direct comparisons private firms tend to be more capital intensive. The conclusions from the 1975 data are broadly similar. (The decomposition for the government joint venture–foreign comparison is of limited relevance because the difference is small and not statistically significant.)

By contrast, the higher ratios for foreign firms, compared to the government and private groups, are explained by both factors, with the first generally being somewhat more important. In other words, foreign firms are usually more capital-intensive within a given industry and, in addition, they tend to be located in more capital-intensive industries.

The results in Table 6.7 also illustrate the limitations of comparisons at the more aggregated (3-digit) industrial classification. In many cases the

TABLE 6.7
Decomposition of Differences in Value Added per Worker

Comparison	Values	Differences	Disaggregated Data I	Disaggregated Data II	Aggregated Data I	Aggregated Data II
(1) 1983						
Government (JV)–Foreign	13,707–7,641	6,066	2.1	97.9	18.6	81.4
Government (JV)–Private	13,707–2,740	10,967	36.6	63.4	56.5	43.5
Government (JV)–Government	13,707–3,881	9,826	38.7	61.3	45.8	54.2
Foreign–Private	7,641–2,740	4,901	56.1	43.9	170.4	−70.4
Foreign–Government	7,641–3,881	3,760	51.8	48.2	212.5	−112.5
Government–Private	3,881–2,740	1,141	−30.2	130.2	30.6	69.4
(2) 1975						
Foreign–Government (JV)	2,318–2,252	66	1,071.0	−971.0	626.1	−526.1
Foreign–Government	2,318–1,288	1,030	55.1	44.9	94.8	5.2
Foreign–Private	2,318– 575	1,743	48.5	51.5	125.7	−25.7
Government (JV)–Private	2,252– 575	1,677	13.4	86.6	68.4	31.6
Government (JV)–Government	2,252–1,288	964	12.5	87.5	9.3	90.7
Government–Private	1,288– 575	713	42.9	57.1	66.8	33.2

Note: Values in Rp '000. Disaggregated data refer to 5-digit ISIC; aggregated data refer to 3-digit ISIC. Terms I and II indicate respectively percentage difference due to choice of technology *within* industry, and due to industrial composition.

differences between the two sets of estimates are very marked. In 1983, for example, the aggregated data suggest industrial composition exerts a large negative influence on the difference in the foreign–private and foreign–government comparisons, whereas the more accurate 5-digit data point to both factors being of similar importance. Contrasting results are also evident in the government–private comparisons in both years, and in some of the comparisons involving private firms in 1975. Clearly the aggregated data are of very little use in explaining differences among firms, and it is surprising how often such classifications have been used in the literature.

The differences were also computed after discarding those industries where scale factors (as indicated by very small average firm size) may explain much of the difference. However, as with the t-tests, the results did not differ greatly from the full data set.

Are the results of the decomposition analysis sensitive to differences within broad industry classifications? This question may be answered by conducting the same analysis for each 5-digit industry within what may be termed 'old' and 'new' industries. The former are the food and textiles industries and related activities (ISIC 31 and 32), which are generally labour-intensive consumer goods industries. The second group comprises mainly intermediate and capital goods industries, which are generally more capital intensive. The results are presented in Table 6.8.

Compared to the disaggregated data in Table 6.7, the figures in Table 6.8 differ considerably, but the fundamental conclusions still hold. Putting aside cases where the absolute differences are small, the higher capital intensity for government and government-associated firms is explained mainly by their location in more capital-intensive industries. This is so for five out of the six cases for which the comparison is relevant in 1983, and for four out of five in 1975. Similarly, the higher ratios for foreign firms are generally explained about equally by both factors, although there are substantial variations.

It is useful to draw attention to some of these variations, since they are indicative of important changes which occurred between 1975 and 1983, and of differences within the manufacturing sector in both years. Once again, we put aside comparisons where the absolute differences are small. The first significant feature is the role of government firms in 'new' industries in 1975, which for all three comparisons exhibit a higher ratio. This is presumably explained by industrial infancy in the earlier year, and by the fact that in many cases the government directly initiated the establishment of new intermediate and capital goods industries. By 1983, both government joint ventures and foreign firms had overtaken these purely state-owned enterprises. Secondly, the differences between private firms and the other three groups in value added per worker are especially pronounced in the new industries, in both years. In the case of old industries, the ratio for private firms actually exceeds that of government firms in 1983; for the other comparisons, location in more capital-intensive industries explains most of the difference. In other words, in those industries in which production technologies are widely available and disseminated, the differ-

TABLE 6.8

Decomposition of Differences in Value Added per Worker, Old and New Industries

Comparison	'Old' Industries				'New' Industries			
	Values	Differences	Percentage Difference Due To		Values	Differences	Percentage Difference Due To	
			I	II			I	II
(1) 1983								
Government (JV)–Foreign	7,558–7,826	–268	–1,874.1	1,774.1	16,490–7,538	8,952	28.5	71.5
Government (JV)–Private	7,558–2,969	4,589	38.3	61.7	16,490–2,493	13,997	39.4	60.6
Government (JV)–Government	7,558–2,282	5,276	39.7	60.2	16,490–6,340	10,150	53.3	46.7
Foreign–Private	7,826–2,969	4,857	44.8	55.2	7,538–2,493	5,045	73.8	26.2
Foreign–Government	7,826–2,282	5,544	45.8	54.2	7,538–6,340	1,198	134.8	–34.8
Government–Private	2,282–2,969	–687	–147.1	47.1	6,340–2,493	3,847	14.0	86.0
(2) 1975								
Foreign–Government (JV)	3,064–2,607	457	179.4	–79.4	1,736–1,902	–166	400.3	–500.3
Foreign–Government	3,064– 902	2,162	48.3	51.7	1,736–2,142	–406	54.5	–154.5
Foreign–Private	3,064– 527	2,537	43.8	56.2	1,736– 683	1,053	65.4	34.6
Government (JV)–Private	2,607– 527	2,080	5.4	94.6	1,902– 683	1,219	28.8	71.2
Government (JV)–Government	2,607– 902	1,705	43.1	56.9	1,902–2,142	–240	–227.6	127.6
Government–Private	902– 527	375	29.3	70.3	2,142– 683	1,459	50.8	49.2

Note: Based on 5-digit (disaggregated) data. 'Old' industries refer to ISIC 31 and 32 (food, beverage and tobacco industries; and textiles, garments, leather and footwear industries). 'New' industries refer to ISIC 33–39 (all remaining industries). See also note to Table 6.7.

ences between the private firms and the other groups are not particularly great. Larger differences arise in the case of new industries, although there is no clear pattern regarding the relative importance of the two explanatory factors.

The general pattern is therefore clear enough. Private firms tend to be located more often in the labour-intensive industries and, within these industries, they are generally more labour intensive than other firms, with the partial exception of government firms. The differentials are, however, narrowing over time. Government firms are on average more capital intensive, but this is mainly due to the government's decision to invest in more capital-intensive industries, rather than to sharp differences within industries. Foreign firms are more capital intensive than either of these two groups, and both explanatory factors exert a broadly similar influence. Finally, it is the government firms with foreign partners which display by far the highest capital intensity, again primarily because of their location in more capital-intensive industries. It is the combination of the government's strategic investment decisions (in these industries) *and* the greater capital intensity of foreign investors which appears to explain the result.

Some of the individual industry results may at first sight appear surprising. One is that private firms are the most capital intensive in transport equipment (ISIC 384) in 1975, and nearly so in 1983; in many subsectors within this group, private firms are also, on average, more capital intensive. The explanation is simply that most of the private firms have licensing arrangements with foreign partners who, though unable to invest directly, do play a large role in technology selection. The enormous differences within the basic metals group in 1983 require little elaboration. There is no breakdown of categories within this industry and, in effect, the ownership groups are producing different products. The high state figure is because of the Krakatau steel plant, while the even higher ratio for the government joint venture groups is due to the Asahan aluminium smelter. The two privately owned groups produce various types of steel products, the production technologies for which are less capital intensive.

Within the heterogeneous, food, beverage, and tobacco manufacturing industries (ISIC 31) there are many cases of non-comparison. The ratio for government firms is as high as it is—especially in 1975—mainly because of the dominance of sugar refining. In other industries these firms are less capital intensive than the privately owned firms. The foreign firms' ratio is high within ISIC 311 mainly owing to the figure for dairy products. The ratios for foreign and joint ventures are especially high for the beverage industry mainly because of brewing, which is entirely controlled by these two groups.[7] The ratios for tobacco products are above average for foreign firms, which employ mechanized technology to produce 'white' cigarettes, and for private firms in the rapidly mechanizing *kretek* cigarette industry.

The higher figure for foreign firms in the textiles industry, by contrast, is due to greater capital intensity within all three subsectors, synthetic fibre, spinning, and weaving. The same conclusion applies in the various wood products industries.

The chemicals industry is dominated by fertilizer and other basic chemicals on the one hand, and a wide range of chemical products (detergents, pharmaceuticals, and so on) on the other. Here also there is some specialization according to ownership: the average for government firms (and joint ventures) is very high because of fertilizer plants; foreign firms are much higher for other chemical products (ISIC 352), in some of which product differentiation is significant.

Large variations occur within the non-metallic minerals industries due to the industry specialization of the ownership groups and the range of factor intensities. Within the cement industry, government firms once dominated and were the most capital intensive. By 1983, however, the government joint ventures had the highest ratio. The glass industry is another example in which foreign firms have both located in the more capital-intensive subsector (sheet glass) and employed more capital-intensive technologies.

Towards an Explanation of Differences

The previous section has demonstrated that the greater capital intensity of foreign and government (joint venture) firms is explained in part by their location in more capital-intensive industries. This location can be attributed both to economic factors, in the case of foreign firms, and to strategic development objectives, in the case of state enterprises.

But there are also significant differences among the ownership groups *within* industries. What accounts for these differences? There are at least four explanations:

1. Firms face different sets of relative factor prices, in some cases resulting from government intervention in factor markets.

2. Access to and knowledge of internationally available technologies vary among ownership groups.

3. Product specifications dictate technology selection for certain groups of firms, even within disaggregated industry classifications.

4. The differences are spurious because of data and conceptual limitations.

The *relative factor price* argument is the most frequently cited among the few studies which attempt to explain differences among firms (for example, Agarwal (1976), Ahiakpor (1986), Forsyth and Solomon (1977)).

The hypothesis is that foreign—and perhaps government—firms face lower capital costs because of preferential access to credit and capital-cheapening fiscal concessions. These firms also face higher labour costs, it is alleged, owing to social obligations, and regulations governing minimum wages and dismissal of employees. Both arguments are a good deal more relevant in explaining differences between firms in the 'organized' and cottage industry sectors than among ownership groups within the organized sector.

Most manufacturing investment decisions in Indonesia during the New Order period were either formulated or implemented in the 1970s. During this period, the capital-cheapening argument was a relatively minor one. All firms, in principle, had access to BKPM incentives. There may have been a slight implicit bias towards large foreign- or government-owned projects in the granting of incentives, through political influence, 'pecuniary scale economies' in dealing with the bureaucracy, or bureaucratic preferences towards these firms. Nevertheless, at least in the case of foreign firms, investors from some countries were sometimes discouraged,[8] and certain industries were simply open to foreign investors without incentives. In any case, it is debatable whether the BKPM incentives had a great impact on investors' decisions because, as we have seen, many domestic firms were established under the BRO system in preference to the BKPM. Such an option was not available to foreign firms.

The segmented capital market explanation is more important. Throughout most of the 1970s both foreign and (domestic) state banks offered credit at negative real interest rates. The nominal rates of the former were generally lower but, allowing for exchange rate risk, there was little difference between the two. Foreign and government firms generally had little difficulty obtaining access to one of these credit sources. Large, well-connected domestic investors also had easy access to the state banks. However, many other domestic investors, not so well placed, obtained finance from private banks or the informal money market at considerably higher interest rates (see McLeod, 1980).

Wage rates among the ownership groups appear to vary substantially. In part this is due to 'non-economic' factors, such as over-staffing in government firms,[9] and community pressures on foreign firms. But the most comprehensive study of wage differentials in Indonesian manufacturing, by Manning (1979), has demonstrated that economic factors also played an important role. Foreign firms, in particular, generally recruit more skilled labour than their domestic counterparts. Rather than necessarily facing a different wage–rental ratio, foreign firms are, in effect, purchasing more human capital.

For all these reasons, the relative factor price argument may be of some relevance in explaining technology differences, especially in the comparison between private firms and the other groups which obtained cheap credit. But the argument is unlikely to have been a major factor in most cases.

The second explanation, *access to and knowledge of technologies*, was probably the most important factor. It is significant that studies of the North-East Asian NICs, in which the domestic entrepreneurial base is comparatively strong, have found little difference between foreign and local investors. The situation in Indonesia has, until recently, been quite the opposite. In the late 1960s, Indonesia possessed only a rudimentary modern manufacturing base and a poorly developed domestic entrepreneurial capacity. After two decades of economic dislocation and minimal international contact, Indonesian investors generally lacked knowledge of the international technology market and the skills to operate technologies purchased 'off-the-shelf'.

With few exceptions, modern technologies in the early years of New Order industrialization were introduced either through government firms, or private firms in which foreigners had a licensing or equity interest. The 1975 SI data indicate the large differences between private firms and the other groups both within industries and in the industry composition. By 1983, the SI data suggest, private firms were rapidly catching up, as technological competence in these firms expanded considerably. Cross-section, 'snap-shot' pictures of technology choice therefore obscure the dynamics of the transition from the adoption of simple to modern technologies on the part of domestic firms. Differences among groups are likely to remain, both because of inherent preferences and imperfect knowledge, but over time these differences will become less important.

A third explanation is that, even within finely *disaggregated* industrial classifications, *product specifications among firms* may dictate technology differences. Several studies have established that the more restricted technology choices are, the more comprehensive the product specifications (Stewart, 1978). Some analyses of technology choice in Indonesian manufacturing (for example, Keddie, 1975) suggest product differentiation is of some importance in brand name consumer goods industries. But this argument is probably not of great importance in explaining differences *within* industries. The domestic market is a highly competitive one, and price is the major basis of competition. As Thee and Yoshihara (1987) have documented, in several industries (soft drinks, detergents, and perfumes) higher priced international brand name products have not been able to compete successfully with cheaper domestic alternatives. Moreover, some domestic firms produce international brand names under licence from foreign firms (for example, batteries and automobiles), and so product specification as a basis for technology differences is not relevant. Product differentiation is more likely to explain differences in inter-industry specialization among investors, to the extent permitted by government entry regulations, rather than differences within industries.

Finally, it is possible that *data limitations* explain some of the differences. Two limitations, in particular, have been highlighted. One is that differences in the value added measure capture more than simply differences in capital intensity. This could be either because the firms with higher value added per employee possess a more skilled labour force; in other words, the differences are due to higher physical *and* human capital intensity. Or, as Balasubramanyam (1984) points out, productive efficiency in foreign (but not government) firms could be greater. Both arguments are valid for Indonesia and the results therefore need to be qualified. The other possible limitation is that even though allowance has been made for scale differences, the industry averages for each ownership group may conceal skewed size distributions which render non-comparable apparently similar aggregate figures.

In sum, putting aside data limitations, no single argument provides a complete explanation for differences among firms. Rather, a combination of factors—inherent preferences, technical competence, and perhaps relative factor prices—appears to be significant. It is important to emphasize that the differences among groups are narrowing over time. In another decade or two, as domestic technological competence expands, the issue will be much less important.

1. In Indonesia for example, Kuntjoro-Jakti *et al.* (1983, p. 47) lament the fact that just a little over 400,000 jobs were to be created by approved foreign investments from 1967 to 1980. Palmer (1978) expresses similar sentiments.

2. The ratio for foreign firms was found to be 30 and 40 per cent higher than government and private firms respectively. The differences were much greater if non-wage value added per worker was used as the measure.

3. Numerous examples may be cited. In the cigarette industry, only private firms produce the more labour-intensive *kretek* cigarettes, while foreign firms are much more important in the production of white cigarettes. Similarly, foreign firms play a significant role in the more capital-intensive spinning and synthetic fibres sectors, while private firms are the major producers in the more labour-intensive weaving and garments industries.

4. The industries were plastic sandals, cigarettes, soft drink bottling, bicycle and *becak* tyres, flashlight batteries, and woven bags.

5. For useful syntheses of the literature, see Caves (1982, pp. 267–70), Lall (1978), Nixson (1984, pp. 109–14), and White (1978).

6. I am grateful to R. M. Sundrum for drawing this approach to my attention.

7. This is clearly a case where the value added ratio is a poorer indicator of factor intensities: the high figure reflects not only high physical capital intensity but, in addition, product differentiation in an oligopolistic industry.

8. Wells (1983) suggests this was the case occasionally for firms from Hong Kong and Singapore.

9. Numerous studies of government enterprises in Indonesia have drawn attention to this fact. See, for example, Gillis (1982), Hill (1982), and McCawley (1971).

7 Technology Diffusion and the Distribution of Gains

The slow process, I would almost say, reluctance to transfer technology to Indonesian firms could have its origin in the Japanese concept of lifetime employment which demands loyalty; in practice the turnover rate in Indonesia can sometimes be high. In any case, while some Indonesian nationals have occupied important posts in production units, there are often considerable discrepancies between stated job description and day-to-day responsibilities. (Soehoed, 1981, p. 135.)

FOREIGN investors introduce a package of highly productive resources into the host country. These include managerial skills, production technology, continuing access to established research and development facilities, proprietory use of international brand names, and knowledge of and access to international product and capital markets. The issue of technology transfer lies at the heart of the debate concerning the costs and benefits of foreign investment. Host governments and firms want access to the technology which foreigners possess. Foreign firms seek to employ their technology abroad and to maximize their returns to it. There is thus a mutuality of interests in increasing the international dissemination of technology. The differences between the two parties arise only in the distribution of the *net benefits* of their technology.

The issue of technology transfer is becoming more important for other reasons. Host governments recognize that the old arguments for foreign investment, which rested on its contribution to capital formation and the balance of payments, are now a good deal less important. In the case of capital formation, net foreign direct investment inflows have rarely been a significant proportion of gross domestic capital formation in Indonesia and elsewhere, as was shown in Chapter 3. Moreover, foreign investment as a percentage of long-term financial flows to developing countries has been declining, from about 19 per cent in 1970 to 8 per cent in 1983 (UNCTC, 1985, 1.25). If it is capital which countries require, it can more easily be obtained through direct borrowing on international capital markets. Similarly, in an era of floating exchange rates, the old balance of payments argument is also a good deal less relevant. At a theoretical level, also, the focus in the foreign investment literature has been changing, and it has come to regard intangible assets as having a larger development contribution than financial assets.

To examine the extent and nature of technology transfer we need to ask three questions. First, to what degree have foreign investment and other forms of involvement contributed to increased productivity in the host country? Secondly, how great have the technology spin-offs (the so-called 'leakages and linkages') to Indonesian factors of production been, and in what other ways have the benefits of new technology (broadly defined) been captured? Thirdly, which groups within the host country have been the prime beneficiaries: particular business groups, consumers, workers, or some other group? Technology transfer also raises questions about the appropriate location of research and development capacity. Over 95 per cent of the world's research and development expenditure is in the industrialized economies, and much of the private sector research and development is undertaken by multinationals. According to the static theory of comparative advantage, research and development is a particularly human capital- and scale-intensive activity, which also requires an advanced supporting scientific infrastructure. It is therefore argued that it is cheaper for developing countries to purchase new technology 'off-the-shelf' than to develop it themselves.

What light does Indonesia's experience with technology imports shed on these questions? We examine first the impact of foreign investment on productivity, and the spin-offs to domestic factors, in the following section. Next the distribution of gains is assessed. Finally, the more general question of research and technology policy is addressed in the latter part of this chapter and in Chapter 8.

Technology Transfer

Detailed estimates of the profitability and productivity of foreign investments in Indonesia are not available. It is widely believed that foreign-owned firms are more profitable than their domestic counterparts, and this in all likelihood is the case. The international data suggest that, at least for United States firms, Indonesia has been a moderately profitable base for operations, although rates of return have been higher elsewhere—notably in Malaysia, Singapore, and Taiwan (see Table 7.1). These figures do, however, have to be treated with caution. The rates fluctuate considerably between years; United States investments in Indonesian manufacturing are relatively small, and concentrated mainly in the chemicals industry; and similar data are not published for other major investors, from Japan, Hong Kong, and the EC.

It is almost certainly the case that joint ventures in Indonesia are more productive than their domestic counterparts. No estimates of total factor productivity are available for manufacturing as a whole, let alone according to ownership. But the much higher labour productivity of foreign firms and joint ventures is strong presumptive evidence of their greater total productivity.[1]

Assessing the indirect effects of technology spin-offs from foreign firms

TABLE 7.1

Rates of Return on United States Direct Investment in Manufacturing
in Selected Developing Countries

Country/Region	1979	1980	1981	1982	1983	1984
Indonesia	20.4	22.9	n.a.	76.3	n.a.	9.9
Other ASEAN						
Malaysia	27.5	31.3	n.a.	26.5	32.8	15.4
Philippines	15.8	13.4	11.0	3.6	−6.1	n.a.
Singapore	34.4	37.5	40.2	25.6	40.2	34.7
Thailand	20.0	16.1	26.9	−4.8	97.1	n.a.
Other Asia						
India	14.6	12.7	10.1	9.9	4.2	n.a.
Korea (South)	18.8	negative	−18.0	11.2	38.2	41.2
Taiwan	34.4	37.5	40.2	25.6	40.2	34.7
Latin America	12.1	14.7	11.1	8.3	1.4	7.2

Source: Business International, 29 November 1985, as cited in Chia (1987).
n.a. = Not available.

is a good deal more difficult. Conceptually these effects might be measured by tracing over time the experience of those associated with foreign firms—workers, suppliers, and customers—relative to that of a control group with no such links. Significant differences in productivity and earnings between the two groups, it could plausibly be argued, are the results of the interaction with foreign firms. In practice, such experiments are extremely difficult to conduct; not only do they require large research resources, but it is also extremely difficult to identify a suitable control group.

In Indonesia, as elsewhere, we are thus left with a series of case studies. Although they do not employ a common framework, they provide much useful information. The general conclusion of these studies is that there is a considerable amount of technology diffusion through training and other activities, but that the spill-over benefits are limited by very low turnover of personnel in foreign firms (in part because of superior working conditions) and by the fact that the training received is often firm or even technique specific. However, it is important to emphasize that, since many of the studies were conducted after a very short period of exposure to foreign investment in manufacturing, the long-term benefits are probably understated. Over time they will almost certainly have risen.

Most studies of technology transfer in Indonesia focus on the training of employees by foreign firms. Foreign firms appear to pay higher wages than their domestic competitors, and this is a result of their higher productivity, their recruitment of more skilled labour, and their internal training programmes. The most complete study of wage differentials in Indonesian manufacturing is the survey of firms in three industries (white and kretek cigarettes, and weaving) by Manning (1979) in the mid-1970s. In a simple comparison within weaving, for example, he found wages in foreign firms to be approximately double those in domestic firms (pp. 240 ff.). This was partly due to the foreign firms' higher capital intensity but, even when controlling for this variable, wages in foreign firms were still substantially higher.

Manning attributed the higher wages mainly to the skill composition of foreign firms' work-force and to the internal labour market policies of these firms. That training is an important component in the latter is illustrated also in a survey of 74 Japanese firms in 1973 by Tsurumi (1980). He cited management reports that Indonesian production workers initially were found to have productivity levels of 50–60 per cent of those of Japanese or Korean workers in comparable industries. However, 'after 12 to 18 months of work experience and closely supervised training', Indonesian workers achieved 80–90 per cent of this level (Tsurumi, 1980, p. 314).

How much training do foreign firms provide? The mere presence of highly skilled personnel in a factory is likely to provide a stimulus to a firm's productivity. In addition, surveys suggest that most foreign companies provide a range of training programmes. For example, Siahaan, Thee et al. (1978) surveyed 23 Japanese companies in 1976 and found that training was considerable (see Table 7.2). For upper and middle management, this training often took the form of special courses conducted by Indonesian institutions, and not infrequently programmes at company headquarters and institutions in Japan. For production workers, it consisted mainly of on-the-job instruction, but there was substantial training outside the factory at supervisor level.[2]

It also appears that foreign firms provide considerably more training than comparable domestic firms. Here also, the most detailed study is that of Manning (1979). Half of the foreign firms he surveyed provided special training courses for production workers, while the other half provided formal on-the-job training (see Table 7.3). As would be expected, these findings contrast sharply with those for domestic, non-mechanized firms. But even among comparable domestic firms (column 3), formal training appears to be considerably less important. Broadly similar conclusions apply, according to Manning (1979, p. 337), for non-production workers.

Although the benefits of these training programmes accrue to Indonesian factors of production (that is, employees of foreign firms), the evidence

TABLE 7.2

Training in 23 Japanese Companies, 1976 (number of personnel)

Level	On-the-job	Company HQ in Japan	Japanese Educational Institution	Indonesian Educational Institution	Other Programmes
Upper management	2	3	1	6	8
Middle management	41	39	2	19	14
Office workers	185	4	0	9	22
Plant supervisors	240	74	0	3	110
Plant workers	3,975	5	0	13	135

Source: Siahaan, Thee et al., 1978, p. 115.

also suggests that foreign firms internalize—and therefore appropriate—a good part of the gains in the short run. One reason is the low turnover of workers in foreign firms, who are reluctant to leave secure and better paid positions. In Manning's survey, for example, labour turnover in foreign firms was about half that in comparable (that is, mechanized, high capital–labour ratios) domestic firms (p. 351). This conclusion confirms that of a large eight-industry survey conducted in 1973 by Rice (1974). Focusing in particular on the movement of skilled labour, he concluded from his survey that there was a net loss of workers to foreign firms (p. 143), although there were instances of several shoe companies being established by former Bata employees (p. 147). This finding is, however, hardly surprising—as Rice recognizes—because the foreign firms in the survey had only recently been established.

The survey evidence, though scattered and somewhat dated, is thus generally consistent: the productivity of Indonesian labour and management has undoubtedly been enhanced by their association with foreign firms. And the spill-over effects, in terms of inter-firm labour movements and the internal dissemination of managerial skills and technologies, must certainly have been increasing over time.

There are other externalities and spin-offs associated with foreign investment in Indonesian manufacturing. One which has received considerable attention in the recent literature is sub-contracting, from large assembling firms to the generally smaller supplier firms which provide a wide range of specialist components. These sub-contracting networks are particularly important in the automotive and appliance industries, in which the final manufacturing process consists largely of the assembly of components, and in which specialization dictates that it is more economic to put out the production of many components than to engage in extensive in-house manufacture. Belief in the desirability of sub-contracting as a

TABLE 7.3

Major Methods of Skill Generation in Indonesian Manufacturing
by Capital Intensity and Ownership
(percentage of firms)

| Major Methods of Skill Generation | Domestic | | | | |
| | Non-mechanized (1) | Mechanized | | Foreign (4) | All Firms (5) |
		Low K/L (2)	High K/L (3)		
Learning by doing	72	—	—	—	25
Help of friends/family	14	59	20	—	28
Formal on-the-job training	14	41	60	50	36
Special training courses	—	—	20	50	11
Total (per cent)	100	100	100	100	100
N (firms)	28	27	10	14	79

Source: Manning, 1979, p. 328.

means of technology diffusion is supported, especially, by the Japanese experience of very strong vertical inter-firm linkages between assemblers and suppliers, and of important technical and other resources from the former to the latter.[3]

In Indonesia, most of these assembler firms are either joint ventures or producing under licence from overseas, and so the appeal of sub-contracting as a means of technology transfer is obvious. But the results of the government's sub-contracting policies are so far not very encouraging. Since the mid-1970s, several measures have been introduced which compel the assemblers not only to backward integrate (that is, to source locally), but also to procure from local firms rather than to engage in in-house manufacture. For example, a Ministerial decision in 1976 (SK Menteri No. 307/1976) introduced a phased-in mandatory deletion programme for several components of commercial vehicles which were previously imported in completely knocked down (CKD) form. The list was extended in 1979 (SK 168/1979), and in 1983 the Minister for Industry announced that full local content would be required for commercial vehicles. Similar programmes have been introduced for motor cycles, and regulations are in preparation for passenger cars. In several cases, the regulations have explicitly required that the components be manufactured by the unaffiliated firms[4] (see Thee, 1985, pp. 225–7).

Several studies of sub-contracting undertaken by Thee Kian Wie and his colleagues (reported in Thee (ed.) (1985)) have concluded that most assemblers have been sub-contracting only because of government pressure. Moreover, in response to the mandatory deletion programme, they have preferred wherever possible (and even if contrary to the spirit of the regulations) to manufacture in-house; most putting-out has been confined to a few insignificant and non-essential items. Consequently, linkages—technical, managerial, and financial—between assemblers and sub-contractors have generally been weak. These findings are consistent with a survey of sub-contractors in the automobile industry in 1977 conducted by Witoelar (1983). He observed that many of the sub-contractors were sizeable firms, including several PMA and PMDN companies, and that the extent of components manufacture (as distinct from assembly) was often limited. Significantly, he concluded that 'almost none [of the sub-contractors] derive their technology from local assemblers'.

These results are hardly surprising. As Caves (1982, pp. 270–2) and others have observed, multinationals often have fewer links with the local economy than do domestic firms. These weaker links are the result of both 'policy' and 'commercial' factors. Policy factors include the establishment of export processing zones (EPZs), which discourage forward and backward linkages, and a cascading protective structure, which encourages overseas rather than domestic sourcing of components. EPZs are still little developed in Indonesia, but the structure of protection has certainly inhibited internal economic integration. Commercial factors include the introduction of new products, for which inputs are not locally available, and the fact that foreign firms are less familiar with the local business environment. Both these propositions are relevant to Indonesian manufacturing; the weak linkages have also been compounded by government policies which have resulted in excessively fragmented markets, in which component manufacturers have been unable to reap the benefits of scale economies.

Consequently, the technology spin-offs through sub-contracting have been minimal, although they may develop over time. It is true that most of the foreign partners may not have approached the development of sub-contracting networks with enthusiasm, but a major cause lies in the inappropriate policy environment in Indonesia. In other developing countries, where the policy environment has been more conducive, stronger links have emerged.[5]

There is considerable evidence on the high import intensity of foreign investors, another factor contributing to low linkages. A Bank Indonesia survey in 1978, cited by von Kirchbach (1982, p. 16), found that the imports of multinationals outside the oil sector were about double their exports. The surprising feature of this finding is that imports were not relatively higher, given the very low volume of *total* manufacturing exports in that year; in any case the results mean little without reference to some bench-mark. More detailed, although also more dated, evidence was provided by Yoshihara (1978, p. 49). He reports a MITI study which concluded that in 1974 almost half of the inputs of Indonesian subsidiaries of Japanese companies were imported from the parent company, a substantially higher figure than for either the Philippines or Thailand. In textiles, where much of the early Japanese investment occurred, the import intensity ratio for Indonesian joint ventures was double that of Malaysian companies and more than six times the comparable Thai figure. The much higher figures for Indonesia were presumably indicative of the country's high domestic cost structure and limited industrialization, rather than the nationality of investors.

It needs to be emphasized that, while linkages in the form of sub-contracting which facilitate technology transfers might be encouraged—especially when much of the modern manufacturing sector is foreign dominated—there is nothing inherently desirable in high linkages of the input–output type. Indeed, they may be undesirable. Recent input–output studies of ASEAN manufacturing (see, for example, van Dijck and Verbruggen, 1983) have found that linkages are lower in the dynamic and open Singapore economy than they are in the inward-looking and uncompetitive Indonesian manufacturing industry. As Lall (1978) observed, export-oriented foreign investments generally have weaker domestic links than those which are primarily import substituting.

But the former type of investment is no less desirable. In fact, although the linkages may be weaker in a formal sense, export-oriented investments generate new information for the host country about international marketing channels. For a country like Indonesia with an inward-looking manufacturing sector, these investments can also constitute a powerful demonstration effect. Scattered evidence suggests that foreign firms have not played a major role in the recent increase in Indonesia's manufactured exports, although foreign trading houses—especially from Japan—have been important. Of the three large manufactured exports, foreign ownership is negligible in garments and modest in the plywood industry. Only in electronics was foreign investment until recently sizeable. However, in 1986, the two foreign companies withdrew from Indonesia, partly in response to the world-wide over-supply in the industry, and partly because—according to the companies—Indonesia is not competitive in the labour-intensive (assembly and packaging) activities compared to neighbouring countries. A majority of firms in the Jakarta EPZ are foreign owned but, as noted, exports are small in aggregate (Warr, 1983).

In the recent push for non-oil and gas exports, foreign firms in Indonesia have been criticized for their allegedly poor export performance. In response to these criticisms, the Jakarta JETRO office undertook a survey in 1984 which suggested that about 80 per cent of Indonesia's textile (that is, cloth and yarn) exports were in the hands of Japanese trading houses. The survey results also indicated that about 27 per cent of these textile exports were produced by Japanese joint ventures, a much higher percentage than their share of industry output (Jakarta JETRO office, personal communication). The export performance of multinationals in Indonesian manufacturing is clearly unimpressive, but here also it needs to be emphasized that the main explanation is the (until recently) unattractive commercial environment rather than the nationality of investors.

The earlier survey by Rice (1974) and a more recent one by Thee (1984c) examined other aspects of technology transfer by multinationals in Indonesia. Focusing especially on the externalities associated with foreign investment, Rice concluded that, although they were 'less than expected', in some cases they were quite substantial. Domestic firms reported experiencing severe competition in three industries, paints, enamelware, and soft drinks. Although Rice recorded these as diseconomies for the firms concerned, they may well have been positive for consumers and workers in the industries. In some industries, also, he found foreign firms were an important source of new ideas about production technology (especially) and products. Thee (1984c) studied intensively twelve firms with either foreign equity or licensing agreements. Many of his findings confirmed earlier studies. Training, especially at management levels, was found to be quite extensive, and generally included some international exposure. Backward linkages were found to be expanding, but the main impetus was government programmes, and in some instances local procurement was unprofitable. As compared to operations in the parent company's home base, there was greater modification of production technology than of products, in part because parent companies were concerned to preserve international brand names.

Thee's survey also addressed two issues which have received much less attention in Indonesia. The first was local research and development activity. He found that most of the firms had extremely limited research and development capacity. In some cases, modest laboratories had been established to conform with Indonesian government requirements or to ensure quality control. But there was little else. This finding is consistent with the results of other case studies and also some source (investor) country data. In the 1977 survey of American overseas affiliates, for example, it was found that manufacturing firms spent $1,785 million on research and development, of which 93 per cent was in other developed countries. For affiliates in Indonesia, research and development expenditure was just $1 million, or 0.4 per cent of sales, compared to 1 per cent for developed country affiliates. In the 1982 survey (United States Department of Commerce, 1985), the percentage for Indonesian manufacturing was even lower, at 0.2 per cent. A similar picture probably applies for investors from other countries. These results, also, are not surprising. Research and development is an extremely skill-intensive activity. Given the shortage of skilled labour in Indonesia, the absence of a supporting scientific infrastructure, and the fact that patents and other protections for proprietory technology barely exist, Indonesia is hardly an attractive base for research and development activities.

The second issue examined by Thee (1984c) was the costs and conditions of technology purchase. He found a variety of agreements. For firms willing to disclose financial details, the costs ranged from 3 to as high as 6 per cent of sales (the latter for a pharmaceutical firm) plus other charges. In several cases, restrictive clauses applied, including a prohibition on exports and exclusive sourcing of some inputs from the parent company.

There has been little serious scrutiny of the terms on which Indonesian companies acquire foreign technology. However, it is probable that Indonesia's experience is not dissimilar to that of Thailand, which was carefully analysed by Santikarn (1981, chap. 5) in the mid-1970s. She found many instances of high royalty charges, generally linked to the licenser's possession of trademarks and brand names, rather than production technology. A range of restrictive clauses was also enforced. In addition, she found that the costs of technology acquisition from Japanese companies were generally lower. This was partly because these companies were mainly offering standardized technologies with less scope for exacting monopoly rents, and partly because, as late comers, these companies were forced to offer more attractive conditions. It is likely that the costs of technology acquisition may be higher still for Indonesian companies given their more limited international exposure and experience, and the less competitive commercial environment (with, consequently, less pressure to minimize costs). But this will have to remain an hypothesis pending further empirical research.

To sum up, the evidence on technology transfer is mixed. There is some evidence to support the former Minister for Industry's assertion, at the beginning of this chapter, about the 'slow process' of technology transfer. Indonesian firms may also have paid too high a price for some technology, especially for the right to use brand names, which may not be central to the development of an efficient manufacturing sector. But if the costs of technology acquisition have been 'excessive', as we will argue in the next chapter, the cause lies as much with the domestic policy environment as any other factor. It is also important to place the role of foreign investment in proper perspective. Many of the fastest growing industries in Indonesia since 1970 have been overwhelmingly owned and controlled by (private or state) domestic business groups. Moreover, *direct* investment has been just one channel—albeit a fairly important one—for the introduction and dissemination of new technologies.

The Distribution of Gains among Investors

Which groups have benefited from the virtual technological revolution which has occurred in much of Indonesian industry over the last twenty years? In many cases the beneficiaries are not easy to identify since these groups are so diffused. But clearly consumers have a wider range of better quality goods from which to choose, and workers and firms associated with joint ventures have acquired new skills. What of the domestic capitalist class, both private and state? Government policy since the mid-1970s has increasingly emphasized the goal of localization in ownership and management. The premise underlying government requirements of increased local ownership and control is that more of the gains from foreign investment will be appropriated by Indonesian citizens, and that they will be more responsive to Indonesia's 'national interests'.

All available information, however, suggests that many local partners participate little in joint ventures, although their role is probably increasing over time, and that local partners are drawn predominantly from a very small group consisting mainly of military officials and non-*pribumi* businessmen. McCawley (1983, p. 50) reflects the generally held view: 'It is in the nature of the relationship between Indonesians and foreign businessmen that it will generally be Indonesians from the Jakarta professional, military and government circles who benefit [from pressures for increased localization].'

The following examples from firm surveys, generally somewhat dated, are indicative of local partners' roles:

1. Tsurumi (1980, p. 304) concluded from his survey that 'a "typical" Indonesian partner in a Japanese venture is an individual Indonesian of Chinese ancestry, who used to be an importer of Japanese goods'.

2. Kuntjoro-Jakti *et al.* (1983, p. 45) cite a report that over 90 per cent of all capital invested by Indonesian citizens with foreign investors up to 1974 was by non-*pribumi* Indonesians.

3. The Indonesian partner is not infrequently chosen on the basis of political connections, as Weinstein (1976b, p. 389) reported: 'One Indonesian army general involved in numerous joint ventures asserted that his actual "capital" contribution was his ability to see the President on a day's notice.'

4. A study of the timber industry by Manning (1971) found that most local partners were from the military.

5. Okada (1983, pp. 120–2) pointed to the prevalence of 'dummy' partners in joint ventures, and also to the much higher proportion of part-time Indonesian directors, as compared to their foreign counterparts. In his survey, Indonesians constituted 37 per cent of full- and part-time management, but only 18 per cent of full-time managers.[6]

Most studies of decision-making structures within joint ventures also conclude that local partners play a limited role. Weinstein (1976b, pp. 390 ff.) characterized the division of responsibility between partners as

TABLE 7.4

Japanese and Indonesian Management Personnel in Japanese Companies (number of personnel)

Level of Management	At Time of Establishment			'Present' (1976)			Targeted		
	Japanese	Indonesian	Ratio	Japanese	Indonesian	Ratio	Japanese	Indonesian	Ratio
Upper	84	36	2.3	94	46	2.0	39	23	1.7
Middle	167	122	1.4	124	198	0.6	28	71	0.4

Source: Siahaan, Thee et al., 1978, p. 84.

follows: foreign partners controlled production, finance and management, while local partners were responsible for public relations, labour relations and (sometimes nominally) domestic distribution. He also asserted that this division appeared to hold independent of equity shares. Tsurumi (1980, p. 307) concurred, concluding that 'with some notable exceptions, Indonesian partners are not involved in the management of the foreign subsidiaries'.

Panglaykim and Pangestu (1983) provide one of the more detailed studies of business relations within (Japanese) joint ventures. They conclude that the local partner's contribution frequently consists only of land,[7] that additional equity shares are financed by internal arrangements, and that even domestic marketing (which the government until recently decreed must be in the hands of Indonesian citizens) is often only nominally under local control. Not only, they argued, are 'the majority of joint ventures still in the hands of the Japanese partners' (p. 74), but local partners often have little interest in increasing their role. They see the obstacles to increased localization as deep-seated and in part culture based, concluding (p. 78) that it is 'very difficult for the Japanese partner of a joint venture company to appoint an Indonesian national as the real top man, because the latter cannot possibly participate fully in the Japanese system of decision-making'.

The results of these surveys are not altogether surprising. They were mostly conducted in the 1970s when there was an especially acute shortage of Indonesian entrepreneurs with capital and technical and managerial skills. The response to increased pressure for localization has been to increase the gearing (debt–equity) ratio of joint ventures, and for more *Ali–Baba* relationships to develop. Moreover, the beneficiaries of these pressures—the 'bureaucratic capitalist' class of Jakarta and the military—have often been the same group which nationalist critics of Indonesia's development strategy allege have gained disproportionately from the last twenty years of rapid growth.

Although no systematic longitudinal studies are available, it is probable that Indonesian participation has been increasing along with an expanded supply of suitable local partners. The survey by Siahaan, Thee *et al.* (1978) suggested such a trend almost a decade ago. At both upper and middle management levels—especially the latter—the ratio of Indonesian to Japanese personnel was increasing at the time of the survey, and it was expected to continue to rise (see Table 7.4). Despite the authors' observation that the increase may be 'more apparent than real' (p. 85), such a conclusion does accord with other, anecdotal evidence. Whether this has resulted in more of the gains of foreign investment being appropriated by Indonesia is another question, however.

1. One exception to this generalization is the finding by Pitt and Lee (1981), from a sample of 50 weaving firms in the early 1970s, that domestic firms were more efficient than foreign firms. However, the authors do not offer an intuitive explanation for this puzzling result, and the secondary data base over this period—on which the authors relied—was rather weak.

2. These results do differ somewhat from those of Okada (1983) who surveyed 171 affiliates of (mainly) Japanese firms in Indonesia in 1978. Ranking the training programmes of firms from 0 (no training) to 4 (four kinds of programmes), he found an overall mean of 0.92. He also concluded that 51 per cent of the affiliates offered no management training. He provided no explanation for the different results, but clearly much depends on the definition of 'training'.

3. The literature on sub-contracting in Japan is very extensive. Useful references include Ono and Odaka (1979), and Watanabe (1983).

4. Following the slump in motor industry sales in the mid-1980s, the government announced that implementation of these programmes has been deferred. But there is no indication of a change in fundamental policy.

5. It is of interest to compare the Indonesian experience with that of India and Singapore. Case studies in these two countries, by Lall (1980) and Lim and Pang (1982) respectively, have pointed to quite strong technical and other linkages in some instances. The weaker links in Indonesia resemble more closely the situation in the Philippines (see Hill, 1985), and for similar reasons.

6. Robison (1986, chaps. 7–10) provides the most thorough analysis of domestic business groups in the New Order, focusing respectively on state, military, non-*pribumi*, and indigenous enterprises. These chapters also provide many interesting case studies, including an analysis of these firms' relations with foreign interests, through trade, licensing, finance, and other channels.

7. In many cases this, also, is simply due to government decree. Except in special circumstances, foreigners may not own land in Indonesia. It is likely that some purchases of land by domestic partners have been financed indirectly by the foreign partner.

8 The Policy Environment

[Developing countries] should try to attract private foreign investment by making their resources (both natural and human) more attractive rather than by making their markets more attractive by tariffs and tax concessions. (Myint, 1972, p. 90.)

The Law is brief and simple, though one should not look at the Foreign Investment Law only, but at the 328 kinds of related legislation as well. (Sumantoro, 1984, pp. 28–9.)

THE previous chapters have been essentially positive in nature. The government's policies towards foreign investment have been outlined, and the pattern and impact of foreign investment in manufacturing have been analysed. It is now time to undertake a critical review of the government's policies, and to adopt a more normative approach. Have the effects of these policies been broadly consistent with the government's industrialization objectives? Could an alternative mix of policies have achieved these objectives more effectively? Is there a case for major policy reform?

It needs to be emphasized immediately that foreign investment policies are only a subset—and a relatively minor subset—of the broader industrial policy environment. The overall impact of foreign investment depends primarily on *general* policies. At the macro-economic level, these policies include monetary and fiscal management, exchange rate policy, and investment in physical infrastructure and human skills. At a micro-economic level, the important policies are those which affect the efficiency with which resources are allocated, and include especially the trade and regulatory regime.

Nevertheless, there is a range of policies in Indonesia which specifically affect foreign investors—where they can invest, how they may operate, and the package of incentives (or, more often, disincentives) which influences the profitability of their operations. Consequently, a proper analysis of the policy environment requires an examination of both general industrial policies and of measures aimed directly at foreign investment.

An assessment of foreign investment policies and options would be incomplete without reference to the general climate of opinion towards the entry of foreign capital to Indonesia. As we have seen, the remarkable change of direction in 1967, and the adoption of a liberal 'open-door' policy, was short-lived. There has been a deep-seated suspicion of foreign

ownership in Indonesia ever since Independence. Not surprisingly, as the
economy recovered from the stagnation of the Sukarno era, and as nationalist sentiment resurfaced, the government began to adopt a more cautious
and restrictive approach to foreign investment in the early 1970s. It is
necessary to reflect briefly on the importance of public opinion in shaping
the policy environment in Indonesia. In many cases, such opinion effectively limits the range of policy options open to the Indonesian government.

Attitudes towards Foreign Investment

Both in élite Jakarta opinion and elsewhere attitudes toward foreign
ownership range from one of considerable reservation to strong ideological
antipathy. It is very difficult to determine how widespread these opinions
are, but two detailed surveys, one at the beginning of the 1970s and the
other a decade later, suggest that suspicion—and even hostility—towards
foreign investment is considerable.

The first survey, of a broad spectrum of élite opinion, was conducted by
Weinstein (1976a, pp. 279 ff.). Of the 44 individuals he interviewed, 30
expressed 'concern' about foreign investment resulting in foreign domination;
15 of these expressed 'serious concern'. Respondents gave a large number
of reasons for their distrust of foreign investment, illustrating the sensitivity
of the issue. The reasons included practically every major criticism of
foreign investment: perpetuating 'colonial' patterns of development,
unreasonable demands (for concessions or privileges) made by foreign
investors, dishonesty and corruption of foreign investors, foreign investors
having different priorities from the government, the existence of Ali–
Baba relationships within joint ventures, the deleterious effects on indigenous entrepreneurship, minimal technology transfer, excessive dependence on powerful developed countries, and limited employment generation.

Clearly, in this survey, a significant element of élite opinion had strong
reservations about the adoption of liberal policies towards foreign investment, and 'dependence' more generally, after about five years of the New
Order. On the basis of his research, Weinstein (1976a, p. 287) argued,
plausibly, that: 'We can hardly escape the conclusion that the sharp
reversal of Indonesian foreign policy in 1966 was accompanied by much
less change than might have been expected in the elite's underlying per-
ceptions of the world and attitude towards aid and independence.'

Have attitudes softened subsequently, after more than a decade and a
half of sustained economic growth? The answer is almost certainly no. In
fact, they may have hardened. After Weinstein's survey was completed,
opposition to foreign investment intensified, culminating in the anti-
Japanese protests (the so-called Malari riots) of January 1974. Although
these protests were directed as much against the government's policies as
they were against Japanese investors, the growing—and very visible—
Japanese presence was undoubtedly an important factor. Thereafter, public
protests subsided, partly because the government introduced more restrictions on foreign investment, and partly because it adopted firmer political
controls over public criticism and dissent. But, more recently, an interest-

TABLE 8.1

Summary of Opinions on Policy Priorities in Domestic and International Affairs
of Various Important Political Groupings in Indonesia, 1981

Policy Priority	Nationalists	New Nationalists	ABRI	Technocrats	CSIS Intellectuals
A. Old Order Policy					
1. Self-reliant economic development	Yes, high priority	Yes, high priority	Yes, to some extent	No or low priority	No or low priority
2. Anti-colonialism/ Anti-imperialism	Yes, high priority	Yes	Ambiguous	No, irrelevant	No
3. Non-bloc grouping	Yes, high priority	No, irrelevant	—	—	—
4. Independent and active foreign policy	Yes, high priority	Yes	Yes	Yes	Yes
B. New Order Policy					
1. Pragmatic–open economic development	No	No	Yes	Yes, high priority	Yes, high priority
2. NIEO via active consultations/ diplomacy	No	Sceptical	Yes	Yes, high priority	Yes, high priority
3. ASEAN regional grouping	Sceptical	Sceptical	Yes	Yes, high priority	Yes, high priority
C. New Issue					
1. Asian–Pacific community	No	Strongly sceptical	Yes, with reservations	Yes, with conditions	Yes, with conditions

Source: Kuntjoro-Jakti et al., 1983, p. 54.

ing survey of opinion by Kuntjoro-Jakti *et al.* (1983) confirmed the continued suspicion of foreign investment and other forms of foreign involvement by significant sections of the community (see Table 8.1).

The study was based on a detailed survey of the press and other forums of public comment, together with the authors' own knowledge of the groups identified. Although it is not based on a formal survey of opinion, it is the most complete analysis of views among the major policy factions. As would be expected, both the technocrats and the CSIS[1] intellectuals attach little importance to such Old Order policies as self-reliant economic development, which included little or no direct foreign investment. But among the nationalist groupings and, significantly, ABRI (the armed forces), there is still a good deal of support for Old Order policy priorities. It is important not to lose sight of the significance of public opinion in shaping the government's policies.

The Industrial Policy Environment

The macro-economic environment and general policies towards industry are far more important than policies which specifically affect foreign investment. There is no need to elaborate on the significance of macro-economic policies, other than to underline their contribution to Indonesia's relatively good economic performance since 1966. The second set of factors—general industrial policies—has also been crucial. We focus on three issues of particular relevance to both industrial performance and the benefits and costs of foreign investment in Indonesia. These are trade and protection policy, the regulatory regime, and state enterprises.

Whilst protection for manufactures in Indonesia has undoubtedly been high ever since Independence, precise estimates of effective rates of protection (ERPs) have been available only recently. The four studies undertaken in the last decade are consistent in their analysis of the fundamental features of Indonesia's trade regime, even if they differ on minor points (for example, precise estimates of ERPs for each manufacturing industry).[2] It is not necessary to examine these studies in any detail, but it is useful to highlight their main findings. There are principally three.

The first is that Indonesia's trade regime is characterized by large intersectoral biases. The most important is that manufacturing has been protected relative to agriculture; another way of looking at the same phenomenon is that importables (mostly manufactures) have received protection at the expense of exportables. Secondly, protection for manufactures is not only high on average, but the ERPs are highly dispersed between sectors. All studies have found that ERPs range from well over 100 for some industries to negative values for others. Moreover, the studies have found several industries with negative value added at international prices. In many instances, there are large differences in effective rates for products within the same broad grouping, although in general a 'cascading' pattern is evident, with low ERPs for capital goods and much higher rates for consumer goods. A third feature of the system is the plethora of non-tariff barriers (NTBs). These include the import sales tax, the withholding tax, import prohibitions, import quotas, and import licensing. As a result of these NTBs, tariffs as protective instruments are relatively unimportant, and the system of protection is opaque. The latter feature is of considerable importance in the emerging policy debate in Indonesia because the magnitude of import barriers is difficult to measure with any accuracy.

The second outstanding feature of the industrial policy environment is the system of licensing and regulation.[3] The system is extraordinarily complex and pervasive, and almost certainly as important an obstacle to the development of an efficient manufacturing sector as the trade regime. The effect of various regulations is that firms in the organized industrial sector have to comply with an enormous range of bureaucratic requirements each time a significant (and in many cases an insignificant) business decision is contemplated. It is virtually impossible to quantify both the extent and consequences of the regulatory system, but its importance is such as to require a broad elaboration of dimensions.

The regulatory system comprises the major instruments of the central government, together with the minor tiers of government. It encompasses laws passed by the People's Representative Assembly (the DPR), and decrees from a variety of government authorities, ranging from the President to Directors-General of the various departments.[4] For foreign and larger domestic firms, the BKPM is often the first official point of contact.[5] Although there have been important simplifications in recent years, the BKPM application and reporting procedures remain extremely complex. For example, the master list which firms must submit in their applications requires an extraordinary amount of detail, much of it seemingly irrelevant to the BKPM's regulatory and monitoring role. Moreover, the BKPM is only part—and in some cases a relatively small part—of the government's regulatory tools. For most large manufacturing firms, licences also have to be obtained from the Departments of Industry, Labour, Trade (both internal and external), and Environment, together with the central bank (Bank Indonesia), the taxation office, urban planning authorities, and the minor tiers of government.[6]

There is not only substantial duplication in these requirements between departments, but also not infrequently differences in emphasis and priorities. Consequently, although the BKPM nominally provides a 'one-stop-service' for new investors, the experience of most firms in practice is that the BKPM is simply the first point in a long list of bureaucratic transactions. In addition to the complexity of these regulatory requirements, their content is not always clear. This lack of clarity is itself a major problem, because enforcement confers a good deal of discretionary authority on implementing officials. Consequently, the impact of licensing requirements may differ between and even within regions depending on the personnel. As McCawley (1983, p. 42) observes: 'Each regulation seems to generate more "elucidating" regulations, so that in the end minor officials in regional offices and harbors feel at liberty—indeed, feel obliged—to "define" certain vague matters by issuing their own regulations.'

A final outstanding feature of industrial policies has been the prominent role of state enterprises. As noted earlier (Chapter 2), state enterprises contribute a significant proportion of manufacturing value added in Indonesia. A recent study revealed there were about 220 of these enterprises on the records of the Department of Finance[7] (Ismangil, 1985, p. 349). This number is probably an understatement of the total, both because some of the very large firms (for example, Pertamina) are effectively beyond the Department's jurisdiction and because others are controlled by provincial governments.

The Indonesian government's motives for establishing state enterprises are similar to those in other countries, and also to many of the objectives of the regulatory regime. They are seen as a means of controlling strategic industries (for example, petroleum refining and fertilizers) and of developing new industries in which the private sector would be reluctant to invest (for example, aircraft). In the words of a group of prominent officials and academics, in December 1985, they should be used as a 'catalyst for development' into the 1990s. They are also advocated by many in an attempt to redress the 'ethnic imbalance' in ownership and entrepreneurship, especially in the context of extensive Indonesian-Chinese and foreign control of the economy. Finally, they have been developed as a potential source of government revenue, an objective which in practice has rarely been fulfilled.

What has been the impact in Indonesia of a large state-owned sector on industrial performance in general and foreign investment in particular? Although many state firms are well managed, perhaps the greatest effect is the presence of a substantial number of inefficient enterprises in the manufacturing sector. Broad aggregate data on these firms are not available, and so we have to rely on a series of detailed industry and firm case studies. The main conclusion of virtually every one of these studies is that state enterprises perform very poorly.[8] It is not entirely clear whether this record is the result of firm-level inefficiencies or government-imposed constraints. In fairness to these firms, the latter appears to be generally the more likely. Consequently, reform of the state enterprise sector depends on the general policy environment, in particular the trade and regulatory regimes discussed earlier.

There are also important implications for the pattern of foreign investment of extensive state ownership. One is, simply, that foreign firms have been excluded from sectors in which they might otherwise have invested. Not surprisingly, the government's strategic imperative to control the 'commanding heights' of manufacturing industry has resulted in large state investments in sectors dominated by foreign investors in other countries. Indirectly, the presence of state enterprises in an industry may have discouraged potential foreign investors, who might fear discriminatory government intervention in support of firms in which they have a direct stake (for example, import licensing arrangements, and price controls). Conversely, many state enterprises have sought technology from overseas, and in the process invited the participation of foreign firms. For example, of the 393 firms with some state equity recorded in the 1983 *Statistik Industri* series, 25 also had foreign equity. It is likely that a good deal of the remaining state enterprises—especially the larger ones—had some technology tie-ups with foreign firms.

Implications for Foreign Investment Policies

What are the implications of the general industrial policy environment for foreign investment in Indonesia? We have already argued that it is these general policies—rather than policies directed specifically at foreign investors—which largely determine the 'foreign investment climate' in Indonesia and the impact on domestic economic welfare. As numerous surveys have demonstrated, foreign investors attach more significance to the general political and economic environment (political stability, commercial infrastructure, supplies of natural resources, and labour), and to the trade regime, than they do to specific foreign investment policies. The development of an efficient and internationally competitive industrial sector also depends, critically, on these general factors. What matters for Indonesian welfare is an industrial base which provides the cheapest goods for consumers, the highest returns to factor inputs, and the greatest return to public sector revenue. Policies, not ownership, are the important determining variable.

Reform of the trade and regulatory regime is therefore an essential prerequisite for increasing the benefits of foreign investment to Indonesia. Were it not for the huge revenue windfalls which accrued up to the early 1980s, the particular policy mix might well have induced immiserizing growth caused by a tariff-induced inflow of capital (see Brecher and Alejandro (1977) and references cited therein for a theoretical discussion of this issue). Contrary to the advice proffered by Myint at the beginning of this chapter, the Indonesian government has sought to attract foreign investors by making the domestic market, rather than domestic resources, more attractive. It is well known—although difficult to document—in Indonesia that 'tariff bargaining' is pervasive. Foreign investors have frequently secured entry on condition that barriers to entry be erected to subsequent entrants, either to import competition (by trade barriers) or to domestic competitors (by licensing).

Consequently, many of the criticisms of foreign investment in Indonesia should properly be directed at the policy environment, rather than foreign ownership *per se*. It is true that foreign investments in manufacturing have been overwhelmingly import substituting in nature (although foreign firms generally have a higher export propensity than domestic counterparts). This is hardly surprising. It reflects primarily the bias in the trade regime against exports, together with the high costs of operating in Indonesia, many of which result from government intervention (see, for example, Kinoshita, 1986, pp. 49–51). In a similar vein, it is frequently alleged that foreign firms in Indonesia earn 'excessively high' profits. While the empirical basis for such an assertion is rarely given, it is in all probability correct. But here, also, the trade regime plays a major role. Foreign investors in Indonesia have introduced superior technology and efficiency into a highly protected environment, and their capacity to earn above normal profits is the expected outcome.

Finally, the trade regime has encouraged indiscriminate import substitution, and fostered the development of industries in which Indonesia does not have an obvious (static) comparative advantage. A stated objective of trade policy has been to promote self-reliance. But paradoxically, at least in the short run, the policy has had the effect of *increasing* Indonesia's foreign dependence, by encouraging the development of industries which have necessitated large capital and technology imports.[9] It is not without significance that foreign ownership is less in the recently emerging export-oriented industries which rely heavily on unskilled labour (garments) and natural resources (plywood).

Estimates of effective rates of protection by industry illustrate the anti-export bias of the trade regime. More difficult to measure, but probably equally important, are the effects of the highly regulated environment. Regulatory policies not only increase the costs for businesses in Indonesia, they also increase the uncertainty. These costs translate into higher costs domestically, and demands for higher compensatory payments (such as the recently abolished *Sertifikat Ekspor* scheme) for exporting firms.

Firm surveys are indicative of the general effects of regulation in Indonesia. One such survey is that of Allen (1979), who conducted a comparative study of foreign firms in ASEAN in the late 1970s (see Table 8.2). Indonesia scored well on a range of general factors, such as political stability and the state of the economy. Foreign investors also found the prospects for market growth, labour costs, and tariff and taxation policies attractive. But on a range of facilitating factors—provision of industrial estates and

TABLE 8.2

Comparative Assessment of the Business Environment of the ASEAN Countries in the Late 1970s (Simple Score System)[a]

Factor	Philippines	Thailand	Malaysia	Singapore	Indonesia
Political stability	3	3	3	5	3
internal	3	3	3	5	3
external	4	1	3	4	4
Government policies, general	3	2	4	5	3
Economic health and policies, general	3	2	4	5	2
Stability of currency	3	3	3	5	4
Government policies on imports	3	3	4	5	3
land ownership	3	3	3	3	3
foreign exchange	3	3	3	4	3
Government restrictions on equity participation	2	3	3	4	3
Other controls on foreign enterprises	2	2	3	4	2
Government incentives taxation	2	3	4	4	3
tariff protection	4	4	3	2	4
other	3	2	4	2	2
Industrial estates	3	3	4	4	2

(*continued*)

TABLE 8.2 (*continued*)

Factor	Philippines	Thailand	Malaysia	Singapore	Indonesia
Availability of required data or information	3	2	4	4	2
Assistance by country in feasibility studies	3	2	4	3	2
Assistance by country in arranging joint-venture partners	3	3	3	4	2
Assistance by country after establishment	3	2	4	4	2
Other assistance by country	3	2	3	4	2
Lack of red tape	3	2	4	5	2
Lack of corruption	2	1	3	4	1
Overall interest of country investors	3	2	3	4	2
Industrial expertise of country	4	3	3	4	1
Support facilities supply	4	2	3	4	2
Training facilities	3	2	3	4	2
Supply of					
skilled workers	4	2	3	4	1
technicians	4	2	3	4	2
unskilled workers	4	4	4	3	4
Existing market size	4	4	3	1	5
Market growth	4	4	3	1	4
Proximity to other markets	3	3	4	4	3
Infrastructure					
ports	2	2	3	4	2
roads	2	2	3	4	2
power	3	3	4	4	2
communications	2	1	3	4	1
Cost of production, general	4	4	4	3	4
Labour costs	4	4	4	3	4
Labour productivity	3	2	3	4	2
Worker attitudes and stability of labour force	3	2	3	4	2
Living conditions for executives	4	3	3	4	2
Joint-venture partners	4	2	3	3	2
Total	132	107	141	159	105
Ranking	3	4	2	1	5

Source: Allen, 1979, pp. 140–1.
[a] Graded on score of 1 to 5 for each country.

assistance with feasibility studies—and negative attributes, such as 'red tape' and 'corruption', Indonesia was generally the least attractive environment in ASEAN.

The US Department of Commerce (1985) survey of all United States affiliates, conducted in 1982, is also illustrative of some of the problems (see Table 8.3). Results from the 133 responding firms for Indonesia suggested a relatively restrictive environment, especially regarding foreign equity, use of local labour, and technology transfer. For these variables, a higher percentage of firms was affected in Indonesia than in either Asia or Latin America as a whole, and in two of the cases the percentage was higher than that for affiliates in India. These results do not detail the intensity of the regulations, but they are at least indicative of the environment in Indonesia compared to other developing countries. This survey, and the earlier one by Allen (1979), were conducted before the recent policy changes which helped to create a more conducive commercial environment. But other countries in the region have also recently liberalized their foreign investment policies, so the country rankings probably remain reasonably accurate.

The regulatory regime in Indonesia also renders entry conditions—for both foreign and domestic investors—more difficult because of the complexity of Jakarta bureaucratic politics. A thorough study of the political factors underlying investment regulatory policies has not been conducted.[10] But the essential feature of the system is that, although the BKPM nominally provides a 'one-stop-service', in practice it has tended to play a co-ordinating role, and in several crucial respects it has only limited authority. Its most obvious weakness is its total exclusion from the huge petroleum sector; even after Pertamina's financial difficulties in the mid-1970s, the BKPM's power did not rise appreciably. In sectors for which it has authority, its influence is often circumscribed. For one thing, it does not have the technical resources to evaluate and initiate new projects. For another, it does not have control over important variables, such as tariffs and import licences. Yet another limitation, perhaps, is that its fundamental objectives have never been fully specified. In the words of Encarnation and Wells (1985, p. 71), '. . . the BKPM had not yet resolved whether its mission was exclusively to regulate foreign investment or simultaneously to promote that investment'.

Recent developments have clarified neither its status nor its authority. On the other hand, its current Chairman, Ginandjar Kartasasmita, is regarded as one of its most influential leaders. Nevertheless, the 1984 tax reform removed most of the fiscal incentives the Board was able to offer investors. Consequently, as with much of the regulatory environment in Indonesia, the decision-making processes which form the basis of policy formulation are not well understood and appear to vary considerably between sectors.

A final general observation on the policy environment, including that directly affecting foreign investment, is warranted. The case for liberal policies towards foreign investment implicitly assumes the presence of an efficient, incorruptible, and 'development-oriented' administrative system

TABLE 8.3

Share of United States Affiliates Subject to Performance Requirements by Host Country, 1982

Region/Country	Total Number of Affiliates	Minimum Export Requirement	Import No More Than Certain Amount	Minimum Local Content	Employ Minimum Amount of Local Labour	Technology Transfer Requirements	Limits on Foreign Equity
Developing countries	5,760	3 (13)	3 (5)	2 (7)	15 (15)	7 (24)	10
Latin America	3,562	3 (12)	5 (6)	2 (9)	18 (21)	5 (18)	10
Asia and Pacific	1,270	3 (15)	1 (0)	2 (4)	10 (22)	10 (23)	13
Indonesia	133	2 (0)	2 (0)	3 (25)	19 (16)	38 (27)	19
Malaysia	107	6 (33)	1 (0)	4 (0)	33 (26)	11 (25)	18
Philippines	156	6 (0)	3 (0)	3 (0)	3 (25)	6 (11)	14
Singapore	202	1 (0)	0 (0)	0 (0)	2 (25)	3 (20)	1
Thailand	77	1 (0)	0 (0)	7 (0)	11 (25)	13 (20)	11
India	891	7 (17)	8 (0)	5 (0)	17 (7)	15 (31)	52
Korea	74	7 (0)	1 (0)	1 (0)	13 (11)	12 (13)	31

Source: United States Department of Commerce (1985).
Note: Figures in parentheses refer to percentages of cases subject to performance requirements which are applicable only to foreign-owned companies. Non-responses have been excluded.

in the host country. In the case of Indonesia, there has obviously been enormous progress in the quality of administration in the last two decades. But to the extent that this assumption is invalid, the benefits of foreign investment (and indeed *any* investment) are diminished.

Perhaps the most powerful and compelling critique of foreign investment in Indonesia has been developed by Weinstein (1976b) and others. This argument invokes the concept of the 'soft state', popularized by Myrdal (1968), to maintain that the benefits of foreign investment in Indonesia have been dissipated and narrowly based.[11] In this view, the benefits are less than what could (and should) have been achieved because 'rent-seeking' and the granting of special privileges are ubiquitous, and because regulations designed to maximize domestic economic benefits are not adequately enforced: taxes are not collected, import licences are awarded selectively, the costs of the provision of public infrastructure are not fully recouped, and barriers to competition are arbitrarily imposed. Clearly, many of these arguments are applicable to Indonesia, and the case for liberal foreign investment entry conditions thereby qualified. Nevertheless, it is important to recognize that Indonesia has become much more of a 'hard state' since the early 1980s, at least with regard to macro-economic policy. There have been major changes in taxation, customs, and banking regulations, for example. Moreover, to the extent that the Indonesian state retains its 'soft edges', the case for general policy liberalization is correspondingly strengthened. If the problem is a bureaucracy which arbitrarily distributes largess, the solution is a smaller government with fewer opportunities to distort the allocation of resources.

Policies Specifically Affecting Foreign Investment

The final section of this chapter focuses on policies directed mainly—but not entirely—at foreign investors. We focus on three: ownership requirements, fiscal incentives, and technology transfer and training.

In the early years of the New Order, domestic *ownership requirements* were minimal. The government began to adopt a more restrictive attitude in the early 1970s, hastened by the *Malari* protests, after which 100 per cent foreign ownership for new investments was prohibited. What is the case for restricting foreign equity shares and for a progressive 'dilution' requirement? The most compelling argument is a political one. Governments can demonstrate their sensitivity to nationalist sentiment by imposing such a requirement. Will this policy increase domestic economic welfare? Here the evidence is a good deal less clear. Advocates of minimum domestic equity in foreign investment maintain that it will ensure greater local control and participation, and increase the host country's share of profits.

In Indonesia, neither of these arguments has so far been persuasive. As discussed in Chapter 7, local equity has not necessarily implied local control. Foreign firms have responded to pressure for increased localization by raising the debt–equity ratio and by maintaining control through long-term licensing and management contracts. In any case, the survey evidence (albeit rather dated) suggests overwhelmingly that local partners do not play an important role in the key areas of finance and technology. Many are simply 'sleeping partners'. The argument concerning Indonesia's share of profits is also a weak one. In many cases, foreign firms may be better 'corporate citizens' when it comes to paying taxes, both because they are more visible (and vulnerable to public criticism) and because of behavioural constraints imposed by their home country.[12] In addition, local equity is an inefficient means of securing domestic control. The appropriate policy is to develop a competitive economic environment and a stronger administrative apparatus.

Moreover, it needs to be emphasized that the imposition of local equity controls is not a costless exercise. The fact that 100 per cent foreign ownership is not permitted in even special sectors of the economy—such as in export processing zones, as offered by most neighbouring countries—has undoubtedly deprived Indonesia of some footloose, export-oriented (and labour absorbing) investments. There is also some circumstantial evidence to suggest that increased restrictions in the mid-1970s and early 1980s may have deterrred potential foreign investors, or induced them to seek quick-yielding projects with a short time horizon.

There is no simple means of reconciling the political goal of extending national control with the economic reality of the superior technological know-how of foreign investors. To the extent that local equity is regarded as a 'public good', the case for ownership restrictions and dilution requirements is correspondingly strengthened. The ultimate solution is, of course, the gradual development of indigenous entrepreneurs who will play an effective role as local partners. Policies to develop Indonesian technical and managerial expertise will be more effective than the mere introduction of regulations which are openly and easily circumvented.

The second policy concerns *fiscal incentives* and the investment priorities list of the BKPM. As Guisinger (1986) has argued, it is more appropriate to regard these as part of the general package of 'investment incentives', which includes also the effects of the trade regime. They are considered separately here only because some incentives and priority listings apply only to foreign investors.

The previous system of fiscal incentives, and some of the present policies, raise at least two questions: Were the incentives excessive? And what effect did they have on allocative efficiency? These questions are now much less important than they were in the 1970s, following the far-reaching 1984 tax reform. Under the new policies, virtually all the fiscal incentives previously offered (see Chapter 3) were abolished, and in their place lower rates of company taxation were introduced. The new tax package is a major improvement, for two reasons. First, there is little doubt that the old incentives distorted factor prices. They introduced a capital-cheapening bias which encouraged firms to adopt excessively capital-intensive techniques. 'At the margin' they may have mattered less than other distortions—for example artificially low interest rates for domestic investors—but they were of some significance. The second reason is that the revenue loss of the incentives was not inconsiderable, and they were probably less important in attracting foreign investors than the general factors discussed earlier. The case for the abolition of incentives rests on the argument that the most efficient means of attracting foreign investment is to reallocate the revenue savings to infrastructure and training investments, and to simplify the regulatory regime. Both measures benefit all firms.

Although the incentives have been abolished, the BKPM's priority listing remains. The basis for this listing has never been clearly articulated, but it derives in a general sense from the broad objectives enunciated in each *Repelita*. The economic rationale for determining priority areas is consequently fairly limited. For example, sophisticated economic analysis— employing measures such as domestic resource costs—is almost entirely absent, both in deciding sectoral priorities and in investigating particular projects. A 'back-of-the-envelope' approach is less of a problem now that substantial incentives are not offered. But it is indicative of the essentially *ad hoc* policies of the BKPM.

The third major issue is *technology transfer and training*. A number of considerations arise in this context, although Indonesian government policy has been primarily directed to one, namely localization of senior management positions. In the mid-1970s, and again under the current Minister of Labour, Sudomo, the government has been pushing foreign firms to hasten the replacement of foreign staff with local personnel. In some cases these firms have been slow to localize senior positions, possibly as a means of ensuring continuing control. But it needs to be recognized that there are already substantial costs for foreign firms in locating foreign staff in Indonesia, in addition to the monthly cost of a work permit imposed by the government, and so there is a strong incentive to keep foreign personnel to a minimum.[13] Moreover, by hastening the departure of these staff, Indonesia is in effect foregoing the potential benefits of highly skilled labour, and associated skill diffusion.[14] Finally, the placement of foreign staff in Indonesia is a two-way process; as senior Indonesian personnel obtain experience, they might be expected to be placed abroad in the other offices of multinational firms for which they work.

Policies which encourage localization and training of staff are therefore politically desirable, and they may have economic benefits. But equally their provision is not costless. The most important issue is the development of training programmes which enable Indonesians to extract maximum benefit from the package of technical and managerial skills which foreign firms introduce. The imposition of training requirements on foreign firms should not be a substitute for the development of local training programmes.

Unlike many developing countries, there is no screening of technology licensing agreements in Indonesia, although it is likely that such a mechanism will soon be established. These regulatory bodies have been created elsewhere on the assumption that potential domestic licensees are in a weak bargaining position relative to overseas suppliers (Panglaykim and Pangestu (1983) emphasize this point), and that the international market for technology is inherently imperfect. While this may be correct in some respects, this market is also becoming larger and more competitive. Just as the number of capital-exporting countries has increased substantially in the last decade, so too has the number of technology suppliers.[15] Whereas twenty years ago the United States and a few European countries were the principal suppliers, first Japan and more recently the NICs and other countries have become quite significant.

The major requirement to take advantage of these developments is competitive local markets which will compel Indonesian buyers to seek out the most competitive technology package. Here also, trade and regulatory policies are critical. There may be some scope for limited government surveillance as a means of enhancing the bargaining power of local firms in the face of intransigent technology suppliers. Also, as Peck and Tamura (1976) have demonstrated in the case of Japan, the government may intervene to restrain competitive bidding among local firms for highly sought-after licensing agreements. But against these possible benefits is the danger that cumbersome administrative arrangements may be established which impede technology flows.

A final technology issue relates to the development of indigenous research and development capacity. Foreign investors, it is alleged in Indonesia and elsewhere, exacerbate the 'technological dependence' of developing countries by centralizing research and development facilities in their home base. It is therefore argued that extensive foreign investment is inimical to indigenous technological development in the host country. While this view may be of some relevance to countries with a developed scientific base, it is hardly so to Indonesia. As was shown earlier, American companies undertake very limited research and development in Indonesia. This is almost certainly because of the virtual absence of an established technological infrastructure, and high local operating costs. The most effective means of developing local research and development competence in Indonesia is for the government to invest in research and training, to develop local skills, and to induce multinationals to relocate some research and development investments—initially in technologically simple activities—to Indonesia. In the process, local firms will develop their capacity to select and adapt imported technology more effectively.[16]

1. CSIS is the important Jakarta think-tank, the Center for Strategic and International Studies. One of the most influential military figures in the New Order, the late Ali Murtopo, was instrumental in the Center's establishment. The Center's supporters also include several prominent government officials and well-known Chinese intellectuals.

2. The four studies are cited in note 7, Chapter 5. Some of the estimates of one of the studies are presented in Table 5.5.

3. The following paragraphs draw heavily on the pioneering analysis of McCawley (1983). For an evaluation of Indonesia in the ASEAN context, see Ariff and Hill (1985, Chapter 4).

4. Those of the President are termed *Keputusan Presiden* (or Presidential Decree), while those from Directors-General are generally termed *Surat Keputusan Direktur Jenderal*.

5. It must be recalled that BKPM licensing is compulsory only for firms with foreign equity. Larger domestic firms generally obtain BKPM approval for the official sanction and protection it implies and for fiscal incentives (which, however, are now relatively insignificant). An indication of the coverage of the BKPM is given in Table A.2. Small and cottage firms rarely seek BKPM approval.

6. Although the minor tiers of government are less important, provincial governors exercise considerable authority in, for example, the selection of land sites. They also frequently interfere in inter-island trade. Two examples in late 1985 illustrate the latter proposition. One was the restriction of cement imports to East Nusa Tenggara province in order to protect a local state-owned cement factory. The other, affecting South Sulawesi, was a ban on the import of second-hand textiles.

7. This figure differs from the estimate in the 1983 *Statistik Industri* of 393. The Department of Finance number refers to corporations, whereas the SI are enumerated on an establishment basis.

8. These studies include McCawley (1971) on the State Electricity Company (PLN, *Perusahaan Listrik Negara*); Dick (1977) on the state shipping company, PELNI, Funkhouser and MacAvoy (1979) on a sample of 150 firms; Gillis (1982) on a comparative study of mining companies in Indonesia and Bolivia; and Hill (1982) on the weaving industry.

9. Glassburner (1978, pp. 38ff.) develops some of these arguments.

10. Encarnation and Wells (1985), in an interesting comparative study of India, Indonesia, the Philippines, and Singapore, come closest to achieving this objective.

11. See also McCawley (1980) who employs the hard–soft state distinction in contrasting Indonesia and Singapore.

12. Foreign investors in Indonesia are frequently criticized on the grounds that they practise extensive tax evasion, but empirical estimates of taxation payments by foreign and domestic firms are not available. (One study (Keuning, 1985), using a Social Accounting Matrix for Indonesia in 1975, found that about half of the profits of foreign firms were transferred to the government, with the other half equally divided between foreign remittances and retained earnings. However, these figures would be dominated by the petroleum sector, and no separate data are available for manufacturing investments.) It is also alleged that they use transfer pricing as a means of evasion (see Panglaykim and Pangestu, 1983, p. 70). These are obviously extremely difficult subjects on which to obtain accurate information. Nevertheless, it is perhaps invidious to single out foreign firms for such criticism, when evasion appears to be so widespread among *all* firms.

13. For example, the annual survey of expatriate living costs in Jakarta, conducted by the American firm, Price Waterhouse, has estimated the cost of maintaining a family of four in Jakarta to be between $90,000 and $100,000 per year, in addition to the executive's base salary.

14. Professor Sadli, in 1985, reflected a widely held view in technocratic circles when he observed: 'We call on foreign investors to take part in our development and to help broaden our export base. But how can they be competitive on the export market if they cannot freely hire qualified personnel for their production and distribution operations.' (*Jakarta Post*, 17 July 1985.)

15. Numerous studies of the international technology market have reached this conclusion. See, for example, Contractor (1981).

16. Two additional regulations directed specifically at foreign investors in Indonesia are the prohibitions on domestic trade and on borrowing on the domestic capital market. These are not examined in detail here, except to note that the same complex interplay of political and economic factors arises. The respective prohibitions have probably resulted in a less efficient domestic distribution network (because barriers to new entrants have been erected), and denied Indonesian banks potentially profitable business. But the government has understandably been sensitive to allegations that it has offered a *carte blanche* to foreign firms.

9 Conclusion

INDONESIA has been a large capital importer throughout the New Order period, despite the oil boom, and it has attracted considerable foreign investment. Few countries have witnessed such a rapid change in policies and economic performance as Indonesia did in the mid-1960s. The change is nowhere better illustrated than in the case of foreign investment. New *direct* foreign investments were almost entirely absent in the first twenty years after Independence, and over the period 1957–65 the Sukarno government adopted an increasingly hostile attitude towards existing foreign property. Following the change in regime in 1966, one of the first new measures was the Foreign Investment Law of 1967. Hostility and nationalization quickly gave way to a liberal, virtual open-door policy.

After initial hesitation, foreign investors responded enthusiastically and by the early 1970s foreign ownership in some industries was quite significant. But it is misleading to see the present regime as one committed to liberal trade and investment policies. Following the restoration of economic and political stability, the government adopted an increasingly restrictive stance towards foreign investment, especially after 1973.

Foreign investment in Indonesia is of interest also because it has been one of the most controversial features of the New Order regime. There is hardly a criticism which has not been levelled at foreign investment in Indonesia (at least until the mid-1970s after which the press was more tightly controlled). Foreign investment, it is alleged, has created a 'Japanese colony', exacerbated Indonesia's 'dependent status', suppressed indigenous entrepreneurship, displaced labour, and contributed very little in terms of new technology and capital.

The purpose of this book has been to address these issues, with specific reference to the manufacturing sector, by asking the following questions: What would Indonesian manufacturing be like in the absence of foreign investment? How important a role have foreign investors played in the manufacturing sector? Are there any special characteristics in the industry distribution and (source) country composition of these investments? What has been the impact of the general policy environment on the costs and benefits of foreign investment? Are there arguments for major policy reform?

Our principal conclusion is that it has been the general economic environment which has been the major contributory factor to Indonesia's rapid industrialization since 1966. Indeed, what is remarkable is how relatively *little* direct foreign investment there has been in the manufacturing sector. 'Foreign involvement' has been extensive—through the introduction of new products, processes, and ideas—but much of it has been through channels other than equity investments. Although in aggregate foreign investment in Indonesia in the last twenty years has been considerable, relative to the size of the economy the inflows have been quite small and directed mainly to the petroleum sector. The important foreign contribution in manufacturing has been technology and skills rather than capital.

Several special features of foreign investment in Indonesian manufacturing have been highlighted. The first is the dominant role of Japan compared to all other countries. In certain important respects it is no exaggeration to say that the story of foreign investment in manufacturing has basically been one of Japanese investment. In almost every major industry where foreign investment is permitted, the largest investors have been Japanese companies. The Japanese have been prominent from the very beginning of the new investment policies, and their share of foreign investments has actually increased over time. Their large role is attributable to proximity, economic complementarity, and a remarkable coincidence in policy reorientation in the two countries. Just as Indonesia began to look outward for new enterprise in the late 1960s, policy and economic changes in Japan led inexorably to the beginning of very large capital outflows over the same period.

The second special feature of foreign investment in Indonesian manufacturing is its industrial composition. According to the theory of direct foreign investment, foreign firms seeking market entry via equity investments will concentrate on those industries in which they can exploit their firm-specific advantages. In an unconstrained policy environment, these usually result in a heavy concentration of foreign firms in industries characterized by technology and capital intensity, and extensive product differentiation. But in many such industries in Indonesia, direct foreign investments are relatively unimportant. The explanation is not that the theory is deficient but that foreign investments are either prohibited or discouraged. One reason is the presence of state enterprises. In some industries—petroleum refining, fertilizers, and others—it is state rather than foreign firms which control the 'commanding heights'. The other reason is investment licensing regulations. In industries such as automobiles and motor cycles foreign brands are ubiquitous, but foreign equity shares are low. Excluded from direct investments, foreign firms have entered the industry through licensing arrangements. A final feature of the industrial composition of foreign investments is that they have been overwhelmingly import substituting in orientation. We shall return to this point shortly.

A third important characteristic of foreign investments has been the nature of the joint venture relationships. Most firms with foreign equity capital have hardly been a 'partnership among equals'. The evidence, though somewhat dated, strongly suggests that majority local ownership has not been accompanied by local control. The sudden push for localization in the mid-1970s, the dearth of local entrepreneurial skills, and the essentially 'rent-seeking' nature of much of the domestic business environment have all produced lop-sided systems of control and management in many firms. Such an outcome is not surprising given Indonesia's very limited industrialization experience before 1966, however, and genuine local participation appears to be increasing over time.

Indonesia's experience thus differs from that of other developing countries in East and South-East Asia. In Singapore, multinationals and a large state-owned sector have responded to an open but heavily regulated business environment to generate a dynamic and outward-looking manufacturing sector, the current slump notwithstanding (Chia, 1985; see also Mirza, 1986, chap. 3). By contrast, a recent study of the role of foreign investment in Hong Kong emphasized its relatively minor role, especially prior to the 1970s, and partly because the colony 'imported' its own entrepreneurs following the Chinese revolution (see Lin and Mok, 1985). Finally, there is the case of Korea, which has combined heavy initial reliance on imported technology with strong local participation. In the words of Westphal et al. (1979, p. 385): 'Korea's export-led industrialization has been overwhelmingly and in fundamental respects directed and controlled by nationals. . . . Though Korea has relied rather heavily on inflows of investment resources, these have largely been in the form of debt, not equity.' The pattern in Indonesia resembles none of these cases. Foreign investment has been a good deal less important, relatively, than in Singapore, but indigenous participation has been less than in Hong Kong or Korea. Indonesia's foreign investment policies have been more restrictive than those of Singapore, but more open than those of Korea. However, the really crucial distinction lies in the general economic environment, and particularly the trade and regulatory regimes.

The most important factor determining the contribution of foreign investment to Indonesian economic welfare has not been the (source) country composition, the industrial distribution, or the particular entry modalities of foreign investors. Rather, it has been the general economic and political environment, and the specific policy parameters to which foreign firms have responded. There are many paths to rapid industrialization, as the experience of East and South-East Asian economies illustrates. The common feature in the case of the industrially advanced NICs is not their policies towards foreign investment, but rather their trade regime and a

	Trade Regime	Regulatory Regime	Foreign Investment Policies
Singapore	outward looking	extensive but efficiency enhancing	very liberal
Hong Kong	outward looking	minimal	very liberal
Korea	outward looking	extensive but generally efficiency enhancing	fairly restrictive
Indonesia	inward looking	extensive and often efficiency impeding	fairly liberal

regulatory system which—whether extensive or not—is what might be termed 'efficiency enhancing' (see Ariff and Hill (1985, chap. 4) for an elaboration). The table on page 152 illustrates the diversity of experiences.

What distinguishes Indonesia from the other countries is not its policies towards foreign investment: these have been in the middle of the spectrum, between the city states on the one hand, and Korea (and Japan in an earlier period) on the other. The really important difference lies in the trade and regulatory regime of Indonesia (and the Philippines, also, for that matter), as compared to the other countries.

Consequently, as has been emphasized throughout this book, many of the criticisms directed at foreign investors in Indonesia should properly be aimed at the policy environment. The trade regime attracted much of Indonesia's foreign investment, since market access through exporting from the home base was effectively precluded by import barriers. It is also the trade regime which goes a long way towards explaining the virtual absence of export-oriented foreign investments and the (probably) above average profitability of foreign firms, particularly in the 1970s. Similarly, weak competitive pressures, and some factor price distortions, have contributed to the selection of inappropriate production technology in some instances. Finally, the underdeveloped scientific and educational infrastructure, as much as foreign ownership, explain the limited technological spin-offs.

Foreign investment inevitably entails a loss of 'economic sovereignty', broadly defined. The compensating benefits to Indonesia, from the intrusion of foreign enterprise, have been diminished by the set of industrial policies pursued since 1970, and by the fairly weak administrative apparatus. The outcome of the current vigorous debate on industrial policies, between the technocrats favouring a more liberal and outward-looking policy environment, and those favouring a more inward-looking approach, will have an important bearing on Indonesia's future industrialization. That outcome will also greatly affect the benefits to Indonesia of foreign investment. An optimistic scenario—difficult to envisage even six years ago but now becoming more and more likely—is that an increasingly 'hard' state and the adoption of more liberal trade policies will together result in more dynamic and efficient foreign enterprise in Indonesia.

It hardly needs to be stressed that foreign investment is simply a means to an end for the host country. Indonesia needs the skills and technology which foreign investors possess. The most important issue is that these attributes be transferred as efficiently, rapidly and 'appropriately' as possible. The *modes* of transfer are less important. In deference to political sensitivities, there might be a case for more emphasis on such transfers while retaining domestic control and ownership, along the lines of the Korean or Japanese 'model'. There might also be a case for such a strategy, based on the rapid development of indigenous technological capacity. But the economic argument for such 'off-the-shelf' technology acquisition is not clear-cut. For the first time in fifteen years, Indonesia's foreign debt has become an issue of some concern, and it will not be ameliorated by increased resort to debt rather than equity capital for industrial development. There is, moreover, some evidence from case studies in other countries (see, for example, Balasubramanyam (1973) on India) that foreign firms may restrict access to technology in arm's length, as opposed to inter-affiliate, transfers. Finally, of course, as Caves (1982, p. 225) reminds us, '. . . there is no presumption that the MNEs [multinational enterprises] themselves undervalue the risks when licensing or placing their technology abroad'.

What matters most in the development of an efficient Indonesian manufacturing sector is a competitive business environment, a strong and supportive government, and ready access to foreign skills, technology, and markets.

Appendix

Data Limitations

THE range and quality of economic statistics published in Indonesia have improved enormously during the New Order period. Indonesian statistics relating to foreign investment and industry compare favourably with those of neighbouring countries. Nevertheless, major shortcomings remain. Discussion of these shortcomings was kept to a minimum in the main text. The purpose of this appendix is to provide more information on data quality and sources, for industry and investment.

Industry

The major BPS publication is the *Statistik Industri* (SI) series, produced annually since 1970. For each 5-digit (ISIC) industry in Indonesia, SI includes production, wage, and employment information, and is usually published with a lag of eighteen to twenty-four months. Unpublished data are also available on ownership, regional location of industry, concentration, and size distribution. In principle, SI includes all large and medium firms (defined from 1974 as employing at least twenty workers), although in practice it is not clear how complete its enumeration is. Up to 1975, it included all large firms and a sample of medium firms. The most comprehensive data source on manufacturing is the now rather dated 1974/5 *Sensus Industri* (Industrial Census), which was intended as a complete enumeration of all firms, large and medium (1974), small (1975), and household (1974/5). The reference period differed in the three cases, but for each its duration was twelve months. BPS also undertook a partial enumeration of small and household firms in 1979.

The main limitations of the SI series are:

1. Coverage of firms: Firms employing fewer than twenty workers are not included regularly. No comprehensive data are available on small and household industry since the 1974/5 Census.

2. Coverage of industries: This is the major weakness of the series, since the huge petroleum refining sector (ISIC 353) and other petroleum and coal products (ISIC 354) are excluded. Their exclusion complicates interpretation of the SI series, because these industries have almost certainly *not* been a roughly constant proportion of total MVA. Pertamina has embarked on a major programme to expand refining capacity in the last decade. Estimates of value added in the missing industries are available, based on production and investment data, but they are very approximate. In addition to petroleum-based industries, several important state enterprises do not participate in the SI enumeration. For example, firms controlled by the Department of Research and Technology, including aircraft, shipping, electronics, and munitions, have not been included until recently.

3. Comparability over time: In 1974, the current definition of large and medium firms (twenty or more workers) was adopted.[1] As a result, SI data before and after 1974 are not directly comparable. In particular, since the definition of large and medium firms is less comprehensive after 1974, the output and employment magnitudes from this time on are relatively smaller.

4. Data coverage: The major omission is that there is no estimate of capital stock.

In addition to the SI, several other sources provide statistics on the manufacturing sector. The major ones are:

1. The national income accounts, published in aggregate and by province.

2. Input–output tables: To date these have been prepared for 1971, 1975, and 1980. Despite minor changes, the three series are broadly comparable.

3. Production data: Physical production estimates are published in the *Nota Keuangan* each January, and in the attachment to the President's annual address to the nation on the eve of Independence Day, 17 August. Since 1975, a quarterly production index covering selected industry groups has also been published. The index is based on a rather small sample of firms, however, and therefore needs to be treated with caution.

4. Trade statistics: Import and export data are published annually on a 5-digit SITC basis with major trading partners. Monthly data are also published. As far as manufacturing goods are concerned, the data are likely to be reasonably accurate, especially compared to those published before 1966. There is, of course, some physical and technical (i.e. under-invoicing) smuggling. Very approximate estimates of the magnitude and composition of smuggling were prepared for the period prior to 1970 by Richter (1970) and Simkin (1970), but no recent studies are available. However, as an archipelago in close proximity to a free trade port (Singapore), smuggling is probably still of some significance, for highly protected and high value-to-volume products, such as electrical goods.

5. Population and labour force data: Since Independence, population censuses have been undertaken in 1961, 1971, and 1980. The census data generate much useful information on the skill, status and duration of employment of the manufacturing work-force. Two inter-census surveys (*Supas*) have also been undertaken, for 1975 and 1985.

There are significant differences between the SI estimates of value added and employment, and the corresponding figures from the national accounts and population censuses respectively. In the case of value added, the comparison can be undertaken for 1974/5 and 1979, when estimates for small and household industry are available, and including approximate figures for petroleum refining given in Hill (1984). In both years, the adjusted SI estimates are only about 74 per cent of the national accounts figure (for ISIC 3).[2] In 1979, the difference totalled Rp 851 billion. It is not clear which estimate is more accurate. But it is likely that under-enumeration in the SI series, of state enterprises, newly established firms, and small and household industry, is the main explanation.

If the SI estimates of MVA appear to be too low, the reverse problem has arisen in the case of employment estimates. The 1974/5 *Sensus Industri* reported total manufacturing employment as 4.9 million, more than one million higher than the 1975 *Supas*, and two million greater than the 1971 Population Census. However, of the 1974/5 figure, 3.9 million was in household industry, and this figure is almost certainly an overestimate of equivalent 'full-time' employment. The adjusted 1979 SI figure (of 4.5 million) corresponds closely to the 1980 population census total of 4.7 million.[3]

Foreign Investment

The limitations of published foreign investment statistics were discussed quite extensively in the text (Chapter 3), and need not be repeated here. The BKPM approvals data bear limited relation to actual foreign and domestic investments. There is little point in using the former, except as a very general indication of investors' intentions within BKPM sectors. Even for this purpose they are of limited value, since the approval estimates are frequently revised, principally when the BKPM learns that approved projects have been deferred or cancelled. The best source of data on realized foreign investments is the unpublished Bank Indonesia monthly report, which is thought to be reasonably accurate. There are no reliable estimates of realized domestic investments, nor are there usable data on the stock of foreign and domestic investment.

It will be useful to examine five questions related to the scope and reliability of Indonesian foreign investment data:

1. Why do the annual totals of different sets of estimates vary so greatly?
2. What is the nature of BKPM and Bank Indonesia reporting procedures?
3. How important are domestic firms in the factory sector which have opted for the BRO system rather than BKPM approval?
4. How significant is foreign investment in the non-BKPM sectors?
5. How should the category 'more than one country' be treated in determining the shares of investment by country of origin in the disaggregated data?

The available estimates of total annual foreign investment vary considerably (see Table A.1). Of the four series, the BKPM figures can be discarded immediately for reasons discussed above. But the other three series also differ greatly, especially in the case of the OECD. Both the IMF and Bank Indonesia data are derived from Indonesia's balance of payments figures. The differences between these two presumably arise from different treatment of certain items, and the fact that the Bank Indonesia data are for financial years, whereas the IMF reports on a calendar year basis. In any case, the differences are not large in most years.

The really large discrepancies occur in comparing the IMF and OECD data. In most years, the figures bear little relation to each other. Why are the differences so enormous? There appear to be two explanations.[4] The first is the definition and scope of foreign investment. The IMF data, based on host countries' flow data, exclude reinvested earnings of foreign firms. These are thought to be substantial in many countries, including Indonesia. For some countries, the IMF makes separate estimates of reinvested earnings, but Indonesia is not among them. Consequently, both the IMF and the Bank Indonesia data substantially understate the real magnitude of foreign investment.[5] The OECD data, based on the reporting DAC group, should in principle include these reinvested earnings, but here also the figures are incomplete.

The second explanation lies in the data sources. The OECD estimates are derived mainly from member countries' *outward* investments. They therefore exclude investment by non-OECD countries, although rough estimates of these flows have, it is understood, been included in some cases. As we shall see, investment by regional developing countries in Indonesia is significant. The IMF data are based on inflows from all sources and therefore do not have this shortcoming.

The puzzling feature of the OECD data is that in spite of their omissions they generally exceed the IMF figures. The reason presumably is their inclusion of reinvested earnings; for example, the very high figure for 1981 is due mainly to Japanese investment of over $2 billion, alone about sixteen times the recorded IMF

TABLE A.1

Estimates of Direct Foreign Investment in Indonesia,
1967–1985 ($ million)

Year	OECD	IMF	BI[a]	BKPM
1985	−295	271	299	773
1984	423	227	245	1,121
1983	303	289	193	2,882
1982	537	226	311	1,800
1981	2,584	133	142	1,092
1980	300	184	140	914
1979	−383	226	217	1,320
1978	418	279	271	397
1977	−67	235	285	328
1976	746	344	287	449
1975	1,289	476	454	1,757
1974	182	−49	538	1,417
1973	348	15	318	655
1972	90	207	240	522
1971	117	139	173	426
1970	49	83	90	345
1969	48	32	39	682
1968		−2	−3	230
1967		−10	−12	125

Sources: Various issues of OECD (annual), IMF (annual), Bank Indonesia (annual); and
BKPM.
[a] Refers to Indonesian financial years, i.e. 1984 refers to 1 April 1984–31 March 1985, etc.

figure from *all* sources. In the absence of more detailed analysis, it is not obvious
which series is preferable. The IMF data are used simply because they are more
widely disseminated and because, using host country data, they should be in a
better position to monitor all inflows accurately.

The second general data question concerns the disaggregated BKPM and Bank
Indonesia figures. Rosendale (1978, pp. 83–4), who examined reporting procedures in the first decade after the enactment of the 1967 Foreign Investment Law,
provides the most detailed assessment. PMA firms are required to report quarterly
to Bank Indonesia, but she found the response rate never exceeded 60 per cent. To
supplement its estimates, the bank uses the value of imports classified under the
PMA (duty-free import) code, together with cash inflows into PMA companies'
bank accounts. In the early years, sales under the Debt Investment Conversion
Scheme (DICS) were also included. Over this period, the BKPM 'implementation'
figures were even more approximate, since they were based on general disbursement patterns and they assumed a given gestation period for manufacturing investments of eighteen months to two years. It is thought that the reliability and coverage
of these estimates—especially those prepared by Bank Indonesia—have improved
considerably in recent years, but they must still be regarded as 'guesstimates'.

The third question concerns the coverage of the BKPM (and realized Bank
Indonesia) data on manufacturing. It may safely be assumed that all small and
household firms are outside the scope of the BKPM, and that all foreign firms are

included (subject to the somewhat fuzzy distinction between 'foreign' and 'domestic' noted above). But what of domestically owned large and medium firms which opt for the BRO system rather than the BKPM? Since obtaining BKPM approval is a lengthy and complex procedure, many smaller firms, and those which do not wish to import machinery (and therefore to take advantage of the duty rebates), have chosen the BRO system. This trend is likely to accelerate now that most of the BKPM incentives have been abolished.

Unpublished data for large and medium firms from the 1980 SI series give some indication of the magnitude of the excluded firms (see Table A.2). Approximately one-quarter of the value added in the organized sector was produced by non-BKPM firms. The share of the latter group in terms of employment and number of enterprises was a good deal higher (44 per cent and 70 per cent respectively), suggesting

TABLE A.2

Shares of BKPM Firms by Industry, 1980

| | | *Percentage of Industry Value Added* | | |
	Industry	*Foreign* (*PMA*)	*Domestic* (*PMDN*)	*Other*
311	Food	54.8	17.9	27.3
312	Food	29.4	38.1	32.4
313	Beverages	11.1	85.3	3.6
314	Tobacco	49.8	16.1	34.1
321	Textiles	48.8	16.3	35.0
322	Garments	47.4	9.4	43.2
323	Leather (excluding footwear)	46.6	2.2	51.2
324	Footwear	18.5	0.0	81.5
331	Wood and wood products	63.5	23.2	13.3
332	Furniture	33.0	13.6	53.4
341	Paper and paper products	56.0	16.0	28.0
342	Printing and publishing	47.7	10.3	42.0
351	Industrial chemicals	81.2	8.9	9.9
352	Other chemicals	20.2	65.9	13.9
355	Rubber products	39.4	24.9	35.7
356	Plastic products	35.6	27.6	36.7
361	Pottery	60.1	34.9	5.0
362	Glass	29.2	0.4	70.4
363	Cement	32.7	56.8	10.5
364	Structural clay products	36.0	0.3	63.7
369	Other non-metallic minerals	61.0	0.0	39.0
371	Iron and steel	68.6	31.4	0.0
381	Fabricated metal products	36.4	42.8	20.8
382	Machinery (excluding electrical)	37.5	41.5	21.0
383	Electrical machinery	28.1	61.8	10.0
384	Transport equipment	43.6	19.4	37.0
385	Professional and scientific equipment	21.3	7.3	71.4
390	Other	69.4	10.0	20.6
All	Manufacturing	46.2	27.5	26.2

Source: Unpublished data from BPS.

Note: In some cases columns do not add in original.

that it is mainly the smaller firms which are excluded. This observation is confirmed also by the fact that the share of non-BKPM firms is generally higher in industries where smaller, domestically owned firms are still significant: these include footwear, leather products, structural clay products, and professional and scientific equipment. By contrast, these shares for industries in which modern technology or international brand names are important (iron and steel in the case of the former, beverages and industrial chemicals in the latter) are very much lower.

Two additional features of the BKPM coverage warrant attention. The first is that the share of PMA firms in total value added was about three times that of the 'collapsed' share of foreign firms in 1975 and 1983 referred to in Chapter 2. The difference arises simply because the coverage of PMA is more extensive, including all firms with foreign equity, whether as joint ventures or sole foreign ownership. The second point is that the 'other' category also includes firms established before the 1967 and 1968 Investment Laws. In aggregate, these firms are probably not of great importance since most of Indonesia's modern industry was established after 1966, and many existing firms also took advantage of the new regulations and sought BKPM approval.[6] But the non-BKPM firms also include a number of state enterprises established during the Old Order period. These older firms, generally termed *perusahaan negara* (PN, or state enterprises), are still quite significant in industries such as food processing (mainly sugar mills attached to government estates). It is thought that the majority of state enterprises established or extended during the New Order applied for BKPM approval in order to receive the investment incentives. They should therefore be included in the SI series as either PMA

TABLE A.3

Gross Foreign Investment, 1968–1984 ($ million)

Year	BKPM Sectors 'Implemented'	Petroleum[a]	Total
1984	388	1,994	2,382
1983	517	2,728	3,245
1982	459	2,708	3,167
1981	379	2,111	2,490
1980	347	1,435	1,782
1979	319	745	1,064
1978	405	593	998
1977	256	600	856
1976	426	766	1,192
1975	547	725	1,272
1974	634	557	1,191
1973	394	271	665
1972	271	197	468
1971	151	161	312
1970	98	96	194
1969	47	54	101
1968	18	26	44
Cumulative Total	5,656	15,767	21,423

Sources: BKPM and United States Embassy (annual).
[a] Refers to exploration, development and capital production expenditures by foreign oil companies.

TABLE A.4

Relative Importance of Foreign Investment in Indonesia and Selected
Developing Countries, 1970–1984 (by sub-period)

	1970–4	1975–9	1980–4
(1) Foreign Investment as Percentage of Capital Inflows			
Indonesia	16.8	34.2	5.7
Other ASEAN			
Malaysia	58.0	98.1	40.0
Philippines	a	9.1	2.5
Singapore	65.4	80.6	74.3
Thailand	32.1	7.1	13.0
Other Oil Exporters			
Mexico	26.4	17.5	18.4
Nigeria	93.9	57.7	24.7
(2) Foreign Investment as Percentage of GDP			
Indonesia	0.5	0.7	0.3
Other ASEAN			
Malaysia	3.6	3.0	4.3
Philippines	b	0.5	0.1
Singapore	8.2	9.3	12.1[c]
Thailand	0.9	0.4	0.7
Other Oil Exporters			
Mexico	0.9	0.9	0.5
Nigeria	4.6	1.9	0.4
(3) Foreign Investment as Percentage of Gross Capital Formation			
Indonesia	3.2	3.4	1.1
Other ASEAN			
Malaysia	15.1	11.9	13.2
Philippines	0.1	2.0	0.4
Singapore	22.8	26.8	27.4[c]
Thailand	4.2	1.5	3.2
Other Oil Exporters			
Mexico	4.6	3.9	3.4[c]
Nigeria	25.7	7.0	a[d]

Source: IMF (annual, monthly), various issues.
[a] = Negligible (less than 0.1 per cent).
[b] = Negative foreign investment.
[c] = 1980–3.
[d] = 1980–2.

or PMDN firms (with the exception, of course, of Pertamina and other firms in petroleum-related industries).

The fourth data limitation relates to the exclusion of the huge petroleum sector and of financial services in the BKPM and disaggregated Bank Indonesia data. In principle, the omitted investments might be calculated as the difference between annual net inflows from the balance of payments estimates of foreign investment and the realized investments for the BKPM sectors. But such an exercise is virtually impossible because the two data sets do not use comparable definitions. As an

TABLE A.5

The Ten Largest Foreign Investors in Manufacturing, 1967–1985 ($ million, or percentage, realized)

Rank		Equity			Equity and Loans	
	Country	Value	Percentage of Total	Country	Value	Percentage of Total
1.	Japan	592	53	Japan	2,667	65
2.	Hong Kong	77	7	Hong Kong	190	5
3.	United States	54	5	United States	143	3
4.	Netherlands	48	4	Netherlands	73	2
5.	West Germany	26	2	West Germany	57	1
6.	Switzerland	21	2	Australia	45	1
7.	Singapore	17	1	South Korea	34	1
8.	Belgium	16	1	Switzerland	30	1
9.	United Kingdom	15	1	United Kingdom	28	1
10.	Australia	12	1	Singapore	28	1
	Subtotal	878	78	Subtotal	3,295	82
	More than one	209	19	More than one	698	17
	Total	1,087	97	Total	3,993	99
	Total, all countries	1,123	100	Total, all countries	4,084	100

Source: Bank Indonesia.

TABLE A.6

Foreign and Local Equity Shares by Country of Origin, 1967–1985

(percentage of total approved equity investments)

Industry	Japan		United States		West Germany		Netherlands		Hong Kong		Australia		All Countries	
	F	L	F	L	F	L	F	L	F	L	F	L	F	L
Food	62	38	81	19	77	23	52	48	67	33	77	23	69	31
Textiles	72	28	75	25	50	50	88	12	83	17	—	—	76	24
Wood	54	46	58	42	61	39	—	—	47	53	—	—	50	50
Paper	59	41	50	50	—	—	70	30	79	21	—	—	59	41
Chemicals	55	45	81	19	64	36	86	14	66	34	54	46	68	32
Non-metallic minerals	55	45	76	24	—	—	—	—	60	40	68	32	62	38
Basic metals	74	26	70	30	80	20	77	23	60	40	60	40	52	48
Metal goods	57	43	66	34	62	38	58	42	65	35	65	35	60	40
Other	75	25	—	—	51	49	50	50	16	84	—	—	37	63

Source: Bank Indonesia

F = Foreign.

L = Local.

alternative it is possible to obtain an approximate comparison of magnitudes by relating the realized BKPM–Bank Indonesia data to estimates of foreign investment in the petroleum sector given in the annual United States Embassy report. These estimates reveal the dominance of the petroleum sector and the importance of its omission in the BKPM data (see Table A.3). Total gross petroleum investment has been about three times the (very approximate) 'implemented' BKPM figure. In fact, a comparison of cumulative totals understates the relative importance of petroleum investments. Up to the mid-1970s, the totals were broadly comparable, but during the 1980s petroleum investments have been about five times that of the BKPM sectors. The figures for both series are gross estimates and they need to be interpreted with caution, but they are at least indicative of broad magnitudes.

Finally, there is the question of the large category—indeed the second largest after Japan in the BKPM sectors—of investments from more than one country in the disaggregated BKPM and Bank Indonesia data. Information on realized projects involving investors from more than one country is not published. In the absence of more detailed data, and to simplify the presentation, these investments have been redistributed on the basis of single country shares in some tables (always indicated in a note to the table). It is possible that this consolidation results in an overstatement of Japan's share, because it is generally believed that fewer Japanese companies have engaged in such joint ventures than investors from other countries. Nevertheless, the consolidation is a great simplification and probably a reasonable approximation.

Little is known about this very large category of investments. It is likely that many of the projects take the form of joint ventures between the head office and a subsidiary of the same company. One motive for such a strategy may be that the head office employs the superior regional knowledge of its subsidiary in the project. Another may simply be risk diversification (if, for example, Indonesia's relations with one of the countries in which the multinational company is based were to deteriorate). Hasan (1981, p. 46) advances a third possible motive: 'maintaining flexibility with respect to interaffiliate transfers'.[7]

1. The definition of large and medium firms before 1974 is given in the note to Table 1.3.

2. McCawley (1984, p. 173) presents another set of estimates which are broadly similar to this.

3. See McCawley and Tait (1979) and Jones (1987) for further discussion of the employment data.

4. See United Nations Commission on Transnational Corporations (UNCTC) (1986) for a recent discussion of the major foreign investment data sources, and on which the following discussion is based.

5. An additional difficulty relates to international comparisons, whatever series is used. For example, in the case of the IMF definition (Chapter 3), it is known that the phrases 'lasting interest' and 'effective voice' are interpreted differently by countries. Some countries take this definition to mean at least 50 per cent interest in local firms, whereas for others a 10 per cent interest is sufficient (UNCTC, 1986, p. 6).

6. Although the exclusion of older firms may explain the above average shares for the 'other' group in such traditional industries as textiles, garments, and structural clay products.

7. The issue of transfer pricing and intra-firm trade was considered briefly in Chapter 8. There are no reliable data on its incidence in Indonesia (or most other countries for that matter).

Bibliography

Agarwal, J. P. (1976), 'Factor Proportions in Foreign and Domestic Firms in Indian Manufacturing', *Economic Journal*, 86, 589–94.

Ahiakpor, J. C. W. (1986), 'The Capital Intensity of Foreign Private Local and State Owned Firms in a Less Developed Country: Ghana', *Journal of Development Economics*, 20, 145–62.

Allen, G. D. and A. G. Donnithorne (1957), *Western Enterprise in Indonesia and Malaya*, Allen and Unwin, London.

Allen T. W. (1979), *The ASEAN Report, Asian Wall Street Journal*, Vol. 1, Hong Kong.

Ariff, M. and H. Hill (1985), *Export-Oriented Industrialisation: The ASEAN Experience*, Allen and Unwin, Sydney.

Arndt, H. W. (1975), 'PT Krakatau Steel', *Bulletin of Indonesian Economic Studies*, 11(2), 120–6.

Arsjad Anwar, M. *et al.* (1985), *Prospek dan Permasalahan Ekonomi Indonesia 1985/86 (The Indonesian Economy in 1985/86: Prospects and Problems)*, Sinar Harapan, Jakarta.

Azis, I. J. (1985), 'Pengembangan Pembangunan Daerah di Indonesia' ('Regional Development in Indonesia'), in M. Arsjad Anwar *et al.*, *Prospek dan Permasalahan Ekonomi Indonesia 1985/86 (The Indonesian Economy in 1985/86: Prospects and Problems)*, Sinar Harapan, Jakarta, 223–54.

Balasubramanyam, V. N. (1973), *International Transfer of Technology to India*, Praeger, New York.

_____ (1984), 'Factor Proportions and Productive Efficiency of Foreign Owned Firms in the Indonesian Manufacturing Sector', *Bulletin of Indonesian Economic Studies*, 20(3), 70–94.

Bank Indonesia (monthly), *Statistik Ekonomi—Keuangan Indonesia (Indonesian Financial Statistics)*, Jakarta.

_____ (annual), *Report of Bank Indonesia*, Jakarta.

Biersteker, T. J. (1978), *Distortion or Development: Contending Perspectives on the Multinational Corporation*, MIT Press, Cambridge, Mass.

Billerbeck, K. and Y. Yasugi (1979), 'Private Direct Foreign Investment in Developing Countries', World Bank Staff Working Paper No. 348, Washington.

Blomstrom, M. (1983), *Foreign Investment, Technical Efficiency and Structural Change: Evidence from the Mexican Manufacturing Industry*, Ekonomiska Studies, University of Gothenburg.

BPS (monthly a), *Bulletin Ringkas (Concise Bulletin)*, Jakarta.

_____ (monthly b), *Indikator Ekonomi (Economic Indicators)*, Jakarta.

_____ (1970), *Pendapatan Nasional Indonesia (National Income of Indonesia), 1960–1968*, Jakarta.

_____ (1970a) *Sensus Perindustrian Tahun 1964 (The 1964 Industrial Census)*, 10 vols., Jakarta.

Brecher, R. A. and C. F. Diaz Alejandro (1977), 'Tariffs, Foreign Capital and Immiserizing Growth', *Journal of International Economics*, 7, 317–22.

Broek, J. O. M. (1942), *Economic Development of the Netherlands Indies*, Institute of Pacific Relations, New York.

Bureau of Economic Analysis (1985), 'US Direct Investment Abroad: Country and Industry Detail for Position and Balance of Payments Flows, 1984', *Survey of Current Business*, 65(8), 30–46.

Bureau of Industry Economics (1983), *Australian Direct Investment in the ASEAN Countries*, Information Bulletin 4, Australian Government Publishing Service, Canberra.

Callis, H. G. (1942), *Foreign Capital in Southeast Asia*, Institute of Pacific Relations, New York.

Castles, L. (1967), *Religion, Politics and Economic Behaviour in Java: The Kudus Cigarette Industry*, Cultural Report Series No. 15, Southeast Asia Studies, Yale University.

Caves, R. E. (1974), 'Causes of Direct Investment: Foreign Firms' Shares in Canadian and United Kingdom Manufacturing Industries', *Review of Economics and Statistics*, 56, 279–93.

_____ (1982), *Multinational Enterprise and Economic Analysis*, Cambridge University Press, Cambridge.

Chen, E. K. Y. (1983a), *Multinational Corporations, Technology and Employment*, Macmillan, London.

_____ (1983b), 'Multinationals from Hong Kong', in S. Lall *et al.*, *The New Multinationals: The Spread of Third World Enterprises*, John Wiley, Chichester, 88–136.

_____ (1983c), 'Factor Proportions of Foreign and Local Firms in Developing Countries', *Journal of Development Economics*, 12 (1/2), 267–74.

Chia S. Y. (1982), 'EC Investment in ASEAN', in N. Akrasanee and H. C. Rieger (eds.), *ASEAN–EEC Economic Relations*, ASEAN Economic Research Unit, Institute of Southeast Asian Studies, Singapore, 256–313.

_____ (1985), 'The Role of Foreign Trade and Investment in the Development of Singapore', in W. Galenson (ed.), *Foreign Trade and Investment: Economic Development in the Newly Industrializing Asian Countries*, University of Wisconsin Press, Madison, 259–97.

_____ (1987), 'Foreign Investment Policy', unpublished paper, National University of Singapore, Singapore.

Chinwanno, C. and S. Tambunlertchai (1983), 'Japanese Investment in Thailand and Its Prospects in the 1980s', in S. Sekiguchi (ed.), *ASEAN–Japan Relations: Investment*, Institute of Southeast Asian Studies, Singapore, 181–225.

Chung, B. S. and C. H. Lee (1980), 'The Choice of Production Techniques by Foreign and Local Firms in Korea', *Economic Development and Cultural Change*, 29, 135–40.

Clapham, M. (1970), 'Difficulties of Foreign Investors in Indonesia', *Bulletin of Indonesian Economic Studies*, 6(1), 73–80.

Cohen, B. I. (1973), 'Comparative Behaviour of Foreign and Domestic Export Firms in a Developing Economy', *Review of Economics and Statistics*, 55, 190–7.

Contractor, F. J. (1981), *International Technology Licensing: Compensation, Costs and Negotiation*, Lexington Books, Lexington.

Corden, W. M. (1984), 'Booming Sector and Dutch Disease Economics: Survey and Consolidation', *Oxford Economic Papers*, 35, 359–80.

Dick, H. W. (1977), 'The Indonesian Interisland Shipping Industry: A Case Study in Competition and Regulation', unpublished doctoral dissertation, Australian National University, Canberra.

_____ (1985), 'Survey of Recent Developments', *Bulletin of Indonesian Economic Studies*, 21(3), 1–29.

Donges, J. B., B. Stecher and F. Wolter (1974), *Industrial Development Policies for Indonesia*, Kieler Studien 126, J. C. B. Mohr, Tubingen.

Dorrance, G. S. and H. Hughes (1984), 'Economic Policies and Direct Foreign Investment with Particular Reference to the Developing Countries of East Asia', paper prepared for the Commonwealth Secretariat.

Drysdale, P. and R. Garnaut (1982), 'Trade Intensities and the Analysis of Bilateral Trade Flows in a Many-Country World: A Survey', *Hitotsubashi Journal of Economics*, 22(2), 62–84.

Encarnation, D. J. and L. T. Wells, Jr. (1985), 'Sovereignty en Garde: Negotiating with Foreign Investors', *International Organization*, 39(1), 47–78.

Evans, P. B. (1971), 'Denationalization and Development: A Study of Industrialization in Brazil', unpublished doctoral dissertation, Harvard University.

Forsyth, D. J. C. and R. F. Solomon (1977), 'Choice of Technology and Nationality of Ownership in Manufacturing in a Developing Country', *Oxford Economic Papers*, 29, 258–82.

Funkhouser, R. and P. W. MacAvoy (1979), 'A Sample of Observations on Comparative Prices in Public and Private Enterprises', *Journal of Public Economics*, 11, 353–68.

Galenson, W. (ed.) (1985), *Foreign Trade and Investment: Economic Development in the Newly Industrializing Asian Countries*, University of Wisconsin Press, Madison.

Gershenberg, I. and T. C. I. Ryan (1978), 'Does Parentage Matter? An Analysis of Transnational and Other Firms: An East African Case', *Journal of Developing Areas*, 13, October, 3–10.

Gibson, J. (1966), 'Production-Sharing: Parts I and II', *Bulletin of Indonesian Economic Studies*, 3, 52–75 and 4, 75–100.

Gillis, M. (1982), 'Allocative and X-Efficiency in State-Owned Mining Enterprises: Comparisons between Bolivia and Indonesia', *Journal of Comparative Economics*, 6, 1–23.

Glassburner, B. (1978), 'Political Economy and the Soeharto Regime', *Bulletin of Indonesian Economic Studies*, 14(3), 24–51.

Grunwald, J. and K. Flamm (1985), *The Global Factory: Foreign Assembly in International Trade*, Brookings, Washington.

Guisinger, S. E. (1986), 'Do Performance Requirements and Investment Incentives Work?', *World Economy*, March, 79–96.

Gurney, P. B. (1983), 'Joint-Venture Investments in Indonesia', *Contemporary Southeast Asia*, 4(4), 522–37.

Hardjono, J. and H. Hill (1986), 'West Java: Population Pressure and Regional Diversity', paper presented to Conference on Regional Economic Development in Indonesia, Australian National University, Canberra.

Hasan, I. (1981), 'Direct Foreign Investment in Indonesian Manufacturing: A Bargaining Approach', unpublished doctoral dissertation, University of California, Berkeley.

Hiemenz, U. (1987), 'Foreign Direct Investment and Industrialization in ASEAN Countries', *Weltwirtschaftliches Archiv*, 123(1), 121–38.

Higgins, B. (1957), *Indonesia's Economic Stabilization and Development*, Institute of Pacific Relations, New York.

Hill, H. (1982), 'State Enterprises in a Competitive Industry: An Indonesian Case

Study', *World Development*, 10(11), 1015–23.

_____ (1983), 'Choice of Technique in the Indonesian Weaving Industry', *Economic Development and Cultural Change*, 31(2), 337–53.

_____ (1984), 'Survey of Recent Developments', *Bulletin of Indonesian Economic Studies*, 20(2), 1–38.

_____ (1985), 'Subcontracting, Technological Diffusion and the Development of Small Enterprise in Philippine Manufacturing', *Journal of Developing Areas*, 19(2), 245–61.

_____ (1986), 'Australian Direct Investment in ASEAN: Patterns and Issues', paper prepared for Development Planning Division, United Nations ESCAP, Bangkok.

_____ (1987), 'Industrial Concentration in Indonesia', *Bulletin of Indonesian Economic Studies*, 23(2), 71–100.

_____ (forthcoming), *Industrialisation in an Inward-Looking Petroleum Economy: Indonesia Since 1966* (tentative title).

Hill, H. and B. Johns (1985), 'The Role of Direct Foreign Investment in Developing East Asian Countries', *Weltwirtschaftliches Archiv*, 121(2), 35–381.

Hoffman, L. and Tan S E. (1980), *Industrialization, Employment and Foreign Investment in Peninsular Malaysia*, Oxford University Press, Kuala Lumpur.

Hymer, S. (1976), *The International Operations of National Firms: A Study of Direct Foreign Investment*, MIT Press, Cambridge, Mass.

Indonesia, Departemen Penerangan (annual), *Nota Keuangan dan Rancangan Anggaran Pendapatan dan Belanja Negara (Financial Note and Planned Budget)*, Jakarta.

Ismangil, W. (1985), 'Badan Usaha Milik Negara' ('State Owned Business Entities'), in M. Arsjad Anwar *et al.*, *Prospek dan Permasalahan Ekonomi Indonesia 1985/86 (The Indonesian Economy in 1985/86: Prospects and Problems)*, Sinar Harapan, Jakarta, 345–62.

Japan, MITI (annual), *Overseas Business Activities of Japanese Firms*, Tokyo.

_____, Office of the Prime Minister (annual), *Report of the Survey of Research and Development*, Statistics Bureau, Tokyo.

Jones, G. W. (1987), 'Labour Force and Labour Utilization', in G. Hugo *et al.*, *The Demographic Dimension in Indonesian Development*, Oxford University Press, Singapore.

Keddie, G. J. (1975), 'Adoption of Production Technique by Industrial Firms in Indonesia', unpublished doctoral dissertation, Harvard University, Boston.

Keuning, S. J. (1985), 'Segmented Development and the Way Profits Go: The Case of Indonesia', *Review of Income and Wealth*, 31(4), 375–95.

Kinoshita, T. (1986), 'Japanese Investment in Indonesia: Problems and Prospects', *Bulletin of Indonesian Economic Studies*, 22(1), 34–56.

Kojima, K. (1978), *Japanese Direct Foreign Investment: A Model of Multinational Business Operations*, Charles E. Tuttle, Tokyo.

Krueger, A. O. (1974), 'The Political Economy of the Rent-Seeking Society', *American Economic Review*, 64(3), 291–303.

Kuntjoro-Jakti, D. (1985), 'Indonesia', in *Patterns and Impact of Foreign Investment in the ESCAP Region*, United Nations Economic and Social Commission for Asia and the Pacific, Bangkok, 69–95.

Kuntjoro-Jakti, D. *et. al.* (1983), 'Japanese Investment in Indonesia', in S. Sekiguchi (ed.), *ASEAN–Japan Relations: Investment*, Institute of Southeast Asian Studies, Singapore, 27–59.

Lall, S. (1978), 'Transnationals, Domestic Enterprises and Industrial Structure in Host LDCs: A Survey', *Oxford Economic Papers*, 30(2), 217–48.

_____ (1979), 'Multinationals and Market Structure in an Open Developing Economy:

The Case of Malaysia', *Weltwirtschaftliches Archiv*, 115, 325–48.

—— (1980), 'Vertical Inter-Firm Linkages in LDCs: An Empirical Study', *Oxford Bulletin of Economics and Statistics*, 42(3), 203–26.

Lall, S. and S. Mohammad (1983), 'Multinationals in Indian Big Business: Industrial Characteristics of Foreign Investments in a Heavily Regulated Economy', *Journal of Development Economics*, 13, 143–57.

Lall, S. *et al.* (1983), *The New Multinationals: The Spread of Third World Enterprises*, John Wiley, Chichester.

Langhammer, R. J. (forthcoming), 'Financing of Foreign Direct Investment and Trade Flows—the Case of Indonesia', *Bulletin of Indonesian Economic Studies*.

Lary, H. B. (1968), *Imports of Manufactures from Less Developed Countries*, Columbia University Press, New York, for the National Bureau of Economic Research.

Lecraw, D. J. (1983), 'Performance of Transnational Corporations in Less Developed Countries', *Journal of International Business Studies*, 14(1), 15–33.

Leipziger, D. M. (1976), 'Production Characteristics in Foreign Enclave and Domestic Manufacturing: The Case of India', *World Development*, 4(4), 321–5.

Lim, L. Y. C. and Pang E. F. (1982), 'Vertical Linkages and Multinational Enterprises in Developing Countries', *World Development*, 10(7), 585–95.

Lin, T-b. and V. Mok (1985), 'Trade, Foreign Investment, and Development in Hong Kong', in W. Galenson (ed.), *Foreign Trade and Investment: Economic Development in the Newly Industrializing Asian Countries*, University of Wisconsin Press, Madison, 219–56.

McCawley, P. (1971), 'The Indonesian Electric Supply Industry', unpublished doctoral dissertation, Australian National University, Canberra.

—— (1979), *Industrialization in Indonesia: Developments and Prospects*, Occasional Paper No. 13, Development Studies Centre, Australian National University, Canberra.

—— (1980), 'Stability, Equity, Growth and Devaluation: A New Direction for Repelita III?', in R. G. Garnaut and P. T. McCawley (eds.), *Indonesia: Dualism, Growth and Equity*, Research School of Pacific Studies, Australian National University, Canberra, 539–53.

—— (1981), 'The Growth of the Industrial Sector', in A. Booth and P. McCawley (eds.), *The Indonesian Economy during the Soeharto Era*, Oxford University Press, Kuala Lumpur, 62–101.

—— (1983), 'Industrial Licensing in Indonesia', paper presented to workshop on industrial regulation in ASEAN and Australia, Australian National University, Canberra.

—— (1984), 'A Slowdown in Industrial Growth?', *Bulletin of Indonesian Economic Studies*, 20(3), 158–74.

McCawley, P. and M. Tait (1979), 'New Data on Employment in Manufacturing, 1970–76', *Bulletin of Indonesian Economic Studies*, 15(1), 125–36.

McLeod, R. H. (1980), 'Finance and Entrepreneurship in the Small-Business Sector in Indonesia', unpublished doctoral dissertation, Australian National University, Canberra.

Manning, C. G. (1971), 'The Timber Boom with Special Reference to East Kalimantan', *Bulletin of Indonesian Economic Studies*, 7(3), 30–60.

—— (1979), 'Wage Differentials and Labour Market Segmentation in Indonesian Manufacturing', unpublished doctoral dissertation, Australian National University, Canberra.

Mason, R. H. (1973), 'Some Observations on the Choice of Technology by Multinational Firms in Developing Countries', *Review of Economics and Statistics*, 55, 349–55.

Mirza, H. (1986), *Multinationals and the Growth of the Singapore Economy*, Croom Helm, London.

Morley, S. A. and G. W. Smith (1977), 'The Choice of Technology: Multinational Firms in Brazil', *Economic Development and Cultural Change*, 25, 239–64.

Mulia, W. (1958), 'The Mechanization of Small-Scale Industries (Second Report)', *Ekonomi dan Keuangan Indonesia*, 11(3/4), 158–217.

Myint, H. (1972), *Southeast Asia's Economy: Development Policies in the 1970s*, Penguin, Harmondsworth.

Myrdal, G. (1968), *Asian Drama*, Pantheon Press, New York.

Newfarmer, R. (ed.) (1985), *Profits, Progress and Poverty: Case Studies of International Industries in Latin America*, University of Notre Dame Press, Notre Dame.

Newfarmer, R. S. and L. C. Marsh (1981), 'Foreign Ownership, Market Structure and Industrial Performance: Brazil's Electrical Industry', *Journal of Development Economics*, 8, 47–75.

Nishihara, M. (1976), *The Japanese and Sukarno's Indonesia: Tokyo–Jakarta Relations, 1951–1966*, University Press of Hawaii, Honolulu.

Nixson, F. I. (1984), 'Business Behaviour in the Private Sector', in C. H. Kirkpatrick *et al.*, *Industrial Structure and Policy in Less Developed Countries*, Allen and Unwin, London, 86–149.

Oei H. L. (1969), 'Implications of Indonesia's New Foreign Investment Policy for Economic Development', *Indonesia*, 7, 33–66.

Okada, Y. (1983), 'The Dilemma of Indonesian Dependency on Foreign Direct Investments', *Development and Change*, 14(1), 115–32.

Oman, C. (1985), *New Forms of International Investment in Developing Countries*, OECD, Paris.

Ono, K. and K. Odaka (1979), 'Ancillary Firm Development in the Japanese Automobile Industry—Selected Case Studies I', Institute of Economic Research, Hitosubashi University, Discussion Paper No. 24, Tokyo.

Organization for Economic Cooperation and Development (OECD) (annual), *Geographic Distribution of Financial Flows to Developing Countries*, Paris.

Ozawa, T. (1979), *Multinationalism, Japanese Style: The Political Economy of Outward Dependency*, Princeton University Press, Princeton.

Paauw, D. S. (1960), *Financing Economic Development: The Indonesian Case*, The Free Press, Glencoe.

_____ (1963), 'From Colonial to Guided Economy', in R. T. McVey (ed.), *Indonesia*, HRAF Press, New Haven.

Pack, H. (1976), 'The Substitution of Labour for Capital in Kenyan Manufacturing', *Economic Journal*, 86, 45–58.

Palmer, I. (1972), *Textiles in Indonesia: Problems of Import Substitution*, Praeger, New York.

_____ (1978), *The Indonesian Economy Since 1965*, Frank Cass and Co., London.

Pangestu, M. (1980), *Japanese and Other Foreign Investment in the ASEAN Countries*, Research Paper No. 73, Australia Japan Research Centre, Australian National University, Canberra.

_____ (1985), 'The Pattern of Direct Foreign Investment in ASEAN: The US vs Japan', paper presented to a workshop on ASEAN–US Economic Relations, Institute of Southeast Asian Studies, Singapore.

Pangestu, M. and Boediono (1986), 'Indonesia: The Structure and Causes of Manufacturing Sector Protection', in C. C. Findlay and R. G. Garnaut (eds.), *The Political Economy of Manufacturing Protection: Experiences of ASEAN and Australia*, Allen and Unwin, Sydney, 1–47.

Panglaykim, J. and M. Pangestu (1983), *Japanese Direct Investment in ASEAN:*

The Indonesian Experience, Maruzen Asia, Singapore.

Parker, S. (1985), 'A Study of Indonesian Trade Policy Between 1980 and 1984', unpublished paper, Washington.

Parry, T. G. (1980), *The Multinational Enterprise: International Investment and Host-Country Impacts*, JAI Press, Greenwich, Connecticut.

Peck, M. J. and S. Tamura (1976), 'Technology', in H. Patrick and H. Rosovsky (eds.), *Asia's New Giant*, Brookings, Washington, 525–85.

Perkins, F. C. (1983), 'Technology Choice, Industrialisation and Development Experiences in Tanzania', *Journal of Development Studies*, 19(2), 213–43.

Pitt, M. M. (1981), 'Alternative Trade Strategies and Employment in Indonesia', in A. O. Krueger *et al.* (eds.), *Trade and Employment in Developing Countries*, University of Chicago Press, Chicago, for the National Bureau of Economic Research, Vol. 1, 181–237.

Pitt, M. M. and L.-F. Lee (1981), 'The Measurement and Sources of Technical Inefficiency in the Indonesian Weaving Industry', *Journal of Development Economics*, 9, 43–64.

Polak, J. J. (1942), *The National Income of the Netherlands Indies, 1921–1939*, Institute of Pacific Relations, New York.

Poot, H. (1981), 'The Development of Labour Intensive Industries in Indonesia', in R. Amjad (ed.), *The Development of Labour Intensive Industry in ASEAN Countries*, Asian Employment Programme, ILO-ARTEP, Bangkok, 77–140.

Ranis, G. and C. Schive (1985), 'Direct Foreign Investment in Taiwan's Development', in W. Galenson (ed.), *Foreign Trade and Investment: Economic Development in the Newly Industrializing Asian Countries*, University of Wisconsin Press, Madison, 85–137.

Rice, R. C. (1974), 'The Interfirm Externalities of Foreign Investment in Manufacturing in Indonesia', *Ekonomi dan Keuangan Indonesia*, 22(2), 127–53.

Richter, H. V. (1970), 'Problems of Assessing Unrecorded Trade', *Bulletin of Indonesian Economic Studies*, 6(1), 45–60.

Riedel, J. (1975), 'The Nature and Determinants of Export-Oriented Direct Foreign Investment in a Developing Country: A Case Study of Taiwan', *Weltwirtschaftliches Archiv*, 111(3), 505–28.

Rix, A. (1980), *Japan's Economic Aid: Policy-Making and Politics*, Croom Helm, London.

Robison, R. (1978), 'Toward a Class Analysis of the Indonesian Military Bureaucratic State', *Indonesia*, No. 25.

—— (1986), *Indonesia: The Rise of Capital*, Allen and Unwin, Sydney.

Rosendale, P. (1978), 'The Indonesian Balance of Payments, 1950–1976—Some New Estimates', unpublished doctoral dissertation, Australian National University, Canberra.

Sadli, M. (1970), 'Difficulties of Foreign Investors: A Comment', *Bulletin of Indonesian Economic Studies*, 6(1), 81–4.

—— (1972), 'Foreign Investment in Developing Countries: Indonesia', in P. Drysdale (ed.), *Direct Foreign Investment in Asia and the Pacific*, Australian National University Press, Canberra, 201–25.

Sakurai, M. (1982), 'Japanese Direct Foreign Investment: Studies on Its Growth in the 1970s', Economic Growth Center, Yale University, Center Discussion Paper No. 397.

Santikarn, M. (1981), *Technology Transfer: A Case Study*, Singapore University Press, Singapore.

Schmitt, H. O. (1962), 'Foreign Capital and Social Conflict in Indonesia, 1950–1958', *Economic Development and Cultural Change*, 10(3), 284–93.

Sekiguchi, S. (1979), *Japanese Direct Foreign Investment*, Allanheld, Osmun and Co., Montclair, for the Atlantic Institute for International Affairs.

_____ (ed.) (1983), *ASEAN–Japan Relations: Investment*, Institute of Southeast Asian Studies, Singapore.

Sekiguchi, S. and L. B. Krause (1980), 'Direct Foreign Investment in ASEAN by Japan and the United States', in R. Garnaut (ed.), *ASEAN in a Changing Pacific and World Economy*, Australian National University Press, Canberra, 421–54.

Siahaan, L., Thee K. W. *et al.* (1978), *Japanese Direct Investment in Indonesia: Findings of an Experimental Survey*, Joint Research Program Series No. 9, Institute of Developing Economies, Tokyo.

Simkin, C. G. F. (1970), 'Indonesia's Unrecorded Trade', *Bulletin of Indonesian Economic Studies*, 6(1), 17–44.

Sitsen, P. H. W. (1942), *Industrial Development of the Netherlands Indies*, Institute of Pacific Relations, New York.

Soediyono *et al.* (1984), *Multinational Corporations and Host Country Technology: A Case Study of Indonesia*, Discussion Paper Series No. 84–103, Council for Asian Manpower Studies, Quezon City.

Soehoed, A. R. (1967), 'Manufacturing in Indonesia', *Bulletin of Indonesian Economic Studies*, 8, 65–84.

_____ (1979), 'Foreign Direct Investment in Indonesia: The Next Five Years', in *Japan–Indonesia Relations: Past, Present, Future*, Center for Strategic and International Studies, Jakarta, 75–81.

_____ (1981), 'Multinational Corporations and the Transfer of Technology', in A. Senkuttuvan (ed.), *MNCs and ASEAN Development in the 1980s*, Institute of Southeast Asian Studies, Singapore, 133–42.

_____ (1983), *Asahan, Impian Yang Menjadi Kenyataan (Asahan, A Dream which Became a Reality)*, Jakarta (privately published).

Stewart, F. (1978), *Technology and Underdevelopment*, 2nd ed., Macmillan, London.

Sumantoro (1984), *MNCs and the Host Country: The Indonesian Case*, Research Notes and Discussion Paper No. 45, Institute of Southeast Asian Studies, Singapore.

Sumitro, D. (1954), 'The Government's Program on Industries', *Ekonomi dan Keuangan Indonesia*, 7(11), 702–36.

Sutter, J. O. (1959), *Indonesianisasi: Politics in a Changing Economy, 1940–1955*, Data Paper Nos. 36 I–IV, Southeast Asia Program, Cornell University, Ithaca.

Thee K. W. (1981), 'Indonesia as a Host Country to Indian Joint Ventures', in K. Kumar and M. G. McLeod (eds.), *Multinationals from Developing Countries*, Lexington Books, Lexington, 133–44.

_____ (1984a), 'Japanese Direct Investment in Indonesian Manufacturing', *Bulletin of Indonesian Economic Studies*, 20(2), 90–106.

_____ (1984b), 'Japanese and American Direct Investment in Indonesian Manufacturing Compared', *Ekonomi dan Keuangan Indonesia*, 32(1), 89–105.

_____ (1984c), 'Technology Transfer Through Transnational Corporations in Indonesia: Evaluation of TNCs Contribution to Technological Development—12 Case Studies', draft report submitted to United Nations Economic and Social Commission for Asia and the Pacific, Bangkok.

_____ (1985), 'Kaitan-Kaitan Vertikal Antarperusahaan dan Pengembangan Sistem Subkontraktor di Indonesia: Beberapa Hasil Studi Permulaan' ('Vertical Interfirm Linkages and the Development of the Subcontracting System in Indonesia: Results from a Preliminary Study'), in K. W. Thee (ed.), *Kaitan-Kaitan Vertikal*

Antarperusahaan dan Pengembangan Sistem Subkontraktor di Indonesia: Beberapa Studi Kasus, Masyarakat Indonesia, 12(3), 219–31.

_____ (ed.) (1985), *Kaitan-Kaitan Vertikal Antarperusahaan dan Pengembangan Sistem Subkontraktor di Indonesia: Beberapa Studi Kasus (Vertical Interfirm Linkages and the Development of the Subcontracting System in Indonesia: Several Case Studies)*, *Masyarakat Indonesia*, 12(3).

Thee K. W. and K. Yoshihara (1987), 'Foreign and Domestic Capital in Indonesian Industrialization', *Southeast Asian Studies*, 24(4), 327–49.

Timmer, C. P. (1973), 'Choice of Technique in Rice Milling in Java', *Bulletin of Indonesian Economic Studies*, 9(2), 57–76.

Tomlinson, B. R. (1985), 'Foreign Investment in India and Indonesia, 1920–1960', paper presented to Project on the Comparative Study of India and Indonesia, New Delhi, January.

Tsao Y. (1986), 'Capital Flows among Pacific Basin Economies', in A. H. H. Tan and B. Kapur (eds.), *Pacific Growth and Financial Interdependence*, Allen and Unwin, Sydney, 68–94.

Tsurumi, Y. (1980), 'Japanese Investments in Indonesia: Ownership, Technology Transfer, and Political Conflict', in G. Papanek (ed.), *The Indonesian Economy*, Praeger, New York, 295–323.

United Nations Centre on Transnational Corporations (UNCTC) (1983a), *Transnational Corporations in World Development*, Third Survey, New York.

_____ (1983b), *Salient Features and Trends in Foreign Direct Investments*, New York (ST/CTC/14).

_____ (1983c), *National Legislation and Regulations Relating to Transnational Corporations: A Technical Paper*, New York, (ST/CTC/35).

_____ (1985), *Trends and Issues in Foreign Direct Investment and Related Flows: A Technical Paper*, New York (ST/CTC/59).

United Nations Commission on Transnational Corporations (UNCTC) (1986), *Recent Developments Related to Transnational Corporations and International Economic Relations*, Economic and Social Council, New York, E/C.10/1986/3.

United States Department of Commerce (monthly), *Survey of Current Business*, Bureau of Economic Analysis, Washington.

_____ (1981), *US Direct Investment Abroad, 1977*, Bureau of Economic Analysis, Washington.

_____ (1984), *International Direct Investment: Global Trends and the US Role*, Washington.

_____ (1985), *US Direct Investment Abroad: 1982 Benchmark Survey Data*, Bureau of Economic Analysis, Washington.

United States Embassy (annual), *Indonesia's Petroleum Sector*, Jakarta.

Vaitsos, C. (1974), *Intercountry Income Distribution and Transnational Enterprises*, Clarendon Press, Oxford.

Van Dijck, P. and H. Verbruggen (1983), 'Export-oriented Industrialisation and Economic Development in Developing Countries', unpublished paper, Free University, Amsterdam.

Von Kirchbach, F. (1982), 'Transnational Corporations in the ASEAN Region: A Survey of Major Issues', *Economic Bulletin for Asia and the Pacific*, 33(1), 12–27.

Warr, P. G. (1983), 'The Jakarta Export Processing Zone: Benefits and Costs', *Bulletin of Indonesian Economic Studies*, 19(3), 28–49.

Watanabe, S. (1983), 'Inter-Sectoral Linkages in Japanese Industries: A Historical Perspective', in S. Watanabe (ed.), *Technology, Marketing and Industrialization: Linkages between Large and Small Enterprises*, Macmillan India, Delhi, for the International Labour Organization, 13–57.

Weinstein, F. B. (1976a), *Indonesian Foreign Policy and the Dilemma of Dependence*, Cornell University Press, Ithaca.

―――― (1976b), 'Multinational Corporations and the Third World: The Case of Japan and Southeast Asia', *International Organization*, 30(3), 373–404.

Wells, L. T. Jr. (1973), 'Economic Man and Engineering Man: Choice of Technology in a Low-Wage Country', *Public Policy*, 21(3), 319–42.

―――― (1983), *Third World Multinationals*, MIT Press, Cambridge, Mass.

Wells, L. T. Jr. and V. E. Warren (1979), 'Developing Country Investors in Indonesia', *Bulletin of Indonesian Economic Studies*, 15(1), 69–84.

Wertheim, W. (1956), *Indonesian Society in Transition*, van Hoeve, The Hague.

Westphal, L. E. *et al.* (1979), 'Foreign Influences on Korean Industrial Development', *Oxford Bulletin of Economics and Statistics*, 41(4), 359–88.

White, L. J. (1978), 'The Evidence on Appropriate Factor Proportions for Manufacturing in Less Developed Countries: A Survey', *Economic Development and Cultural Change*, 27(1), 27–59.

Willmore, L. N. (1976), 'Direct Foreign Investment in Central American Manufacturing', *World Development*, 4(6), 499–517.

―――― (1986), 'The Comparative Performance of Foreign and Domestic Firms in Brazil', *World Development*, 14(4), 489–502.

Witoelar, W. (1983), 'Ancillary Firm Development in the Motor Vehicle Industry in Indonesia', in K. Odaka (ed.), *The Motor Vehicle Industry in Asia*, Singapore University Press, Singapore, for the Council for Asian Manpower Studies, 17–84.

World Bank (1984), *World Tables*, 3rd ed., Washington, 2 vols.

Yoshihara, K. (1978), *Japanese Investment in Southeast Asia*, University Press of Hawaii, Honolulu.

Young, A. S. (1978), 'Factors Affecting Flows of Direct Foreign Investment to Southeast Asian Economies', *Journal of Philippine Development*, 5, 75–96.

Subject Index

Author Index